Tiger 2.0

...AND OTHER GREAT STORIES FROM THE WORLD OF GOLF

THE BEST OF JOHN GARRITY
FROM THE PAGES OF SPORTS ILLUSTRATED

SPORTS ILLUSTRATED BOOKS

This book is dedicated to my beloved enabler, my wife, Pat.

CONTENTS

Introduction

By David Feherty

JOHN GARRITY IS AN IMPOSING SPECIMEN FROM A DISTANCE, standing as he does at what seems around nine feet tall, but when you sit down with him for an interview, he is considerably less intimidating. In fact he seems like the gangling, nerdy sort to whom Tiger Woods might well give short shrift in such a situation. This is, of course, not an insult. As one who has been the first MMH (Mobile Microphone Holder, a facetious term used by smelly techs back in the CBS compound) in line to interview Tiger more often than any other, no one knows better than I how much of a challenge it can be to extract anything other than that which we already know from the man known as Goldenballs by the mortals in the world of professional golf. No one who has ever played the game has been subjected to the kind of shock and awe media assault that Tiger has to face after his every sortie to the links, no matter what he has scored. If Jim Furyk or Chris DiMarco shoot 74, there is no forest of microphones to greet them outside the scorer's area, and no obligatory hourlong visit to the press tent. This cannot be said for Mr. Woods. Not since Bill Clinton has a public figure had so intense a flashlight pointed up his kilt, or seen so many absurd interpretations of his remarks in print, and as a result, getting something of substance from he-who-will-be-the-greatest-ever is, to say the least, something of a conjuring trick. For my own part, if I can get him to show his teeth during an interview, I consider it a roaring success.

Perhaps it's the Irish in him, or the height from which he is forced to approach, but it seems to me that John Garrity always seems to find a different angle in his writing. He has an ability to make his subject unconsciously comfortable, which often leads to the interrogator's dream—the guard being dropped. If only they could fit him into one of the cages, I'm sure he'd do a great job with the boys down at the Guantánamo Bay Country Club. It's kind of like being asked questions by Geoffrey, the Toys 'R' Us giraffe. He's just so damned nice, I think people tend to spill their guts to him for perceived therapeutic value alone.

Of course this compilation is not just of interviews, it's a slice of life, viewed from Garrity's altitude, otherwise known as Garritude, from which both the wood and the trees are set in perfect contrast. I have no idea how he accomplishes this, considering the fact that despite his size, he blends like a chameleon into the crowd of drunken, bitter and jaded hacks of which I am now one of the bitter, jaded and ex-drunken.

Here's the thing: I almost never see Garrity, the sonofabitch. A more cynical observer (and let me know if you find one) might suggest that he spends half of his time slithering on the ground, like some pencil-squeezing serpent, scratching out pieces of scabby fluff from the crusty bellybutton of sports, but the truth is, this is the one place he never seems to visit. Trust me, I know this for a fact, because we would have bumped into one another. That's why the rest of the guys never see me. In fact, the more I think about Garrity, the walking one-iron is starting to piss me off.

Yes, that's it! I've also been searching for an angle, a way to describe the articles that follow, which, against my usually even worse judgment I actually read, and it's just come to me. Hell, I'm trying to sell books myself, so why am I promoting this giant invisible asshole who churns out quality writing in such prolific quantities that this book is no doubt a mere fraction of what will appear in later volumes, thereby knocking my own work off the shelves of booksellers everywhere and into the two-buck bargain bins? He's done it to me, the bastard, and he used the very same technique he uses on all of his other victims—he asked me, and I immediately agreed, because I like him, and his writing, goddammit. The worst part about this is, I wasn't even off my meds when he asked me, so I don't even have my normal excuse. The notion of having my name associated with his work was intoxicating enough, and of course, he's known all along of my addictive personality and history of substance abuse, because, don't you know, several years ago, he interviewed me!

Holy crap, but that was a close one, and I almost fell for it. The man is a genius all right, and the book is great, but in the interests of self-preservation, I cannot recommend that anyone should read it.

I only hope that I'm not too late.

❧

Tiger 2.0

With his new swing grooved, his father gone and a new baby on the way, Tiger Woods embarks on the second phase of his professional life

Some years ago, I retired from the Tiger Woods beat. "He won't sit for interviews," I explained to my editors at SPORTS ILLUSTRATED. *"He's muzzled everyone around him. You can't hang with him off the course, and his press conferences are so scripted you can jot down his answers before the words are out of his mouth." So I wasn't exactly thrilled, in the autumn of 2006, when SI managing editor Terry McDonell asked for a long piece on Woods to run before the '07 Masters.*

"Think 'Frank Sinatra Has a Cold,'" said Jim Herre, SI's longtime golf editor, referring to a famous magazine profile by Gay Talese.

"I'll try," I said. "But if Tiger doesn't blow his nose, I'm screwed."

"I AM, BY NATURE, A CONTROL FREAK," TIGER SAYS WITH a smile.

The smile is sheepish. It says, *I get teased about this all the time.*

Tiger sits on one side of a conference table. I sit on the other. A Nike Golf executive, a longtime acquaintance of mine, stands by the door. She checks her watch every minute or so to make sure I don't take more than my allotted 10 minutes.

Outside, on the tarmac, a Gulfstream 5 waits with its stairs lowered. It is parked not far from a chain-link fence topped with barbed wire, beyond which the L.A. traffic whooshes by in hazy sunshine.

So when Tiger confesses that he is a control freak, I have to fight the impulse to snort derisively. *You think?*

I've opened with a few seconds of small talk. I've told Tiger how much I enjoyed playing with him last week in the pro-am of the PGA Grand Slam of Golf. ("Cool," he says, his expression giving no indication that he remembers.) We then get down to business. Or rather, we talk about business. For 9½ minutes.

When my time is up, I reach across the table and shake Tiger's hand. Nodding to my friend, I walk out of the room, down the hallway, out the front door of the terminal, across the tarmac, and up the stairs of the G5.

What? You thought the plane was Tiger's?

THINK OF ME as an auditor. My assignment: Tiger Woods 2006. I've got the ledgers right here, and the numbers are great. He won eight PGA Tour events last year, including the British Open and the PGA Championship. He topped the money list for the seventh time and was voted the Tour's Player of the Year for the eighth time. He beat Ernie Els in a playoff at the Dubai Desert Classic. He won his last six PGA Tour events and then mopped up the season with unofficial wins at the Grand Slam of Golf and his own Target World Challenge.

But there are some anomalies. A 22nd at the Players Championship, won by Stephen Ames. Thirty-three putts and no final-round kick at the Masters, won by Phil Mickelson. A missed cut—Tiger's first in a major as a professional—at the U.S. Open, won by Geoff Ogilvy.

I explain these in a footnote: "Earl Woods dies of cancer, May 3."

It's not my job as auditor to coax a tear out of you with the details. You saw the lost look in Tiger's eyes when he rejoined the Tour for the Open at Winged Foot. You saw Tiger sobbing on the 18th green after his victory at Royal Liverpool. I'll simply remind you that golf's greatest player, in the months since his father's death, has taken direct control of his nonprofit, started a business, begun construction on a new house, negotiated sponsorship of his own PGA Tour event and conceived an heir, whose birth is expected in July.

I submit the words of the Japanese poet Kenji Miyazawa: *We must embrace pain and burn it as fuel for our journey.*

WHEN I FIRST MET Tiger Woods, he had nothing. No bankable assets, anyway. His bedroom was full of schoolbooks, posters and the usual detritus of Southern California teen life. He had just gotten a puppy, but it wasn't one of those pricey pedigree pooches. It was a mutt. When a friend of mine played a friendly round with the 14-year-old phenom, Tiger suggested that they play for a stick of ABC gum.

"What's ABC gum?" my friend asked.

The kid grinned. "Already Been Chewed."

Tiger wasn't much better off two years later, at the 1992 Los Angeles Open. His cap was swooshless, his clothes were off the rack. In fact, he still answered to the name Eldrick. Reporters crowded around him, wanting to know what it was like to be the youngest golfer ever to play in a PGA Tour event. With his proud father at his side, Tiger smiled bashfully and helped the reporters by spelling the names of his teachers at Western High in Anaheim. He said he wanted to go to college, and he'd already picked a major: accounting.

I conducted my own appraisal of Tiger near sunset on the eve of the tournament. We stood behind the practice range at Riviera Country Club, making small talk, getting acquainted. My eyes kept darting to his golf bag—a skinny carry model with no corporate logos. "It won't be long," I told him, "before you have a bag with your name on it."

Tiger flashed the big grin. "That'd be cool."

FIFTEEN YEARS and 65 pro tournament victories later, Tiger, now 31, has a foundation with his name on it. And a learning center. And a street (Tiger Woods Way, Anaheim). Last year he quietly took the helm of the Tiger Woods Foundation, which, since its inception in 1996, has awarded more than $30 million in grants. He keeps a close eye, as well, on the 14-acre Anaheim campus of the Tiger Woods Learning Center, where in 2006 some 8,000 kids, grades 4 through 12, enhanced their public-school education by tackling subjects such as rocket science, software design and crime-scene investigation. In November he hung out a shingle for Tiger Woods Design, a golf course architecture firm.

In keeping with his changed circumstances, Tiger lives large. He circles the globe in Citations and Gulfstreams supplied by a sponsor, NetJets. When he wants to calm his mind, he cruises the Caribbean on his 155-foot yacht, *Privacy*, which set him back a cool $20 million. And while Tiger continues to reside with his wife, Elin, in a relatively humble Orlando-area mansion, he flies down to Jupiter Island, Fla., from time to time to monitor developments at the 12-acre, $44.5 million waterfront estate he bought last year. Workers will soon demolish the 13-year-old, 23,000-square-foot main house, but Tiger and Elin can bunk at either of two guest houses or chill out on the yacht, tied up at their private dock, while they supervise construction of a new domicile worthy of a neighborhood that *Forbes* describes as "the world's most expensive zip code." Last year *Golf Digest* estimated that Tiger had already earned roughly half a billion dollars in endorsements and appearance fees on top of tournament winnings of $66 million over nine seasons. The magazine projected that by the end of 2010 Tiger will become the first billionaire athlete.

But they're guessing, aren't they?

TIGER AND I, talking in the conference room, dance around the net worth issue. (I think he is too polite to ask.) He does speak frankly about his fading youth and the impending demands of fatherhood. "I'm not going to always play golf," he says, leaning forward. "Eventually the body gives out, and you can't play any more. But there are other avenues you can take that will keep you competitive, keep you interested and keep your mind working."

I nod, but I wonder if he is putting me on. Tiger makes commercials for Buick, but he is not an "avenues" guy. Tiger is more your helmeted speed freak in a 6,500-horsepower Top Fuel dragster going 330 mph with header flames flying off the manifold. Since he turned pro in 1996, Tiger has been racing due north toward Jack Nicklaus's career record of 18 major-championship victories. If he wins at the Masters, Tiger will have won three straight majors, 13 overall and will have a chance, at the U.S. Open in June, to reprise his "Tiger Slam" of 2000–01.

But here is Tiger, elbows on the table, working me like a cold-call broker. His business goal, he says, is to get to "a place where my family can be financially secure." His course design work will be "a partnership between me and the owner of the property; I'm trying to provide a product that they'll be happy with." His brilliantly successful endorsement deal with Nike, recently renewed for a reported $100 million plus, is about "providing products that consumers will enjoy."

He sums up: "We are in the providing business."

I wonder, for an instant, if Tiger is trying to sell me a fixed-rate annuity.

"It all depends on how much risk you want to take on," he continues, flattering me with his use of the second person. "The things I do are very conservative. They're one-offs here and there with people who are very good at what they do."

Tiger smiles. "I guess you don't become billionaires by making bad decisions."

LATER, STRAPPED INTO a comfortable leather armchair on the G5, I stretch my legs and sip a cold 7-Up. The brown expanse of the Mojave Desert, 44,000 feet below, resembles an unrolled bolt of tanned leather.

Tiger's talk about risk and reward has left me vaguely discomfited. I think back a decade to one of his more memorable golf shots—the 213-yard six-iron from a fairway bunker that he smacked over a guarding pond to 15 feet to beat Grant Waite on the final hole of the 2000 Canadian Open. If you asked me to review that shot in a PowerPoint presentation, I'd draw a graph with a flat reward line (because the $594,000 first-prize check meant nothing to Tiger) and a risk line as steep as Everest (because his ball figured to make a splash before settling on the pond's murky bottom). But I'd be misstating the risk, because Tiger knew he could hit that shot.

That leads me to ruminations on Nicklaus, who in his prime was famously strong yet paradoxically cautious, an actuary in spikes. "To watch Nicklaus putt," I once wrote, "is to watch a diamond cutter at work—three minutes of scrutiny and analysis followed by a single sure stroke resulting in something sparkling."

I share these thoughts with Nike Golf president Bob Wood, who sits in the facing armchair. Wood is an interesting man, an iconoclastic Californian who collects vintage guitars and maintains an impressive wine cellar. He makes the pertinent observation that Tiger, a fitness freak, embraces a diet of chicken breasts and broccoli. "Only it's four chicken breasts and a bucket of broccoli."

Tiger's famous discipline, in other words, is not grounded in abstemiousness.

I am also puzzled by Tiger's mention of "billionaires"—plural—not making bad decisions. I assume he is close to Nike Sports founder and CEO Phil Knight, who ranks 69th on the FORTUNE money list with an estimated net worth of $9.5 billion. But Tiger also has the ear of Sheikh Mohammed bin Rashid Al Maktoum, vice president and prime minister of the United Arab Emirates and ruler of Dubai. Sheikh Mohammed, who owns the famed Godolphin racing stables and whose family has a reported net worth of $10 billion, outbid Chinese interests last year for the honor of building the first Tiger Woods–designed golf course. The course, dubbed *Al Ruwaya* (meaning "serenity"), will anchor an upscale housing development featuring 20 homes and 300 luxury villas called the Tiger Woods–Dubai. It's just one element of a gargantuan enterprise called Dubailand. Tiger's cut, if you buy into the rumors, will be as much as $45 million.

It suddenly occurs to me that Tiger, with his line about billionaires, might have been talking about himself.

IT'S A LOVELY DAY at the Emirates Club. Palms rustle, birds chirp, pile-drivers hammer, tractors roar, construction cranes rattle, saws whine, Dumpsters clang, trucks groan, and traffic on Sheikh Zayed Road lays down an ambient layer of white noise. It's February 2007, the week of the Dubai Desert Classic, and Dubai is growing. What was vacant desert on my last visit is now a construction project to beggar the imagination. Dozens of skyscrapers are springing up around the Emirates Club course. Twelve-lane freeways coil in serpentine interchanges jammed with backhoes and bulldozers.

I'm seated at a table in a skybox overlooking the 18th green, chatting with a distinguished-looking gentleman dressed in the traditional white robe and *gutrah* of the desert. He tells me that Tiger and Sheikh Mohammed share certain qualities of character and mind. "They both have vision," he says. "They are decisive. They enjoy the things they do." Both men, he adds, are uncompromising. "In his book Sheikh Mohammed writes, 'Second is a loser.'"

I ask the man in the desert robe if Tiger the businessman is more sociable than Tiger the golfer.

He nods and says, "I sit with him, we eat together, he's very friendly. Maybe a lot of people think that he's . . . . " He hesitates. "It's not easy for Tiger. Everybody wants something—an autograph, a photograph, an interview, a business deal. His day starts when he comes out of his hotel room, and it doesn't end until he's back in his hotel room. Before people judge him, they need to put themselves in his position."

The man in the desert robe looks uncomfortable, so I change the subject to Al Ruwaya. His smile returns. The deal, he says, has been in the works for more than two years. He says the original site was Palm Jumeirah, a cluster of man-made islands in the Arabian Gulf sculpted to look like a palm tree from the air. He says Sheikh Mohammed vetoed that plan, arguing that it would be redundant to put one landmark—the first Tiger

Woods course—on another landmark, the islands. Better that it be built at Dubailand, which will make Disney World look like a petting zoo.

I get nowhere, however, when I press for details about Tiger's contract with Tatweer, a subsidiary of Sheikh Mohammed's Dubai Holding. Will Tiger be paid up front, or will he collect a royalty on properties in Tiger Woods–Dubai? What is his design fee for Al Ruwaya? Does the contract include his multimillion-dollar appearance fees for playing in the Dubai Desert Classic?

"Money is not a big issue for Tiger," says the man in the desert robe. "Nor for us."

TIGER COULD USE a banana. Or a deck of cards. Or a PlayStation2 running *Tiger Woods PGA Tour 2007*.

"I hate sitting still," he says from across the table. "I hate being stale. I've always got to be moving. I've always got to be challenged."

He says this while sitting still, but I have no reason to doubt him. Tiger in a conference room is a cat in a cage. Tiger at a press conference is a schoolboy writing *I will not talk in class* a hundred times on the blackboard.

"Tiger, you're about to become a father for the first time," says the reporter in the third row. "Is that going to affect your preparation for the majors?"

"Tiger, you're an expectant father," says the perky blonde, waving a foam-covered microphone in his face. "Are you ready for diaper duty?"

"Tiger, the way you were raised by your father is the stuff of legend," says the long-form writer with crumbs in his beard. "If your firstborn happens to be a son, will you raise him to be a champion or take more of a laissez-faire approach to child-rearing?"

"Tiger...."

"Tiger...."

If, as Tiger likes to say, "a day without adrenaline is a day wasted," then a day of meet-and-greet must be pure hell. But those who chart his business course say that Tiger is as competitive wearing a tie as he is in a Sunday-red polo. "He's a real pro in either environment," says Cindy Davis, domestic general manager for Nike Golf. "He's got endless energy. Everything to Tiger is an adventure."

That must be why Tiger is partial to stunts. A few years ago he smacked balls off the helipad of Dubai's 60-story Burj Al Arab Hotel. Another time he livened up a golf ball commercial by smashing factory windows with precisely aimed five-iron shots.

It is a stunt, in fact, that has drawn a bevy of us faux-auditor types to L.A.'s Hawthorne Airport. On Nov. 28, 2006, the press release promises, Tiger Woods will christen Nike's squarish Sumo^2 driver by hitting balls down the runway. (Hoped-for headline: TIGER CRUSHES DRIVE 1,900 YARDS!) But when he finally saunters out on the pavement and starts launching rockets, there is a bit of a letdown. A runway, it turns out, makes drives look *less* impressive than usual, owing to the absence of a backdrop.

Tiger, though, takes pains not to disappoint. Speaking from a stage in a vacant hangar, he praises Nike across the board— "Now we are a leader in the golf industry"—but concedes that he probably won't use the Sumo^2 in competition. "I do hit it farther, but I launch it a little too high." He points to the golf division's dramatic growth since 1996, the year Nike, Acushnet and American Express plucked him off the Stanford golf team with $12 million of inducements. "Back when we started," he says, "I think we had a red shirt, a yellow shirt, a blue shirt and a black shirt." And gosh, when he beat Davis Love III at the '96 Las Vegas Invitational, Love was still using one of those old clubs with a wood head and a steel shaft. "We've come a long way," Tiger sums up, giving particular credit to Knight, his billionaire mentor. "It starts from the top. We have a leader that everybody's excited to work for."

Ninety minutes later, as our gleaming white G5 banks over Catalina Island and turns tail on the sun, the Nike executives toast each other and sink into their comfy chairs. It will be a short, happy flight to Scottsdale.

YOU GET TOO CLOSE to Tiger and he disappears. Which is ironic, because getting close to Tiger is the reason SI brokered a deal to put me on Tiger's pro-am team at the PGA Grand Slam of Golf. It's November 2006 and I've just started my Tiger audit. "You guys can talk, get reacquainted," says one of SI's top ad sales execs. "Maybe he'll give you a few minutes on the side."

So here I am, Mr. 12 Rounds a Year, standing with Tiger and

our scramble partners in the fairway of the par-5 2nd hole at the Poipu Bay Golf Club in Poipu Beach, Hawaii. We have a bit of a hanging lie, and I need to fly my five-wood about 225 yards to an elevated green, employing maybe 10 yards of fade against a right-to-left crosswind to fit my ball into an opening between a half dozen bunkers. I also have to consider the influence of Tiger's gallery, hundreds strong, clutching cameras and pens, whom I imagine to be debating the identity of the beanpole senior with the mainland pallor and green golf glove.

Tiger? He and caddie Steve Williams are a few feet away, but if they were to don ponchos and fly into the Mexican hat dance, I wouldn't notice.

I misplace Tiger again on the tee of the par-3 3rd, where he smacks a short iron pin-high while I'm trying to choose between a hybrid four and a garden weasel. On another hole a smiling Tiger walks by, saying, "Give me a 6." (I won't learn until nightfall that's he's just yanked his drive out of bounds.) Mostly, though, Tiger is merely a disembodied voice saying "Good swing there," when you hit a nice shot.

Any Tour player could have told me: You don't learn about Tiger when you play golf with him. You learn about yourself.

SO IT HAS to wait until the following week, when we meet in that little room at the airport. How, I ask him, does he find time for his business pursuits? How does he keep the orbits of Mark Steinberg, his agent at IMG, and Hank Haney, his swing coach, from crossing?

"It's a matter of keeping a balance," Tiger says, his eyes locked on mine. "Sometimes in the late evenings I may have to sit down and do some figuring, make a bunch of phone calls, work different avenues. It's basically nonstop. But it's mentally stimulating to work like that. The practice time, the tournaments, doing things with my friends and family, the business side . . . it all blends in."

I picture Tiger in his home office at midnight—signing documents, firing off faxes, checking his bank statements to make sure Steinberg hasn't bought Belize without his permission.

He says, "There's no class to teach you balance. You have to learn on the fly."

A THUNDERSTORM interrupts second-round play at the Dubai Desert Classic, so I drive my rented SUV into the desert for a look at Dubailand. There isn't much to see—a rough expanse of coarse sand and gravel dotted with patches of dusty-green scrub and the occasional stunted tree. But then that's what the area around the Emirates Golf Club looked like a decade ago. If Dubailand is built according to plan, it will have 55 hotels and the infrastructure to accommodate 200,000 visitors a day.

Tiger had been coy the other day when a European reporter asked if he planned to spend part of his week in the desert, stepping off yardages and planting little red flags. ("I'll probably go out to the site and take a look," Tiger said.) His nascent design team, however, is huddling with the Tatweer staff at the Emirates Club. Tiger's man on the ground is his childhood friend and high school teammate Bryon Bell, who caddied for Tiger on occasion before going to work at the Tiger Woods Foundation.

There is understandable curiosity about Tiger's foray into course design. Typically, a champion golfer either partners with an established golf architect—Arnold Palmer with Ed Seay, for example, or Ben Crenshaw with Bill Coore—or hires a staff of practiced landscape engineers and architects a la Jack Nicklaus, whose design company has produced 310 courses in 30 countries. Tiger would seem to be leaning toward the latter model (he took advantage of Nicklaus's generous offer to let Bell visit his North Palm Beach offices to study the golf course operation), but he turns vague when asked who will actually read the topographical maps and produce the construction drawings.

In L.A., Tiger had assured me, "I will not be hiring some guy to design a golf course. I'll be hands-on and involved in it."

He was more forthcoming about his design philosophy. "My tastes are toward the old and traditional. I'm a big fan of the Aussie-built courses in Melbourne, the sand-belt courses. I'm also a tremendous fan of some of the courses in our Northeast." Tiger didn't name those courses, but I mentally ticked off some classic layouts that he probably likes: The Country Club, Shinnecock Hills, Merion, Baltusrol, Winged Foot.

"I'm not one who thoroughly enjoys playing point B to point C to point D golf," he continued. "The courses I like are the ones where you have the option to play different shots. I enjoy working the ball on the ground and using different avenues."

"Like Royal Liverpool?" I asked, naming the English course on which Tiger won the 2006 British Open using a 19th-century arsenal of low, scooting tee shots (played almost exclusively with irons and fairway metals) and ground-hugging approaches.

He smiled at the memory. "Liverpool this year and St. Andrews in 2000 are the only times I've seen the fairways faster than the greens. You hit a putt from the fairway, it was running one speed. It got to the green, the putt slowed down." His smile broadened. "That's not like most golf courses, but that's what I like to see. It fits my eye."

Now, walking on the Arabian desert under dark, roiling clouds, I pause to squint, to fit my eyes to the scrubby slopes and narrow washes of Tiger's blank canvas, trying to see a golf course.

Pretty soon, I see it.

TIGER SAYS the two years he spent at Stanford are starting to pay off. "I was majoring in econ, but the econ I was learning was your supply-and-demand curve, monetary policy. It was mostly math," he says. "I was never going to be an economic analyst or anything like that, but some of it is starting to become applicable now, as I start to get into the business."

I want to dazzle Tiger with some of my own financial acumen—how I bought Garmin at 17.50 and Apple at 21 before the split—but I'm afraid he might have heard that I drive a hail-damaged '94 Volvo. Instead I ask if he has ever sought business advice from Nicklaus, Palmer or Gary Player, the original Big Three of ancillary income. "I have not talked to them," he says.

I can tell, though, that he knows what I know—that the Big Three, while wealthy and widely admired in business circles, have found commerce to be a cruder and meaner game than golf. Nicklaus suffered losses to his bottom line and reputation in the late 1990s when his publicly traded Golden Bear Golf Inc. tanked because of accounting irregularities at a course-construction subsidiary. Palmer got dragged into ugly litigation in the late '80s when his partner in a chain of Arnold Palmer car dealerships was brought down on fraud charges, and again in '90 when homeowners near Florida's ritzy Isleworth community (where Tiger would later move) won a $6.6 million judgment against Palmer and his development partners over lakefront pollution and flooding. Player, too, has had setbacks, most notably with Gary Player Direct.com, an e-commerce company that lost millions in the dotcom fever of the late '90s. And while all three have ventured into the golf equipment business, none of their signature club lines has ever captured more than a tiny share of the U.S. market.

"It all depends on how much risk you want to take on," Tiger says. "Arnold has dibble-dabbled in a bunch of different things, but he's never put himself at complete risk, where the other two basically have. You can reap the rewards by doing that. Or you can get shelled." He shrugs. "Obviously, I don't go into much risk."

The next day, as we leave Scottsdale and fly in the Nike jet, I ask Bob Wood for an appraisal of Tiger Woods, businessman.

"Tiger is a sponge," he says. "He has an incredible memory, and he's had years to soak up information from people who work for large companies." Wood pauses, as if waiting for a presentation graphic. "Whatever he gets into, he gets into all the way. Right now, it's skiing. He's a nut for skiing, and every time I talk to him he knows more about skiing. That's how he is." He pauses again, letting me savor the mental image of Tiger in goggles pursuing his wife, an accomplished skier, down a black diamond.

"He's a complete control freak. He always wants to determine the outcome."

I nod.

"He's very comfortable in his own skin. He doesn't have a posse. He doesn't walk around with a bunch of yes-men."

I nod.

"He's smart enough to know that every strength is a weakness."

That one is sufficiently Zen to stop my nodding. "Is he a new Tiger?" I ask. "Is he playing more than one game?"

"Well, he's running the foundation, now that his father is gone. That's a pretty daunting part-time gig for a 31-year-old." Wood shakes his head. "But no, he's still focused on winning majors."

OF COURSE he is. But Tiger doesn't sleep a lot, and if he can use those otherwise wasted hours that come before dawn to, say, plot a white-knight takeover of a PGA Tour event. . . .

Or perhaps I should call it a coup, inasmuch as the AT&T National, scheduled to debut in or near Washington, D.C., around the Fourth of July, will be played within eavesdropping range of the White House. "If you ever have to choose between announcing a golf tournament sponsorship or testifying before Congress," AT&T chairman Ed Whitacre says at a March 7 press conference with Tiger and PGA Tour commissioner Tim Finchem, "my advice to you is to take the golf tournament." The new event, hosted by Tiger and run by and benefiting the Tiger Woods Foundation, replaces the International in Castle Rock, Colo., which folded in February after 21 years.

Here's where an auditor has to get creative. Looking at the first quarter 2007, I see that Tiger's seven-event PGA Tour winning streak ended on Feb. 23, when he lost to Nick O'Hern at the Accenture Match Play. But there's no compensating line item for Tiger's 10-and-8 reaming of International founder Jack Vickers in the Who-Gets-to-Host-a-Tour-Event Classic. The 81-year-old Vickers, a onetime oil tycoon, is the guy who complained that Tiger's failure to play in his tournament since 1999 had halved television ratings and made it impossible to land a title sponsor. "If something isn't done," Vickers tells me over a bowl of asparagus soup at Castle Pines Golf Club in February, "you're not going to have a Tour. Right now, it's a one-man show."

Yes, I think, and as an astute Wall Street analyst once shouted at Tiger, "You da man!"

In any event, I'm checking out the commodity prices on Bloomberg TV the other day when the network runs video of Tiger, in coat and tie, paying courtesy calls to House speaker Nancy Pelosi and Senate majority leader Harry Reid. Then Tiger is behind a nest of microphones, explaining how he and his dad had always dreamed of running their own Tour event. And because Earl had been a Vietnam veteran and a career soldier, Tiger's thrilled to be hosting a tournament celebrating America's birthday while honoring America's warriors who, by the way, will be offered free admission to the tournament, as will children under 12. At this point there must have been a technical foul-up, because there is no video of fireworks bursting over the Washington Monument. But Finchem and Whitacre are practically floating off the dais, and I'm reaching for my checkbook to contribute to the Tiger Woods for President exploratory committee.

Bloomberg moves on, but I picture Tiger stepping back from the podium and delivering one of his signature fist pumps.

I THUMB A MESSAGE to Vickers on my BlackBerry, quoting Andy Grove, the cofounder and former chairman of Intel.

Success breeds complacency. Complacency breeds failure. Only the paranoid survive.

Maybe I should send it to Finchem instead.

JASON GORE likes the view from 45,000 feet. The feel of it too. He's a big man, so the padded armrests and generous legroom provide a level of luxury he could only dream about two years ago, when he was driving his wife and infant son to Nationwide tour stops in a car packed with practically everything the family owned. One night, at a motel in Asheville, N.C., someone broke into the car and took everything. But, hey, this is America. A week later Gore's mug was as familiar as Suze Orman's—thanks to his play at the U.S. Open. Three months later Gore had three straight Nationwide wins, a promotion to the PGA Tour and a stunning victory at the 84 Lumber Classic. So now he's a winner, like Tiger, and can cross his legs as he soars above Ohio in the G5.

"We're all little kids at heart," says Gore. I think of Tiger at 16, excited about a puppy and eager to join Pops and his mom for a chain-store pizza.

An hour later the plane touches down in Teterboro, N.J., and we pile into a shuttle for the ride to lower Manhattan and the World Financial Center. It's the last stop on the Sumo^2 tour, and Gore's job is to answer reporters' questions and then smack balls in one of two cages set up in an atrium bright with Christmas lights and potted poinsettias. He's a natural at this, and hundreds of brokers, executives and office workers stop to watch on their way out, some of them stepping into the cages to hit a few balls. I watch for a while and then stroll over to the glass wall to take in the big view of New York Harbor and the Statue of Liberty. *Give me your tired, your poor, your huddled masses. . . .*

I wonder where Tiger is and what he's doing.

SO HERE'S MY final accounting: Tiger Woods, in fiscal 2006, earned $11,941,827 in prize money and roughly $90 million from appearance fees, endorsements, corporate outings, bonuses, speaking engagements, books, licensing fees, instructional videos and Tiger Woods–branded products ranging from wine to grass seed. His income from stocks and other investments is harder to gauge; based on the results of my own closely managed portfolio, I estimate that he made another $600, minimum.

Working, then, from an estimated income of $101,942,427—and basing my calculations on a 52-week year and a federally mandated five-day work week of eight hours a day—I value my 10 minutes of Tiger's undivided attention at $8,168.46.

Past performance, of course, does not guarantee future results.

POSTSCRIPT: *A few months after the publication of my Tiger write-around, a major U.S. newspaper, in an otherwise well-reported feature on star athletes' incomes, cited my goofy estimate of Woods's annual take. I thought that citation was funny. Less amusing was my return to flying commercial. Now, every time I take off my shoes for airport security I pine for my two days of Gulfstream bliss.*

᠙

Home on the Range

The author, an avowed range rat, learned plenty about a mostly mom-and-pop business while searching in vain for his swing

For several years I wrote a web column called "Mats Only." The premise was that I had lost my swing—which was true—and like a modern-day Odysseus I roamed the world, trying to get it back. The column led to the following feature, which should be read under driving-range lights with mosquitoes and love bugs flitting about your head.

YOUR RANGE RAT IS A MAN WITH A PAST. HE'S BOGIE—NO pun intended—bent over a bottle of bourbon in the dark of Rick's Café. He's James Stewart in *Vertigo*, tailing a beautiful woman through the streets of San Francisco because she reminds him of a lost love. Your range rat can be charming, even debonair, but golf has made him cynical. Like Sean Connery in a Bond flick, he has wakened too many times with a dead blonde sharing his pillow.

I speak from experience. For more than a decade I have haunted driving ranges from Minneapolis to Miyazaki, searching for a lost swing. I have hit balls off carpet squares, vinyl strips and gravel. I have hit off moldy mats into a night rain and watched the ball vanish above the lights and reappear as a splash in black water. I have aimed at trees, tractors, trampolines, yardage signs, fire trucks, bull's-eyes, pinball pods, rainbows and rafts. I have watched low-compression pitch-and-putt balls swoop and dart like june bugs in the floodlights. I have hit balls from wire buckets, drawstring bags and plastic paint cans. I have pushed computer cards into slots and watched balls pop up from underground. I have picked the gleaming white fruit of those elegant ball pyramids at golf schools and resorts.

Being a range rat is an interesting life, but it changes a man. Some years ago I was hitting balls at 2 a.m. at the Randall's Island Golf Range in New York City, when the cry of a baby distracted me. Turning around, I discovered that a Korean family had taken over a nearby bench. The mother was juggling baby bottles and blankets. A preschool girl slept on her grandmother's lap. Between shots, the father—who looked like a middle manager for Samsung—turned to his family and spoke in Korean. The women shook their heads vigorously and used their hands to show that his club face was closed on the takeaway.

A man wearing a sweatshirt and a ball cap walked up with two wire buckets of balls and took the station to my immediate right. The new arrival and I practiced for a while in silence, until he accidentally kicked over one of the buckets, sending balls bouncing down the concrete sidewalk behind the tee line. "Stop!" he yelled at the runaway balls. He turned to me and said, "I can hit O.K. when I'm a little buzzed. How about you?"

He then told me the story of his life. He was 39, married and childless. He loaded trucks for a living and drank beer most nights at a lounge. He said he had been playing golf for two years and, oh, yeah, he hoped someday to play on the senior tour. "I don't hit it as good as Nicklaus and those guys," he said unnecessarily, "but I used to hustle pool, so maybe I can hustle golf."

He had a 7 o'clock tee time, and that's why he had come to Randall's Island when the bar closed instead of going home. He said, "I could use a few hours sleep, but when my head hits the pillow, I'm gone." He coughed. "Watch this. I can make the ball suck back like Greg Norman." He made a short, choppy swing and hit an ugly knuckleball that flew about 100 yards and hopped down the range like a jackrabbit. He shook his head and said, "Sometimes that's a *hard* sonofabitch to hit."

That's why I say the driving range life changes a man. You start as a kid, swinging so hard with a cut-down five-iron that you stagger off the mat. You celebrate adolescence by taking your girl to the range and showing her how to hold the club while smart guys yell "Fore!" from passing cars. Before you know it, you're a character in a campy poster, smacking balls at the towers of the Triborough Bridge in the wee hours with James Dean on the mat behind you and Marilyn Monroe just up the tee line hitting soft wedges to the 50-yard sign.

YOUR RANGE RAT is afraid of commitment. He's John Cusack in *High Fidelity*, tallying the women who have left him. He's Hugh Grant in *Four Weddings and a Funeral*. Your range rat loves driving ranges, but he knows it's dangerous to invest too much emotion in any particular range. The two formative ranges of my youth in Kansas City—Smiley Bell's and Sam Snead's—gave way decades ago to a television studio and tract housing, respectively. (Range balls, oddly enough, linger for years, transmigrating through the soil by a process understood only by geologists. When bulldozers plowed up Smiley Bell's in 1969, old golf balls were found to a depth of eight feet.)

In Ireland this July I found the Ennis Driving Range padlocked and shuttered. In downtown San Diego, in August, I spied the high nets of a range from the window of my harborside hotel. When I drove to the site, I found a closed range overrun with weeds and trash. Even *The Wall Street Journal* keeps track of driving range morbidity. In May, Family Golf Centers, Inc., which operated 111 golf centers and 19 skating rinks in 23 states and three Canadian provinces, filed for protection under Chapter 11 of the U.S. Bankruptcy Law. Among the Family Golf assets were 21 Golden Bear Driving Ranges, operated under license from Jack Nicklaus's Golden Bear Golf Inc.

This bleak picture notwithstanding, driving ranges are thriving. A National Golf Foundation study found that range rats spent $722 million for balls at stand-alone ranges in 1999, up more than 50% from '94. The number of tee stations climbed 16% in the same period, to 73,158; the number of customers rose by 56% to 17.8 million; and the number of range visits jumped from 71 million to 96 million. "Practice has never been so popular," writes NBC golf analyst Roger Maltbie, co-author of the book *Range Rats*. "The culture is growing like some giant sci-fi creature oozing up out of the ground. It's Range Ratzilla!" A trade publication calls ranges "the golden child of golf."

It's just that driving ranges have remained unalterably small-time, defying the standardization and consolidation of other businesses. "There's a reason why only 12 percent of ranges are part of multisite operations," says Mark Silverman, editor of *Golf Range* magazine. "The minute you have to start paying other people to run the property, a lot of the money goes out the door in overhead."

The Rocky Gorge Golf Fairway of Laurel, Md., is one of my favorite ranges, and it is successful because its owners understand that range rats don't care about corporate balance sheets and economies of scale. "I'm the only corporate structure here," says co-owner Gus Novotny. "It's a mom-and-pop business."

Novotny is a legend. He was the first range operator to offer heated stalls to golfers. He was the first to design a mechanical ball conveyor to deliver washed golf balls to the shop. He was, and is, the only range operator to walk the aisles of the annual PGA Merchandise Show wearing a black bowler. That's why I made a special trip to Rocky Gorge—to talk to Gus and to take a shot at his junked car.

First the car. It's parked about 160 yards from the double-deck tee line, a battered '94 Dodge with a giant bull's-eye painted on it. Hitting from a mat on a crisp weekday morning, I launched seven-irons at the car, wondering what a direct hit would sound like. (I am sadly familiar with the sounds that a golf ball makes when it strikes stucco, tile, aluminum siding, brick, concrete, wood decking and various items of lawn furniture, but I had never hit a car.) "We had a green out there," Novotny said, watching me take a few swings, "but if you hit the flag, you didn't hear anything."

So in 1978 Gus parked his '73 Olds convertible on the hillside and invited customers to rain on his parade. The new target was an instant success, and now Gus has to change the car every year. "Newer cars aren't as good as the old ones because there's too much plastic in them," he told me. "You need a '70s car to get that good old clank sound when it hits, instead of a thud." I finally planted one squarely on the driver's side door and was rewarded with the resonant peal of surlyn on sheet metal. "Bingo!" he said.

Novotny is semiretired at 63, but his mark is everywhere at Rocky Gorge. He designed the tractor-drawn baseball/softball picker. It was his idea to build the world's longest miniature golf hole, a downhill, 185-foot par-2. The workshop where employees build everything from animatronic figures to benches? Gus again.

"I genuflect in front of Arnold Palmer and Walt Disney," he said, giving me a tour of the facility and introducing me to everyone from the Korean golf pro to the married couple who paint the complex in carnival colors. "Palmer for making golf so popular. Disney because he was so smart. Disney took every dollar out of your pocket and made you happy."

Rocky Gorge used to be a farm. Novotny and a partner leased the land back in 1964, when Gus had to decide whether he would be an industrial engineer (he has an engineering degree from Maryland) or a golf pro. "I thought this would be the ideal business," he said. "Open in the summer, off in the winter." He laughed. "I found out you have to be open in the winter and on rainy days too. You have to start at 6 a.m. and work until 1 a.m."

During his first five years, Gus had no income from the range, getting by only by teaching at a technical high school in a rough area of Washington, D.C. Now he has 23 employees, 13 of them full-time, and he boasts that he pays 100% of their benefits. "There will always be Chevrolet, apple pie and driving ranges," he told me, "but to make a living at it you have to love golf, and you have to give up your life."

YOUR RANGE RAT is a wanderer, an adventurer. He's Steve Mc-Queen in *The Sand Pebbles*, wooing a beautiful schoolteacher while Chiang Kai-shek's soldiers riot on the Yangtze. He's Alice in *Alice's Adventures in Wonderland*, drinking from the container labeled DRINK ME.

I was driving a desolate stretch of California 371 between Temecula and Palm Desert. The late afternoon sun hit a peeling wooden sign by a ranch gate, and I caught the words . . . LF RANGE. I didn't hit the brakes until I was a quarter mile down the road. Making a U-turn, I drove back to the gate and turned in at the sign, which read, L C VENTURES GOLF RANGE. No range was visible, but a gravel road ran down the fence line. I followed it, raising a plume of dust. A few hundred yards later, the road turned left into a cluster of sheds and mobile homes. I parked the car between a pickup truck and some rusty barrels and stared out the windshield. A field of sparse prairie grass climbed gently to the south, bisected by a row of decrepit yardage signs. Unpainted and cracked tee markers pointed up the hill toward a small cinder-block house.

I wandered onto the empty tee line, picking my way between a broken-down clothes dryer, a lawn sprinkler and a discarded sofa. I called out, "Hello?" but no one answered. When I looked back at the closest trailer, a red curtain moved in the window—or was it my imagination? A weathered shed caught my eye. I walked over and stared in disbelief. On the counter were a half-dozen wire buckets of old golf balls and a sign: $3 Bucket. I felt a sudden chill. I had stumbled upon a ghost driving range.

I left my $3 under a hunk of rusted metal, got my clubs out of the trunk and, in the setting sun, began hitting balls up the hill. A cool wind blew out of the mountain shadows, making the tufts of grass shake and my skin crawl. I swung mindlessly, slapping balls up the hill with no regard for form or outcome. When the balls were gone, I took the pail back to the shed and put my clubs in the trunk. The curtain in the trailer seemed to move again. Minutes later, speeding down the highway toward the Coachella Valley, I took a deep breath and turned on the radio.

YOUR RANGE RAT is a put-upon consumer. He's Jack Nicholson in *Five Easy Pieces*, sweeping the dishes off the table when the waitress won't bring him a side of toast. Your range rat loves driving ranges, but he knows that most of them are sadly deficient. One range has Heinz 57 golf balls with hand-painted stripes that leave red blotches on a club face. Another range faces the setting sun, so you can't see the ball in the afternoon. Two years ago in Seattle I visited a range that had protective netting that extended out about 10 feet between stalls. You could only aim straight ahead, like a hunter in a hallway. Two months ago in Canada I hit balls at a range advertised as 'One of the Top 100 Ranges in America'; the target greens and landing areas were covered with synthetic turf, causing balls to bounce 100 yards or more.

My experience is universal, judging from the e-mails I get from readers of my *Mats Only* blog. "I absolutely refuse to hit off mats," writes a worked-up Steve Killebrew of New York City. "What a joke they are! They cause you to hit it fat and are hard on the joints." Max Hill of Baytown, Texas, writes that the "absolute worst driving range is Hacker's Haven, here in Baytown. No grass on the teeing areas, just hardpan, and we have been hitting the same balls for about eight years now." Pat Larkey of Pittsburgh describes a range near Cambridge, England, as "early chicken coop" and says it is tended by a middle-aged woman in curlers and a floral housecoat. "The balls are remarkably dirty, cut and ranging in compression from about five (like a Ping-Pong ball) to 150 (a cross between fieldstone and a ball bearing)."

Mats are the bête noire of range rats. Hit your shot a little fat and the sole of the club bounces into the ball, producing a misleadingly decent shot. Hit too steeply into the mat and the elbows rebel with tendinitis. Hit from the outside or toe down and the mat keeps it a secret—there is no divot to analyze to correct one's swing faults. Still, mats have improved exponentially since the 1950s, when all-rubber surfaces caused sprained wrists and left black streaks on the soles of clubs. The nylon top cloth caught hold in the '60s, and the late '80s saw the introduction of the brush insert of artificial grass—a sort of porcupine pelt that simulates real turf. The best mats today, such as the $300 Wittek Quatro, have an air-cushioned underpad that softens impact and minimizes bounce. "There isn't one best mat," says Dennis Tull, owner of Smiley's Golf Complex in Shawnee, Kans. "It depends on the climate. In the desert, adhesives can fail and certain materials will quickly fade. Here in Kansas it gets pretty windy, so you don't want a lightweight mat that blows away in a storm."

Balls are next on the list of range-rat complaints. Though many ranges buy factory-striped two-piece balls from Spalding or Titleist, some economize with smooth, low-compression spheres that perform like petrified marshmallows. Others buy balls from ball hawks—those brave souls who dive into water hazards and scour the woods for lost balls—and paint on their own stripe. "The problem with range balls is not so much the balls as the quality of the landing area," says *Golf Range*'s Silverman. "If they land in a hardpan dirt field, the abrasion grinds off the clear coat, and it's the clear coat that makes the ball durable."

Finally, you have the problem of floodlights. A fancy range opened in Pittsburgh a few years ago with lights that *faced* the golfers, blinding them at night. Other ranges have experimented with berm or ground-based lighting (the Karsten Test Facility in Phoenix) or just plain bad lighting (Surf 'n' Turf Driving Range, Del Mar, Calif.), with varying degrees of success. My man Novotny studied the lighting issue some time back. Observing that the interchange of I-95 and Maryland 216 was made brilliant at night with lights on 100-foot poles, he went out at 4 a.m. and hit golf balls across the highway. "It was really bright," he says. "You could throw a quarter on the ground and see if it was heads or tails."

Unfortunately, you couldn't see a ball once it got airborne because the lights illuminated only the top half of it. That experiment, along with trial and error, convinced Novotny that range lights should be on 30- to 35-foot poles aimed at a central point 150 yards out. It also helps to have covered tee stations with fluorescent lights in the ceilings to eliminate clubhead shadows. "The ideal situation would be a little of each," says Tull. "Pole lighting, bunker lighting and canopy lighting."

Sad to say, even the ideal situation is never quite ideal. Get everything right—the best mats, the best balls, state-of-the-art lighting, landscaped parking, a sushi bar—and your range rat will still sigh and stare at the round rubber tee protruding from his mat. The rubber tee is *always* too high.

YOUR RANGE RAT is a caring individual. He's Bing Crosby in *White Christmas*, organizing a scheme to save the General's country inn. He's Jackie Chan in *Rumble in the Bronx*, delivering kicks to the jaws of the thugs who wrecked a young woman's market.

I, for example, lose sleep over the situation outside Halifax, Nova Scotia, where two driving ranges, no more than a mile apart on Highway 333, compete for a very finite customer base. The Goodwood Family Golf Center, the spiffier of the two, faces east on an appealing tree-lined site. The west-facing Halifax Golf Center, by way of contrast, rubs against gritty workyards filled with chemical tanks and stacked lumber.

I was in the Goodwood shop on a Saturday morning, talking with owner Barry MacDonald, when a woman came in to buy a gift certificate for her husband. She looked as comfortable as a kindergarten teacher at a gun show. She said, "People are content to just stand there and hit those golf balls, are they?"

MacDonald chuckled. "Well, I wouldn't say that they're content."

MacDonald is 53. He was a barber and then a fireman before he took up golf a decade ago. "I got hooked on the game," he told me, "and stupid entrepreneur that I am, I decided to start a range with a fellow fireman." The partner split after three years, but MacDonald soldiers on with the help of his wife, who moonlights as a bank clerk; his daughter, Candace; and golf pro Kevin Reid, a former Mountie. During the golf season MacDonald works 14- to 16-hour days, seven days a week. He picks balls, he mows the range—"I know every rock in the field"—and when the season ends around Nov. 1, he starts right in on equipment repairs and maintenance. "I'm like a lobster fisherman in the Maritimes," he said. "I spend the winter preparing for the season."

I asked about the other range down the road, and MacDonald answered with a tale that sounded like an episode of *Northern Exposure*. He said he and his partner had bought their land in 1992, but the bank needed time to act on their application for a $40,000 business loan—like, two years. The partners cleared the property and put up a sign that read GOODWOOD FAMILY GOLF CENTER. Without warning, a wealthy contractor launched a preemptive strike, opening a range on acreage he owned in the industrial district. Just to draw the line more clearly, the rich guy opened a bar in his shop. "That's something I don't believe in," MacDonald said. So this formerly golf-free stretch of highway suddenly had *two* driving ranges: MacDonald's family-oriented facility (flowers in window boxes, soft drinks in the fridge, Dudley Do-Right on the lesson tee) and the contractor's place (pool cues on the wall, bikers on the tee line, Snidely Whiplash behind the register).

Two years ago, the Halifax Golf Center went out of business and Goodwood seemed to have won. But when spring rolled around a new owner, a Mr. Kim, took over, prolonging the struggle. MacDonald had to consider the possibility that a disciplined Korean businessman might put in the long hours necessary to compete in a range war. "The hours are a killer in this business," MacDonald said.

Goodwood is a delightful driving range and MacDonald is an amiable, hardworking man, so I pledged that I would give him my business whenever I am in Nova Scotia—which is more or less never. I then drove down the road to meet Jae Hang Kim, the new owner of the Halifax Golf Center. I found him in his shop moving boxes, a gray-haired man of 60 with searching eyes.

Kim's story was familiar. He, like MacDonald, had decided to pursue golf as a kind of exit strategy, in his case from a career as a chemist. "I like golf," he told me. "After retirement, it's something to do." He, too, was putting in long hours—in at 7:30 a.m., out at 9 p.m.—and like MacDonald he was getting help from his wife. (Kim's son, a dental student at New York University, planned to work at the range between terms. Kim's other child, a daughter, is a doctor.) "I don't think that I can make any money this year," Kim admitted. "I have to spend more to make the place better."

Moved by his sincerity and his love for the game, I promised I would give him my business whenever I was in Nova Scotia.

YOUR RANGE RAT is an American original. He's John Wayne. He's Bette Midler. He's Jim Reed, a 52-year-old industrial engineer from Lake Linganore, Md. I discovered Reed one morning at Rocky Gorge. A balding man with spectacles, he caught my eye by stripping to an undershirt, stacking his wallet, keys, watch and cellphone by the corner of his mat, and then hitting golf balls with a swing that might charitably be called eccentric. With his feet close together, he picked the club straight up, maneuvered his elbows so that one pointed toward Annapolis and the other toward Baltimore, and then whirled into the ball with a move so vigorous that I felt a shock wave. Remarkably, he hit most of his shots solidly and far.

Passing through the golf shop on my way to the pop machine, I asked the clerk if she knew the fellow. Nancy Ferreira told me that Reed was a Rocky Gorge icon, a regular for more than 25 years. She said, "You wouldn't believe how many people comment on him. They see him swing and say, 'How does he do that?'"

I watched Reed hit balls for another 10 minutes before I introduced myself and asked that very question—how did he do that? He laughed and said, "I hit the ball with a violent wrenching of my hips. My whole swing is violent, but that's the part that really works." Other parts, he conceded, didn't work. "Sometimes I hit myself on the head with my backswing. But if I don't hit myself too hard, I'm O.K."

Reed plays to a 10 handicap at daily-fee courses, and he has taken his game to England, Scotland and Wales. A photo sequence of his swing would show that he manages to compensate for a severe across-the-line position at the top by twisting his pelvis ahead of his arm drop and holding on for dear life. "I often practice with my feet together," he says. "It's a great drill for learning how to move your body under a still head."

I waited for him to leave before trying it.

YOUR RANGE RAT is on a quest. He's Ronald Coleman in *Lost Horizon*, looking for Shangri-La. He's Diogenes with his lantern, the Prince with his glass slipper, Don Quixote with his impossible dream. The range rat knows there is one perfect place to practice, and someday he will find it: El Dorado Driving Range. Holy Grail Hit 'n' Sit. The tees will be sod cut from Augusta National's fairways. The balls will be Titleists, right out of the sleeve. The target green will resemble the 16th at Cypress Point, with pounding surf and sea lions.

Bill Scott, an East Coast lawyer who has taken more than 250 lessons from more than 40 teachers, has practiced at a number of ranges that he classifies as mystical—places like Pine Valley in Clementon, N.J., or Muirfield Village in Dublin, Ohio, where the range grass is as green as Ireland and the air smells like watermelon in the summer. "Some go to the range to correct swing flaws," he says. "I go to the range because there I am free to hit balls in quiet seclusion for the pure pleasure of feeling that solid hit and watching the flight of the ball against a blue sky to a landing place not as carefully selected as it should be."

A surprising number of these mystical fields are open to the public. Albuquerque, for instance, is a destination resort for range rats. You can hit off Tour-quality grass and gasp at sunsets at the city-run Puerto Del Sol Golf Course, the state-owned University of New Mexico Golf Course and the Native American–owned Isleta Eagle Golf Course. Pass through California's Coachella Valley and you can pig out on range balls at the Westin Mission Hills Resort—$7 for a day ticket to either of two scenic, double-ended ranges—or at the new Cimarron Golf Resort, where a range attendant rebuilds your ball pyramid, gives you exact yardages to the target greens and cleans your clubs, all for $10.

Or you can call off the search and go straight to World Woods. I heard about this place last fall when I was in Florida. The assistant pro at a club in Sarasota told me about an emerald city of practice where you could hit shots from all points of the compass to natural greens; where the all-grass tees were smooth enough for lawn bowling; where forest creatures crept out of the woods to watch you swing. "It's in the middle of nowhere," he said, "but that's part of its charm."

I set out the next afternoon in a rental car, driving north into Florida's hill country. It was raining and I got lost, but I finally found the little town the pro had told me about. I asked for directions to the course at gas stations, and glassy-eyed clerks shook their heads. I drove for almost an hour in a hardwood forest, looking for a sign. Then, without really understanding how, I found myself parked in front of the modest clubhouse at World Woods. The rain had stopped, and a handful of golfers were motoring out to resume their rounds on the two championship courses and the nine-hole short course.

Minutes later, I was driving a cart through a haunt of moss-draped trees, following signs to the west tee of the practice range. I emerged behind two large, perfectly turfed tee grounds overlooking a tree-bordered valley. The middle of the magic field was dotted with mature trees and steep-faced bunkers filled with white sand. There were greens at various elevations, set into slopes the way they are on real courses. The mowed area extended into the woods and curved around hillocks, suggesting fairways.

The two west tees had about 20 stations each, but no one was hitting balls. I emptied my two drawstring bags onto the perfect, springy turf and looked in all directions. No one was visible. No balls flew from the north, south or east tees, which were hidden in the distant trees. No tractors chugged back and forth, picking up balls. This empty Eden was all mine.

I hit balls for more than an hour in the long shadows and the golden glow of sunset. After 20 minutes or so, a young woman and her swing coach joined me. "Do you think we could camp here?" she asked. "This is heaven." I hit eight-irons at a hillside green for 10 minutes straight, loving the way each well-hit shot cleared the front bunker and hopped around the hole. My divot field formed a neat rectangle of square, shallow cuts. The exposed soil, sandy and yellow, gleamed like simmering porridge.

Then the sun went down.

YOUR RANGE RAT moves on. He's Mel Gibson in *The Patriot*, putting away his guns and raising what's left of his family on a barrier island. He's Mel Gibson in *The Road Warrior*, cruising down a postapocalyptic highway in a bullet-ridden Mack truck. He's Mel Gibson in *Payback*, driving to Canada with the money, the blonde and a couple of broken toes. He's Mel Gibson at the end of *Lethal Weapon 3*, already thinking up dialogue for *Lethal Weapon 4*.

I saw . . . ING RANGE out of the corner of my eye and whipped my rented car into the parking lot of the Emerald Court Hotel and Resort, a motel-*cum*-driving range in Rancho Mirage, Calif. Barrels of sorry-looking balls were lined up in the sun. The tee line consisted of mats laid right on the desert floor. The target field had no grass at all, but dozens of painted yardage signs were set out in 10- and 20-yard increments, like airport landing lights. You couldn't hit a shot without hitting a yardage sign—unless your ball landed in one of the crumbling concrete target ponds, which had no water in them.

It was the pits. No, it was the pits *squared*—ring four of Dante's Inferno and Family Fun Center. A dozen old farts in shorts and sunglasses were hitting balls under the merciless midday sun.

I joined them.

POSTSCRIPT: *I never found my old swing, but I reached a point where the swing didn't matter any more, just the game. So now I'm a retired range rat. But I still feel the urge, when I pass some hardscrabble driving range, to turn the car around and blow an hour or two on the mats.*

Past Tense

Fiji's Vijay Singh has always been reluctant to discuss his
early years as a pro, and for good reason

*I read mysteries to pass the time on airplanes, and sometimes I stumble
onto a real-life mystery. This detective story began when I asked an editor,
"How come Vijay Singh, who hails from Fiji, doesn't represent his country
in the World Cup? Why do they send two guys who can't break 80?"*

The answer, I learned, was on the other side of the world.

They must be dancing in the streets in Fiji.
—TV VOICE AT THE PGA CHAMPIONSHIP, WHERE FIJI'S VIJAY SINGH
CAME WITHIN AN EYELASH OF BECOMING THE FIRST PLAYER OF COLOR
TO WIN A MAJOR CHAMPIONSHIP.

IT'S JUNE 1996, AND NO ONE IS DANCING. IN FACT, THE PRIME
minister of Fiji looks exasperated. Like many in his Polynesian
island republic, Sitiveni Rabuka appears torn between admira-
tion for Vijay Singh—"Fiji's only sports millionaire"—and peeve
that the expatriate golfer seems not to care what anybody in his
homeland thinks. "Don't pay too much attention to the negative
feelings we have," says the prime minister, looking fresh after 18
holes at Fiji's Denarau Island resort. "I know Vijay personally;
that's why I can't say more nice things about him."

Anyone looking for a hint of irony in the eyes of Fiji's strongman
will be disappointed. But Rabuka (pronounced ram-BOO-ka)—

described in that morning's *Fiji Sunday Post* as "the world's most dashing coup leader"—is a golfer himself, an almost daily visitor to the Fiji Golf Club in Suva, the capital. He is also honorary president of the Fiji Professional Golfers Association. So while he might bristle when he hears that Singh has set foot in Fiji only twice in 16 years and fume when he reads that Singh thinks Fiji is no place to raise his six-year-old son, he must consider also that the tall, handsome Singh hits a two-iron about as well as anybody on earth.

That's why Rabuka recently sent Singh a Fijian diplomatic passport—an honorary device allowing one to sweep through immigration channels and past border guards. Rabuka wonders, however, if he will get even a thank-you note from Singh, who now splits his time between homes in Ponte Vedra Beach, Fla., and London.

"He's flying the Fiji flag out of convenience, I think," says Rabuka, who seized power in a 1987 putsch and quickly raised himself from the rank of lieutenant colonel to brigadier general. "He's not very keen on coming back. He said Fiji was a nice place to visit, but he didn't want to live here."

The prime minister, barely sweating after shooting 76 on the two-year-old Denarau course, breathes deeply of the trade winds cooling the open-walled club bar. He stares out at the palm-lined fairways and green mountain backdrop as if intent on discerning what would keep a true Fijian away. Specifically, he wonders why Singh's last visit, in February, was only a whirl-wind stop for a farcical skins game organized by Vijay's older brother, Krishna. "I wish Vijay could come back and live here,"

Rabuka says, "so our people could see and learn from a man who approaches his sport with such professionalism."

That seems unlikely. Opportunities for professional golfers are few in the Republic of Fiji, which has a population of 750,000 and only 11 courses, most of them scruffy nine-hole tracks. But surely, an overseas visitor ventures, the prime minister is heartened by Singh's recent promise to fund a junior golf program in Fiji, a national system to identify and train the Vijay Singhs of the future. Rabuka snorts. "I'll believe it when I see it," he says. "I don't think he's sincere."

LET'S GO BACK TO May of this year. Vijay Singh, 33 and prosperous, is having an iced tea in the grill room of the Tournament Players Club in Ponte Vedra Beach. He would rather be out under the high sun hitting balls on the practice range—this is not surmise, he *says* so—but he has agreed to an interview. This is an act of extreme sacrifice for Singh, who is known for curt replies, or no replies, when reporters approach him at a tournament. But here he is, pleasant and well mannered. His voice is soothing, an amalgam of colonial English and tournament player *patois*. Then the interviewer asks about Fiji, and Singh's shoulders pull back reflexively.

"I've been asked a hundred times how I started golf," he says, obviously reluctant to rehash what is, in fact, a pretty good tale. But as Singh slaloms through the interview, answering some questions in depth and skirting others, one gets the picture of a man with plenty to say, but reasons not to say it. Is it because he anticipates the questions that must inevitably be asked? About Jakarta, 1985? The cheating allegation and his subsequent suspension from the Asian tour? His two years in exile as a club pro in the rain forests of Borneo? The Australian debts he took years to repay?

Singh couches his defensiveness in clichés. He says, "I like my clubs to do the talking." Well, of course. Singh is comfortable with what his clubs say about him. They say he has won tournaments in Australia, Asia, Africa, Europe and North America. They say that he has won three tournaments on the U.S. Tour in three years, that he was PGA Tour Rookie of the Year in 1993 and that he has climbed as high as 12th in the World Ranking and is currently 17th. His tie for fifth in last week's PGA Championship was not his first close call in a major. He finished in a tie for sixth in the 1995 British Open and was 11th at Royal Lytham and St. Annes this year. He was fourth in the 1993 PGA Championship and tied for seventh in this year's U.S. Open.

"I don't like to talk about my private life," he says, not making a clear distinction about what parts of his past he regards as private. "The media"—and here the exasperation shows on his face, the same look the prime minister displays when talking about Singh—"the media knows *everything* about a player."

If only it were so. Actually, Singh is golf's international man of mystery, a ball-bashing cipher with no deep friendships and an emotional life known only to his wife, Ardena, and son, Qass. Reporters in Europe and North America, far from being intrusive, have written off the Fijian as bad copy—a boring man, a loner. His tag as "the hardest worker on the PGA Tour" frames the picture, and his crankiness with the press discourages reframing. Most profiles of Singh make no mention of his suspension by the Asian tour when he was 22. Those writers who *do* cite the cheating allegation usually print without challenge Singh's assertion that he did not, in fact, alter his scorecard to make the cut in the 1985 Indonesian Open but simply took the fall for "the son of an Indonesian VIP" who he says made the change.

Hardly anyone inquires as to why Singh has never represented Fiji in the annual World Cup of Golf. Asked why he hasn't played for his home islands, Singh points to "some jealousy" among the selectors and says he was very hurt in 1993 when the Fiji PGA shunned him and chose two club pros who could barely break 80 at Lake Nona in Orlando. "It's hard to explain," he says. "Fiji is a poor country. There's a lot of envy."

Rabuka, on the other hand, insists Singh has never been available. According to the prime minister, all three golfing Singh brothers—Vijay, Krishna (who plays the Asian tour) and Mira (who this year opened a golf shop in Nadi, near the Singhs' hometown of Lautoka)—declined invitations to represent Fiji in the 1995 World Cup, in China.

To comprehend this apparent estrangement between golfer and archipelago, one must know more about Singh and more about Fiji. The most relevant fact is that Singh is not an indigenous Fijian, but a Fijian of Indian extraction, a descendant of the Hindus and Muslims from the subcontinent who came to work

Fiji's cane fields between 1879 and 1916. Vijay's father, Mohan Singh, was a refueler at the Nadi International Airport, a busy passenger and cargo hub on the west coast of Viti Levu, Fiji's largest and most populous island. (Nadi, which is pronounced NAN-di, used to be a necessary refueling stop for aircraft crossing the Pacific; thus the doggerel, "We stop in Nadi because it's handy.") Mohan Singh was also an accomplished golfer, a nine-time club champion at the seaside Nadi Airport Golf Club.

The story that Vijay has tired of telling—the Singh legend—has him learning the game from his father on the scenic, rain-tree-dominated hills of the 18-hole airport course. The young Vijay jumped the airport fence after school and raced across the huge runway to the course, where he practiced and played for hours, usually alone. From the shade of a large mango tree by the 14th fairway he hit hundreds of balls a day, stopping only to grab a mango off a branch or drink from a nearby tap. At low tide he hit balls on the flat, firm sand of the beach, a good place to learn the crisp contact needed to spin the ball off Fiji's water-grass fairways. At home the young Singh studied photographs of Sam Snead and watched films of Tom Weiskopf, whose swing tempo he copied. "My brothers would go to the hotels and bars," Singh recalls. "I would never do that, even when I was 15 or 16. Golf was what I did."

By the time he was 16, Singh was hitting his driver prodigious distances and winning island competitions. At 17 he was the Airport Club champion, Fiji amateur champion and owner of practically every other cup and medal the islands had to offer. "Vijay was cocky as all hell," says Michael Lenz, the secretary-treasurer of the Fiji Golf Association, who ran events in the late '70s in which Singh competed. "He used to sell the prizes before he even played the tournament. He was that sure of winning."

Tony Cooper, a former secretary-treasurer of the FGA who directs public relations for the Westpac Bank in Suva, remembers Vijay fondly—but with no illusions. "He was a bit of a villain in those days," Cooper says with a chuckle. "He was raw, never been out of Fiji."

Never, that is, until Cooper took the 17-year-old Singh and three other players to Pinehurst, N.C., for the 1980 World Amateur Team Championship. Vijay shot 84-80-80-81, and the Fijians did not fare especially well, finishing 123 strokes behind a U.S. team led by Hal Sutton, Bob Tway, Jim Holtgrieve and Jay Sigel. But the Fijians *did* beat Papua New Guinea for the first time, allowing them to claim the championship of the South Pacific. That had Cooper on cloud nine—until he got a bill from Pinehurst that showed Singh with $700 in charges for phone calls to Fiji. "There was no malice in it," Cooper hastens to say. "Vijay was a very young fellow, totally naive, always well mannered. But I had to break the news to his father, and his father had to pay the bill to get me off the hook."

The lesson that Singh took away from Pinehurst, however, was not one of fiscal responsibility. His poor play, measured against that of the Americans, convinced him that he needed stiffer competition than Fiji could offer. So he set out in 1982 to play professional golf in Australia: not the big tournaments but the mini-tour events and pro-ams in dusty outback towns like Kalgoorlie and Alice Springs. By his own account Singh was not ready when he hit Australia. That may explain why, to get by, he put the touch on various golf officials and stuck numerous pro shops with big phone bills. Cooper, visiting in New Zealand a couple of years later, met an officer of the Australian Golf Union whose eyes flashed when he heard the name Vijay Singh. "Well, every place he stayed he ran up these enormous bloody bills," the official fumed.

"Vijay was banned from playing the PGA tour in Australia," confirms Ray Graham, administrator of the South Pacific PGA. "He owed me money, and a lot of others, too. He was told he couldn't play here again until those debts were settled." It wasn't so much the money, says Graham, but the seeming lack of gratitude. "He didn't endear himself to people. Vijay wasn't a boy who sent you a card or anything afterward." Graham says that he and the others were finally repaid by Singh about four years ago.

Having been "given the flick" by Australia, Singh—now traveling with his wife-to-be, Ardena—moved on to the Asian tour. There, at 21, he won his first professional tournament, the 1984 Malaysian PGA Championship. But his progress was halted in the second round of the 1985 Indonesian Open in Jakarta, where he was in a threesome with Canadian pro Jim Rutledge and Ruswin Ali, an Indonesian amateur who was keeping Singh's score. The tournament director of the Indonesian Golf Association, Rudy Lisapaly, ruled that Singh improved his score by one stroke before signing his card and was therefore disqualified. Edmund Yong, the secretary general of what was then called the Southeast Asia Golf Federation, notified Singh that he was indefinitely suspended from the Asian tour.

In recent years Singh has described the incident as a "misunderstanding" and blamed Indonesian golf officials for punishing him unfairly. Ardena, who is far more outgoing and spontaneous than her husband, takes the same line, saying that Vijay repeatedly wrote letters to Yong pleading his innocence but got no indication when the suspension might be lifted. "Now that Vijay's somebody," Ardena says with a hint of a smile, "Mr. Yong comes up and says, 'Hello, how are you?' " She adds, "We are extremely courteous but very cold."

Yong suffered a serious illness and cannot comment, but an American pro who played the Asian tour at the time contradicts Singh's account. "I was there," says the player, who asked not to be identified. "It was *not* a misunderstanding. Vijay was accused and suspended for altering his own card. All of us who were around are very upset that Vijay denies this."

Graham says he always accepted the charge at face value, and not just because of his own experience with Singh. "That's quite typical on that tour," he says. "Players can't count." In Nadi, Brian Eastgate, the course superintendent at Denarau, describes the Asian golf culture as more tolerant of rules-stretching—like that of American baseball, for instance, where spitballs and corked bats are winked at. Says Eastgate, "Putting something over on your opponent is almost more important than the golf."

In any event, the suspension from the Asian tour stopped Singh in his tracks. Casting about for a way to survive, he took a series of club-pro jobs in Borneo—the tournament player's equivalent of Devil's Island. Curiously, when Vijay and Ardena talk of this period of exile, they describe it as the happiest time of their lives. At Keningau, where Vijay gave lessons to lumberjacks and to truck drivers from a Shell Oil drilling operation, civilization and its discontents were 2½ hours away on a dirt road. "You'd get up in the morning and hear the birds, the sounds of the jungle," Vijay recalls. "Nothing to worry about. You had a roof over your head and something to eat. And we had each other. I learned a lot about life."

At 500 Malaysian dollars a month—roughly $150 to $200 U.S.—Borneo could have been a *sentence* of life. But Singh took advantage of the steamy hours between nine and three, when only mad dogs and Englishmen wanted lessons, to refine his game. To maintain his competitive edge, he played high-stakes handicap matches with timber tycoons and Shell executives, games that prepared him for the pressures of major championships.

On one occasion Singh played the last hole with $10 in his pocket and $700 on the line. "It was a par-5 where you had to hit over water to an island fairway," he recalls. "Everything was riding on it, and I hit my drive OB. And the feeling I had when I stood over the next drive was the worst feeling I've ever had in the game. How would I pay if I lost? Would I lose my job? What would I tell my wife?" Despite the pressure, Singh found the fairway with his second ball and made eagle—a par, with the penalty—while his opponent dunked one in the water and made 7. "So I won the hole and a lot of money. Now, whenever I'm in contention in a tournament, I think about that." With a guilty smile, he adds, "I never told my wife, either."

The story of how Singh escaped from paradise is somewhat less dramatic but illustrative of his determination. Hoping to qualify for the 1987 British Open, Singh arrived early and played Luffness, his qualifying course in Scotland, every day for a month. When that didn't work out—he shot 75–70 and missed qualifying by eight strokes—he quit his job in Borneo and joined Africa's Safari tour, playing tournaments in smoky, chaotic outposts like Nigeria's Benin City, which he describes as "unbelievable, a Mad Max kind of place." His victory in the 1988 Nigerian Open catapulted him to the top of the Safari tour money list, and by the end of the year he had won a Swedish tour event and tied for second at the European tour qualifying school. He won the Volvo Open in 1989, his rookie year in Europe, then four years later earned $657,831 in the U.S. while becoming the rookie of the year.

"It's a great success story," says Steve Cook, a former Asian tour player who now runs the South American tour. "I hear very nice things about Vijay today." In the same vein Graham describes the post-Borneo Singh as "a greatly transformed man" and gives credit to Ardena and the career shapers at International Management Group who signed Singh to a management contract in 1989. "He's still a bit of a loner," says Graham, "but you can't blame him for that." Rabuka, who obviously has his differences with Singh, says he has "a lot of respect" for the golfer's work ethic and praises him for boosting Fijian tourism. "Vijay's a very easily misunderstood man because he's so quiet and reserved," the prime minister says. "People think he's antisocial, and he's not."

Singh is not much concerned about the bridges he left burning in the Antipodes. The Australian debts were eventually paid, Graham says, but letters of remorse were never written. In Southeast Asia, meanwhile, resentment flares every time Singh casts himself as the victim in the Jakarta episode. "I think he's been very stupid about that," says Cooper, his old World Amateur Team coach. "Wouldn't it be nice if Vijay just dropped a line and said, 'I've done some silly things, and I'd like to make it good'? To my knowledge, he's never cleaned the slate. He's always had a chip on his shoulder about it."

THERE IS, OF COURSE, a larger context. The former British Commonwealth country that Singh left when he was 19 no longer exists, thanks to Rabuka and his armed cabal. Since 1990 the Fijian parliament has been gerrymandered along racial lines, with ethnic Fijians guaranteed a majority. Fijians of Indian extraction cannot hold the offices of president (a figurehead post) or prime minister (a Rabuka sinecure). What's more, although Hinduism and Islam are accepted, the official religion is Christianity, with Sunday laws enforced for everyone except tourists. Predictably, some 40,000 professional and middle-class Indians have voted with their passports since the coup. Singh's mother, three brothers and one of his sisters now live in Australia. His father resides in New Zealand, and another sister lives in the U.K. Rabuka may be a congenial and approachable strongman, but he hews to a Fiji for Fijians course.

Singh, from a distance, has made comments on Fiji's progress—or lack of it—that can be taken as unpatriotic or merely provocative, depending on one's point of view. His beef with the media, he says, derives in part from the way his views are distorted by the time they reach the South Pacific. "I told *Golf Digest* I would not bring my son up in Fiji," he says, "because it's a different environment, there's no opportunity now. It came out, VIJAY DOESN'T HAVE ANY USE FOR FIJI." He grimaces. "You wonder if you should talk to the press anymore."

Fair or not, the gossip washing up on Viti Levu's beaches gives many Fijians the impression that Singh is a haughty millionaire. In June a fledgling Fijian golf magazine, *Top Shot*, reprinted a Jacksonville columnist's blistering critique of the media-dodging Singh—"a man with all the personality and pizzazz of a chicken potpie"—and left even his supporters at the Nadi Airport Golf Club shaking their heads. "Vijay's a naughty boy," says family friend Paras Naidu. "He shouldn't ignore the media. He's not *that* good."

Every Singh misstep provides ammunition for those members of the Fiji PGA who don't want him representing them in the World Cup. And he does have enemies among the FPGA's 15 or so club pros. "The professional setup in Fiji is a joke," former

Denarau pro Ian Roberts told *Top Shot* recently after taking a club job in Indonesia. "Everyone is in it for themselves." Roberts learned this the hard way in March, when he won the Fiji Bitter Open Pro-Am in a playoff with FPGA member Dharam Prakash —only to be told afterwards that he could not have the winner's check because he was no longer a member himself. "The fact that Ian organized the tournament and secured the sponsorship and prize money," *Top Shot* commented dryly, "probably added salt to the wound."

The prime minister insists that he, personally, wants Singh on the World Cup team, but others see racism and parochialism in the FPGA's selections. "Three years ago it was sheer, pigheaded bigotry," says the FGA's Lenz. "The guy who was the head said, 'We don't want that Indian bastard representing us. We want Fijians.' When Vijay got word of this, I think he said, 'Why bother?' "

It's clearly not just a case of Singh's being difficult. The FGA put up Singh's name twice for Fiji's sportsman of the year, and each time the selection committee rejected his nomination, ostensibly because Singh was not a member of a local golf club. Two years ago Mohammed Aziz, president of the FGA and of Indian descent, offered to make Singh a lifetime member of the Nadi Airport Golf Club, but the sportsman of the year selectors still rejected the nomination. "And Vijay," Lenz notes with dismay, "is the only sportsman who's ever done anything for Fiji."

And so the controversy devolves into farce. In June 1995, Krishna Singh announced that his brother would return to Fiji for only the second time in 16 years to play in a half-million-dollar skins game sanctioned by Rabuka and televised by Rupert Murdoch's Star TV. By January the purse had shrunk to $100,000 and television was no longer mentioned. In February, two days before the match, the *Fiji Times* ran a front-page photo of Vijay with his mother—VIJAY SINGH BACK HOME—and reported that Vijay, Krishna, former PGA champion Wayne Grady and a local player would compete for $67,000.

By Friday—the day the prime minister hung a Commemorative 25th Independence Medal around Vijay's neck at a $35-a-plate dinner—the purse had puckered to $50,000, and the local pros were grumbling that Krishna had made them pay an entrance fee to compete for the local pro slot and then asked them for an additional $10 to watch the skins game. (All but one of the unsuccessful pros boycotted Denarau on Saturday.) The actual prize money turned out to be a mere $27,000, $22,000 of which was won by Vijay.

To make matters worse, an incident on the 14th hole had spectators clucking. With $14,000 on the line, Krishna had a putt for birdie from the fringe—that is, until Grady saw him nudge the ball with his foot. Embarrassed, Grady pointed out the infraction, at which point Krishna snatched up his ball and stalked off to the next tee.

Four months later, as he cooled off in the Denarau lounge, the prime minister was still peeved. "I don't believe a professional could have that kind of 'accident,' " Rabuka said, his voice heavy with sarcasm. And surely it didn't help that Krishna had reneged on his promise to pay the FPGA $1,500 and that he had skipped the country without paying his $3,000 phone and fax bill at the Sheraton Fiji Resort. From Rabuka's hangdog expression, one got the idea that being a dictator is no picnic these days.

EXPATRIATES TEND not to be nostalgic; for them, the ties of family and village provide no more comfort than a cage. So those in Fiji who wonder why Singh seems to have forgotten them should consider that his best friend, when he was a boy, was a mango tree. Even now he can conjure up only two names when asked which Tour players know him well—Jim Thorpe and Jesper Parnevik. ("He's very forthright, very honest," says Parnevik. "He says things that other people think but will never say.") It would be a stretch to say that Singh doesn't care where he lives, but his sense of place is circumscribed by his practice needs: Paradise is a 350-yard-long range with a private tee at the far end, away from the chatterboxes and glad-handers. ("It's mindless," 1995 PGA champ Steve Elkington says of Singh's practice sessions. "He just hits his driver all day.") For solace and support Singh has only Ardena, and she admits she sometimes wonders "when he's going to sow that wild oat. It isn't possible for a man to be satisfied with only two things"—i.e., a wife and golf.

"Golf has been a gift to me," Singh said at Ponte Vedra Beach, where the muggy summer afternoons must remind him of Nadi. "Without golf, my loneliness would not have allowed me to succeed." And Viti Levu, he acknowledged, provided the tranquility that made his development possible. "It's a beautiful island. It's my home."

But not really, not anymore. Not with his family gone and ethnic prejudice the law of the land. Fiji, as Singh sees it, is a palm-strewn hideaway where the clock runs 120 minutes to the hour and cows stand in the roads. "The water's blue," he says, "and you spend a week there."

Or less than a week, if you're Vijay Singh—a man who seems to have become an island unto himself.

POSTSCRIPT: *When Singh won the 2004 Masters, a well-known Tour pro said, "Once a cheater, always a cheater." I immediately wrote a column defending Vijay, quoting a PGA Tour rules official who said that Singh's on-course behavior was beyond reproach and that he was "a perfect gentleman." But that column did nothing to salvage my relationship with Singh, who still blames me for digging up his past. He hasn't talked to me since this story appeared.*

⸎

Magic and Magoo

From cosmic to comic, the author discovered common ground
between the Shivas Irons Society and the Goat Hills Gang

*I was a noncombatant in the turf war between the two leading schools of
golf nuts. Then I got simultaneous invitations to the Shivas Irons Games
of the Links, played on California's breathtaking Monterey Peninsula, and
the Dan Jenkins Goat Hills Revival, played on the equally breathtaking
strip-mall verges of Fort Worth, Texas. Dazzled by the prospect of five
company-paid rounds of golf with two of the game's leading literary lights,
I accepted both invitations.*

---

*There are people who actually scoff at the idea of golf as a trans-
formational experience.* —Steve Cohen

*I cling to this theory that if Michael Jackson had ever taken up golf,
he would never have felt the need to have lunch with orangutans,
or even with Elizabeth Taylor.* —Dan Jenkins

"HAVE YOU EVER BEEN ON A SNIPE HUNT?" THE SKEPTICAL
voice, a man's, came from somewhere ahead in the darkness.

Our guide had disappeared into the trees with his flashlight, leaving us to negotiate the root-strewn trail by following
a ghostly chain of bobbing, lime-green, luminescent golf balls.
My own ball, glowing in my left hand like a firefly, served as a

pale beacon for the truth seekers behind me. I say *truth seekers* to distance us from the merely inebriated, a couple of whom were giggling and thrashing through the Del Monte Forest, using their five-irons to ward off aggressive trees.

Ultimately, our column straggled out of the woods onto a moonlit sward. A dozen players were already collected there, murmuring among themselves and nudging the glowing balls along the ground with their clubs. A parapet of Pacific Ocean fog hovered above the trees and below the moon, casting us as witches and warlocks. A woman from the adjacent coven, a Southerner by accent, asked, "What hole is this?"

No one knew.

"I can't see the club head," a man complained good-naturedly. "I can't see my hands. To tell the truth, I can't see why I'm here."

He was joking. We all knew why we were there: to shape space, to open windows on the paranormal, to invite contact with unseen dimensions—and, most important, to get to the distant flagstick, glowing in the dark, in fewer strokes than our mangy, scum-sucking, dog-assed opponents.

Sorry about that last part. Since my midnight round of golf at Spyglass Hill, back in August, I have played daytime golf with certain Texans—boisterous men with booming voices and large, American-made cars. These men speak a language spiced with jalapeno and redolent of tobacco; they pay their gambling debts with soggy currency.

My hat's a little tight these days because I am the only person to have played this year in the two preeminent mind-expanding events in golf: the Shivas Irons Games of the Links—a three-day, 54-hole spiritual ramble over the courses of California's Monterey Peninsula—and the Dan Jenkins Partnership, an 18-hole event otherwise known as the Goat Hills Glory Game Reprise and this year as the Fourth Annual Meatloaf Sandwich Invitational.

To be invited to both these tournaments is extraordinary. The two-year-old Shivas Irons Society is a loose confederation of souls who suspect that golf is a window to metaphysical realms and paranormal experience—"a mystery school for Republicans," in the words of writer and metaphysician Michael Murphy. The Dan Jenkins Partnership, by way of contrast, is a bunch of guys who get their kicks by driving golf carts through flower beds and betting which drop of sweat will outrace another down the exposed crack of a carpenter's butt. "Thieves, gamblers and whoremongers" is Jenkins's description of his invitees, who invade Fort Worth for one day each October to play a raucous two-man scramble over the notorious Z Boaz Golf Course.

The only obvious link between the two sensibilities is that each grew out of a work of literature—Murphy's 1972 novel *Golf in the Kingdom* and Jenkins's comic story *The Glory Game at Goat Hills*, first published in Sports Illustrated in '65. The two works command an international following of high- and low-handicap literary cultists who are quick to quote passages from memory and eager to swap swing tips and bar tabs with the respective authors.

There are differences in tone. My invitation to play in the Games of the Links was printed in two colors on elegant card stock, listed an entry fee of $2,995 for "player and guest, double occupancy" and was signed "warmest regards" by society founder and president Steve Cohen. The steep tariff went for posh accommodations, meals, entertainment and greens fees, and it included a $600 tax-deductible contribution to the nonprofit society, which also sponsors activities around the country "to further the pleasures [of golf] and to explore its many mysteries."

My Jenkins invite, handed to me by his ownself in the press room of the PGA Championship at Southern Hills in Tulsa, was a flyer headlined MEMO TO SEMI-LIGHTWEIGHT DOGGED VICTIM DEAD SOLID DUCK HOOKERS. "It'll cost you $125 to play," the notice said bluntly. But it would be worth it, because "Z Boaz, carrying on the great Goat Hills tradition, has been honored again, named recently as one of America's Worst Twenty golf courses. . . . Hurry! First 120 get to play." Who could refuse?

The first morning at the Shivas Games belonged to Fred Shoemaker. It was bleak dawn when he led some 30 of us, bundled in windbreakers and heavy sweaters, into the fog and dew blanketing the treeless Links at Spanish Bay. He steered us around sand dunes and toward the gray ocean, stopping in a fairway now and then to hit some balls and exclaim over the sea breeze about how Scottish the scene looked.

The purpose of the walk, he said, was to prepare us mentally for what might be an extraordinary day of golf. "One thing I've noticed when a person approaches the 1st tee," he began, "is that they're uncommitted to anything except looking good and not being embarrassed. It surrounds them the way air surrounds the bird and shapes the flight."

A handsome, dark-haired teaching pro of 42, Shoemaker was preternaturally calm and spoke with the soothing mellifluousness of a suicide counselor. When a point needed illustrating, he dropped a ball onto the dewy fescue and heedlessly swatted a perfect draw down the fairway. With the same effortless swing, he changed shot shapes and trajectories, sent the ball soaring or running like a rabbit.

Clearly, he was meant to impress us the way the fictional pro from Burningbush, Shivas Irons, for whom the society is named, had impressed the narrator in *Golf in the Kingdom*. We looked at one another—each of us wearing a cap with the society logo, a flagstick planted in a green formed by the symbol for infinity—and pondered whether the game could be mastered from the mind out instead of from the body in, or whether mastery was even relevant. Golf is a game, Shoemaker told us, "the purpose of which is to teach you something that's not in the game."

Later, as we played our first 18 over the Spanish Bay course, I had occasion to reflect on what that purpose might be— particularly when I stared at my ball, perched on a dune behind an unpainted lath fence labeled ENVIRONMENTALLY SENSITIVE—KEEP OUT. The image of the ball, barely out of arm's reach but unrecoverable, corresponded to the average golfer's conviction that good golf is tantalizingly close, if only some swing defect can be corrected. My playing partners—a bearded, small-town Michigan newspaper reporter; an African-

American baseball publicist; a widow who had retired to the Monterey Peninsula to play golf—seemed open to possibilities, but similarly and cheerfully resigned to golf as most of us know it, peppered with frustration and poor execution.

The most magical aspect of the round was the scoring. We had been encouraged to divide the 18 holes into thirds, with six holes being played for score, six for "the centered swing," and six dedicated to "true gravity," an exalted state described in *Golf in the Kingdom*. Our subjective scores could be alphanumeric, hieroglyphic or simply cryptic. I put down the number of good shots I made on each hole, filling my scorecard with 1s and 2s (and a couple of zeros). One scorecard that I saw had the infinity symbol inserted in three boxes. Another showed a treble clef for the 2nd hole, where a harpist and violinist had plucked and bowed by the green.

Nothing out of the ordinary occurred until the 6th tee, where we blundered into the 19th century. Actually, we were summoned down the fairway by a wildly gesticulating Scotsman in a tweed jacket and knickers, who issued us wooden baffing spoons and replica feathery balls and ordered us to tee off from the fairway, a mere 140 yards from the green. "Get th' whyte thingy off yer hand!" he sputtered at Jim, the newspaperman, who obediently shed his glove. The Scotsman then showed him how to elevate the lopsided feathery on a pinch of sand.

The antique clubs called for a flat, round-the-body swing, and while the others advanced their balls about as far as they could spit, I whacked a knuckleball that flew a good 100 yards.

("My middle name is Stuart," I explained, counting on everyone to know the role that Mary, Queen of Scots, had played in the development of the game.) A pitch-and-run and a long putt later, I had 2½ feet left for a 4. "A 6 is the best of the day," growled a burly, black-bearded galleryite in boots, kilt and embroidered vest. So advised, I made a smooth stroke and watched my feathery veer right and then sharply left before missing the cup by a good foot. "The Stuart curse!" I wailed, dropping the club.

"Aye, laddie," came a sarcastic voice. "Blame yer betters fer yer fawts at gowf!"

Amazingly, no one had spotted me as metaphysically impaired. If pressed, I would have had to confess that I had never witnessed anything remotely paranormal, on or off a golf course. In fact, when windows to the occult seemed to be opening, I quickly slammed them shut. As for golf philosophy, I halfway subscribed to the view of Kenny Lee Puckett, the narrator of Jenkins's novel *Dead Solid Perfect*, who said, "Golf will keep you outdoors and maybe even put you next to rich people."

This shallowness had never seemed to handicap me on the golf beat, but when we filed into the Troon Room at the Inn at Spanish Bay that afternoon, I expected—what? A séance? A fortune reading? Forty chairs were arranged in an oval; at one end was a drawing pad on an easel. "Is this your first Amway meeting?" I asked the woman on my right. She rewarded me with a nervous laugh.

Cohen, a glowing, bearded man of substantial girth and great warmth, quickly put us at ease. A gestalt therapist who quit his

East Coast schoolteaching job in 1978, Cohen moved with his wife and son to Carmel, Calif., where he conducts golf mystery workshops for the Esalen Institute. He spoke to us briefly about how *Golf in the Kingdom* had seized the imagination of so many readers—over 100,000 copies sold in '93 alone—and how the Shivas Irons Society had been formed to explore the hidden dimensions of the game. "That's what these sessions are about," he said, beaming with anticipation. "To me, it's as important as the golf."

Cohen then turned the meeting over to Murphy—world traveler, metaphysician and cofounder of Esalen, an institute in nearby Big Sur dedicated to "transformational practice" and personal growth. Looking younger than his 63 years, the author greeted us with a wry smile and launched into an enthusiastic discourse about "the magic, the mysticism, the occult dimensions" of golf.

"I happen to have written or channeled this book," Murphy said, "and for 22 years not a week goes by without my getting a letter about the mysterious dimensions of the game. It's convinced me that ordinary life is shot through with 'the Zohar.' In Jewish mysticism, this is the tradition that if you get something right, the Zohar, the splendor of God, manifests. The philosophers talk about it, the principles of alignment, attunement, at-oneness, atonement—*something*—but it happens. It can happen around the dinner table; it can happen in the wedding bed, making love; and apparently it really can happen a lot on the golf course."

What did he mean by *it*? Murphy responded by going to the

easel and drawing a graph with one axis labeled Frequency of Report and the other, Degree of Strangeness.

"I've found it useful to talk about something called the Strangeness Curve," he said, drawing a classic bell curve, low at either end and humped up in the middle. If a phenomenon was very strange, he said while pointing to one of the low points on his curve, such as God's voice on the telephone or a car passing through a pedestrian without causing harm, one tended not to report it, fearing ridicule. But he had received hundreds of letters from golfers reporting strange phenomena—streamers of light, space warps, leprechauns, levitation, psychokinesis.

Murphy had recently discussed such phenomena with Clint Eastwood, who owns the film rights to his novel. One category of experience, he had told Eastwood, was the ability to sculpt or shape space. ("Nicklaus says he sees where he wants the ball to land, then he'll play it backwards like a movie.") Another involved the transparency of matter. ("In Tibetan yoga there is a practice where you visualize your ability to walk through walls.") Eastwood had been intrigued—mostly for the special-effects potential—but he had one basic question for Murphy: "What's the book really about? What's the central parable?"

Murphy told Eastwood, "It's that there's a guy named Murphy who thinks you have to go to India to an ashram to find enlightenment. And on his way he goes to a golf course in Scotland, and it's all presented to him—what he's looking for—on the golf course. But the poor schmuck thinks that he has to go to India. And so he leaves."

Murphy shook his head. "I told Clint I intended the book to be a parable of missing what's right under your nose. And Clint nodded and said, 'That's kind of what I thought it was about.' "

I played golf with Murphy the next morning at the Pebble Beach Golf Links, as magical a golfing ground as exists in the world. The thought struck me that the Shivas Irons Society stacked the deck in favor of the sublime by playing at Pebble instead of, say, Z Boaz, where the most notable sightings of recent years were of underdressed damsels sunning on the back porch of New Orleans Nights, a topless joint just off the 4th fairway. But I was glad for the opportunity to share the beauty of Pebble with a man who, if he couldn't shape space, could certainly shape prose.

Ours was a 6:45 tee time, and Murphy was waiting by the pro shop when I arrived. He was dressed in cotton dockers, jogging shoes, a windbreaker and his Shivas Irons cap. He introduced me to the rest of our foursome: Steve Wille, vice president of marketing for the Pebble Beach Company, and Andy Nusbaum, the managing director of the New York Times/Sports Leisure Magazines and a member of the Shivas Irons board. "Maybe we'll levitate," Murphy told a photographer.

We all walked and Murphy had a caddie, so there were opportunities during the round to talk. I found Murphy's conversation, like his game, to be mainstream and accomplished; there were no exhortations for seagulls to talk or sand to rise out of sand traps. The biggest surprise, for me, was that Murphy plays golf only once or twice a year. "It's such a sacred experience, it's all I dare," he joked. "It would destroy my nervous system, otherwise."

The Murphy golf résumé consumed no more than a couple of minutes waiting time on the 4th tee. He had taken up the game at age 14, he said, and by his senior year at Salinas High School played to a four handicap. One notable opponent was Palo Alto's Grant Spaeth, who would go on to become president of the United States Golf Association; another was U.S. Open champion-to-be Ken Venturi, who beat Murphy in the finals of the loser's bracket of the Northern California Juniors Championship. Murphy played at Stanford too, "but when I got hooked up in all this Eastern philosophy, I gave the game up." Years later, "going on 40," he wrote *Golf in the Kingdom* and took up the game again. But then he discovered running (and, presumably, "runner's high"). At age 53, he ran a 4:35 1,500-meter, good for third place at the National Seniors meet.

The golfer in Murphy was rusty—he chunked a couple at Pebble—but his good hits displayed the desired flight, a tight little draw. "I don't keep a conventional score any more," he said. "I just try to see how many pars and birdies I can make. I hit enough good shots that the magic is there for me."

Murphy's comment was a reminder that we were supposed to be looking for magic. I started searching in earnest as we came out of the trees and climbed the magnificent rise of the 6th fairway, which took us simultaneously toward roiling clouds and land's end. From the cliff's edge, we gazed down on boats rocking gently in seaweed-dappled Stillwater Cove and out at the great curve of rocky shore stretching to the Lodge and the forest beyond.

At the par-3 7th the society had laid on the atmosphere. A fiddler and flutist occupied a corner of the tee, playing the allegro section of Thomas Morley's *When Lo' by Break of Morning*. The tweed-coated Scot from the previous day had just arrived when Nusbaum, our best player, launched a soft, high wedge from the precipice. The ball rose against the gray sky, fell like an artist's brush stroke, hit the green a few feet short of the flagstick and rolled into the hole.

We levitated.

And yelled. The musicians looked up from their music, baffled. Up and down the shoreline, heads turned toward our promontory. "Laddie!" the bogus Scotsman shouted, rushing up to embrace Nusbaum. Murphy was almost dumbstruck. "I've never seen one!" he blurted. "I've never seen one!"

Nusbaum's ace gave our foursome scores of 1, 2, 3 and 4 on the hole—a scale. "Numerology is the bargain basement of the sciences, a notch below astrology," Murphy said at that afternoon's seminar. "Nevertheless, there is this peculiar play of numbers that Jung called 'synchronicity.' "

A comical gleam lit his eyes when he said, "Nevertheless. . . ." When I mentioned it to him later, Murphy said, "That's it, that's the way I am. Obviously, a lot of this stuff is just silly, but . . . *but*!" He laughed at the emphasis. "But there's this realm of the mystical that intervenes in our lives, and I've gotten so many reports from sober people—lawyers, doctors, judges, *Republicans* . . . people to be trusted. I would have to be a complete ostrich with my head in the sand to deny these things."

Three weeks later I got my own lesson in denial. Or maybe it was an experiment in sensory overload. All I know is, I was hunched over my ball on the 9th tee at Z Boaz, trying to maintain my balance in gale-force wind and torrential rain. My blown-out umbrella lay twisted in a puddle behind me; my sodden clothes clung like plaster. A rivulet of rainwater ran off the bill of my cap.

"Tempo," one of the semidrowned rats in our sixsome called out facetiously.

Closing my left eye to shut out the stinging rain, I squeezed excess water from the grip of my driver, drew the club back with a couple of discreet jerks and blasted a powerful pull hook into the tempest. So miraculous was this drive, given the conditions, that I could have led a metaphysical seminar on the spot. But of course, they don't conduct postround seminars at Z Boaz; they change shoes in the parking lot and drive somewhere for a beer.

The Dan Jenkins Partnership is a fund-raiser, the profits going to sportswriter scholarships at the author's alma mater, Texas Christian. What sets it apart from other charity scrambles is the Goat Hills imprimatur. Jenkins's story recounts the exploits of a gang of grown men and teenagers who played sprawling, low-stakes golf 40 to 50 years ago on the rock-strewn fairways of the old Worth Hills Golf Course. Many of the characters from the story—Matty, Magoo, Moron Tom, Foot the Free, Grease Repellent—return for the scramble and one of the pleasures, for the stranger, is to connect a youthful nickname to a weathered face. Matty, who in the story "had a crewcut and wore glasses" and played "tunes on his upper front teeth with his fingernails," is now Dr. Donald Matheson, former chief of staff at Fort Worth's All Saints Episcopal Hospital. Magoo, the threadbare caddie who used to join Jenkins in reckless trespass upon the fairways of exclusive Colonial Country Club, is now Vance Minter, retired industrialist and former president of Colonial.

Storytelling dominates the agenda when Jenkins and his pals get together. "They used to have this grass median on Camp Bowie Boulevard," Magoo said, "and one day Walter Rainwater and Don Mack and Johnny Gibson—who was Grease Repellent—and I were carrying our bags back from Z Boaz. There must have been 20,000 cars on both sides of the street. I hadn't hit a fairway all day, and that median's only about 10 yards across, but I teed up and hit one as hard as I could. And it landed right in the middle of the median, on the grass." He laughed. "If it hadn't landed on the grass, I'd still be in jail."

The thin line between respectability and outlawry was a recurring theme in these tales. Whether they were the genesis of Jenkins's novels about well-meaning rogues and adulterers, I could only guess; what was clear was the regard in which Jenkins himself was held. "He was my idol then, and he's my idol now," said Magoo. "I've never seen him in a group where he was not the center of attention. He has that magnetism."

Affection was tempered with concern. Three weeks earlier the 64-year-old Jenkins had undergone triple-bypass heart surgery at a hospital in Jacksonville. (A quadruple bypass had been scheduled, prompting Jenkins's pal Dave Marr to quip that the writer had "birdied the bypass.") That he was in Fort

Worth to host the scramble surprised many; that he looked ruddy and fit was a bonus. The evening before the scramble, Jenkins's familiar deadpan countenance greeted revelers at Juanita's, the downtown Fort Worth restaurant co-owned by his wife, June. The next day he was at Z Boaz to critique the meatloaf sandwiches and pass out trophies to the sandbaggers. He assured us he would be playing golf again in a matter of days, but he did not minimize the operation. "They try to calm you by saying the doctor does this procedure as routinely as he makes two-foot putts. And I'm thinking, Yeah, great, except this particular doctor is a dermatologist with a 28 handicap."

My scramble partner at Z Boaz was Jerry Danford, a retired television executive. Also in our sixsome were former PGA Tour player Lindy Miller and his father, Gene; *Dallas Morning News* golf writer Jeff Rude; and occasional Tour player J.C. Anderson. Anderson proved his Goat Hills mettle during the round by performing trick shots, one of which involved popping a ball out of his mouth and driving it before it hit the ground. I showed I belonged by reaching the par-5 18th with a topped drive and a smoldering four-wood and then barely saving par with three uncommitted putts.

No one promised magic. On our very first hole, the 11th, someone asked, "Is this a shotgun start?" And Anderson, looking out at the strand of transmission shops, karate schools and fast-food joints that surrounds Z Boaz, said, "I don't think you want to fire a gun in this neighborhood." Four hours later, the wind freshened and all the water sucked up from the Gulf of Mexico over a five-day period fell on Z Boaz in one hour. The Firth of

Camp Bowie, a murky pond by the 2nd green, rose dangerously.

Trying to make sense of the experience afterward, I asked several of the Goat Hills guys if they were familiar with Murphy and his novel. Most were not. "I haven't read *Golf in the Kingdom*," Jerre Todd replied, "and I can assure you that Hippie and Rat haven't read it, either." (Hippie and Rat—a shirtless longhair and his geezer pal—are two latter-day Goat Hills types who play at Z Boaz. Rat came up to the golf shop counter at lunchtime, peeled the top off his meatloaf sandwich, and whined, "I got to have another sandwich. That god-damned Hippie took two bites out of mine, and I ain't gonna eat after that contaminated slime.") But Matty—Dr. Matheson—had read it and thought it "a marvelous, marvelous story." He said, "I don't remember the exact quotation, but Murphy has this thing about 'the green of the grass, the blue of the sky, the flight of the ball.' I had occasion to read *War and Peace* not too long ago, and when Nicholas was shot on the battlefield, he woke in a daze and made some of those same allusions—the blue of the sky, and so on. I wondered if Michael Murphy was inspired by that."

I thought Matty had said, "Nicklaus was shot on the battlefield," but we quickly got that straightened out. And it was interesting to find a connection between Goat Hills and Shivas Irons. I had already noticed parallels in the lives of Murphy and Jenkins. Both were acclaimed writers in their sixties; both had been accomplished players as youngsters—Jenkins was a scratch amateur in his TCU days—and both had quit the game in their twenties. ("I started writing books," Jenkins told me, "and was drunk half the time, living in Manhattan, and it was a pain in the ass to rent a car and drive out to Winged Foot. One day I woke up and couldn't break 90. So I quit.") Both had returned to the game in mid-life.

They even shared the same living icon: Ben Hogan. Murphy had stopped during our round at Pebble to point out the old practice area near Stillwater Cove. "Hogan used to practice here by the tennis courts," he said, "and pros would sit for two hours, watching. He had that presence. I watched him in the '65 U.S. Open, and about 10,000 people lined the fairway. And the silence of those galleries was just tremendous." Earlier, Murphy had said, "People who have a big presence are shaping space just by walking around. They say Buddha had an aura a mile wide."

Hogan, for what it's worth, is the Navajo name for a hut or dwelling, which is traditionally built with its entrance facing east.

IT'S ALL ONE event to me now: the Shivas Goats Games of the Meatloaf. If it's possible to keep a foot in both camps, I plan to do so. I'll return to Fort Worth next year for Glory Game V, and if they drop the tuition in California by about $3,000, I'll play there again, as well. I have even suggested that the two organizations set up an exchange program. A foursome of Magoo, Grease Repellent, Murphy and Shoemaker could test the Strangeness Curve and inspire someone to write a new book.

The words, after all, are what matter. No one in Fort Worth got arrested; no one in Monterey reported a paranormal event. The golfers were there to wrap themselves in a beloved piece of literature and to meet the author, nothing more.

On our last night at Spanish Bay we were bused into the Del Monte Forest, where we ate, drank and sang golfing songs around portable heaters. On a makeshift stage, actors performed the pivotal McNaughton Dinner scene from *Golf in the Kingdom*. "Fascination is the true and proper mother of discipline," a flesh and blood Shivas Irons told us. "And gowf is a place to practice fascination."

Later, watching luminescent golf balls streak like shooting stars up and down the moonswept fairways of Spyglass Hill, I felt 15 years old again. In that wind, I was open to suggestion, be it from the enigmatic Irons ("Let the nothingness into your shots") or the unenigmatic Magoo ("Golf was it. Golf was life. You always went back to golf"). We played on, the voices in the dark and I—trespassers who might one day preside.

All we needed were nicknames.

POSTSCRIPT: *Steve Cohen and his mind-expanding pals are still going strong, and they now publish an award-winning periodical, the* Journal of the Shivas Irons Society. *The Goat Hills gang, on the other hand, has gotten out of the charity scramble game. "We all got old and cranky,"* Jenkins tells me. *"Even Hippie and Rat won't play with us any more." After the story came out, I joined the Shivas Irons Society—$50 a year—but I haven't found the time or the scratch for a follow-up golf retreat. I did attend another half-dozen or so of the Goat Hills romps, and I singled out Z Boaz in my hard-to-find best seller,* America's Worst Golf Courses. *Jerre Todd was so proud that he had* HONORED AS ONE OF AMERICA'S WORST *printed on the tournament invitations.*

Happy Warrior

Back on the job after a whirlwind of celebration, Phil Mickelson savored the delights of being Masters champion

No one has ever weighed the proverbial monkey on the back of the poor sap who carries the label "Best Player Without a Win in a Major." I'd say that unloved simian must top the scales at 100 pounds or more, based upon the lighter-than-air demeanor of Phil Mickelson after his first Masters win.

———————

THERE IS GOLF, AND THEN THERE IS TOURNAMENT GOLF, AS Bobby Jones used to say. But there is also celebratory golf, and that's what Phil Mickelson played last week at the HP Classic of New Orleans. *Les bon temps* began to *rouler* on the very first tee at 7:40 a.m. on April 28, when the pro-am starter announced, "Ladies and gentlemen, the 2004 Masters champion. . . ."

"Hey!" interrupted a beaming Mickelson. "Will you say that again?"

What followed was 4½ hours of Mardi Gras for the pasture-pool set. The 2004 Masters champion joked with fans, sampled bayou cuisine and schmoozed with his pro-am partners. ("Mike, how long have you been involved with Hewlett-Packard?") He signed autographs, posed for pictures, handed out golf balls to children and, finally, in a nice bit of stagecraft, thrilled spectators at the 17th hole by making a hole in one.

Mickelson's rollicking round had tournament officials nervously thumbing through the rule book, but they could find no regulation against having fun on a golf course. In fact a little-known subsection of USGA Rule 25-b (Behavior and Sportsmanship) specifically grants "any tournament professional of 12 or more years' experience with at least 22 PGA Tour victories not otherwise deemed major championships the right to celebrate a first victory in one of those four major championships with a period of high spirits and frivolity, not to exceed three weeks." The rule clearly applied to Mickelson, who was making his first appearance in competition since the evening of April 11, when he birdied five of the last seven holes at Augusta National to nip Ernie Els, then the world's second-ranked player, by a stroke.

Do they rank smiles? Mickelson's had spread across his face the instant he completed that preposterous, froglike victory leap on the 18th green at Augusta. It was still on display in New Orleans, even though he had to be getting tired of people asking him if he slept in the garish green sport coat he got for winning the Masters.

Some would call it a practiced smile, but there's nothing wrong with that. Unlike the fantasies of most Tour players, Mickelson's childhood dream did not end with his making a putt to win the Masters or the U.S. Open. His dream had him going on to be a public man, a warm and gracious champion like Bobby Jones, Byron Nelson or Arnold Palmer. His Masters victory was special, Mickelson said last week, because "I'll always be the 2004 Masters champion, and I'll be able to be part of that event for the rest of my life."

So yeah, Philly Mick showed more teeth at Wednesday's pro-am than the Crescent City had seen since Satchmo left town, and he pressed more flesh than a working girl on Bourbon Street. (MICKELSON COMES IN ON HIGH NOTE, punned a headline writer for *The Times-Picayune*, playing off the coincidence that the HP Classic shares its week with New Orleans Jazzfest.) And never did Mickelson drift into unscripted reverie or slip out of character. On the 14th tee, where there was a short wait, he pulled up a camp chair and settled into it with a sigh of contentment meant to be heard by the gallery. His caddie, Jim (Bones) MacKay, sat on a tee marker.

"Who won here last year, Bones?" Mickelson wondered.

"Steve Flesch."

Mickelson nodded. "K.J. Choi won here, too, didn't he?"

"Year before last," volunteered a spectator.

Looking to his left, Mickelson grinned at a television cameraman creeping in for a close-up. "Pretty exciting, eh?" he declared. "Guy sitting in a chair?"

A curious observation, that—considering that's how Mickelson had spent much of his time since the Masters. Sitting in a chair next to David Letterman. Sitting in a chair next to Jay Leno. Sitting in a chair next to Craig Kilborn . . . Bob Costas . . . Dan Patrick. The 2004 Masters champion also did some stand-ups, most notably at the New York Stock Exchange, where he rang the bell to open the markets on April 16. "I was very flattered," he said, "which is why I did all those things. How often do you get those opportunities?"

Week 2 of the Masters fallout saw Mickelson pulling back a

bit. He flew with his wife, Amy, and their three kids to Phoenix to visit old friends. While there, he spent a day with swing coach Rick Smith on the practice range at Scottsdale's Whisper Rock Golf Club. Neither Mickelson nor Smith would discuss their technical work with outsiders—"It's our secret," Smith joked—but the coach said he had never seen his student more confident or upbeat about his game. "Phil's really enjoying this, and nobody deserves it more."

When asked in New Orleans if winning the Masters had taken a load off his shoulders—the weight of that ponderous tag, Best Player Never to Have Won a Major—Mickelson insisted that he didn't feel any different, either as a player or a person. "I don't think anything changed over four or five days, other than my gaining the experience of a lifetime," he said. He didn't deny that 2003, with its succession of scares and insults, had depressed his spirits. Early last year, after all, he had nearly lost Amy and son Evan during a delivery gone wrong. That was followed by the worst season of his pro career: no victories and a plummet to No. 38 on the money list after three straight years at No. 2. The year bottomed out in November at the Presidents Cup in South Africa, where the usually reliable team player failed to win a single point in five matches. Says Mickelson, "It's not a year I want to dwell on."

Now the old, buoyant Mickelson is back. It's not often that you see a Tour player so carefree that he needs to be tethered with four long ropes, like a Macy's Parade balloon. That's probably why the 2004 Masters champion spent much of his New Orleans pro-am round adding ballast. On the 4th tee he sampled crawfish étoufée. ("Just a little bowl," he told the volunteer servers. "I can't pass it up.") On the 10th tee he downed about a dozen of his favorite dish, grilled oysters, seasoned with butter, parmesan and romano cheeses, garlic and a drizzle of lemon. Behind the 15th green he stopped for a cup of spicy catfish court bouillon. "Remember the alligator last year?" a server asked.

"Yeah," Mickelson said, "that was excellent."

What came next was also tasty. On the 17th hole, a par-3 playing about 195 yards to a front-right pin position, the 2004 Masters champion put a smooth swing on a six-iron and holed it to shrieks of joy from about 100 spectators watching from mounds. When he got to the green, Mickelson retrieved his ball with a grin and turned to the gallery. "How'd it go?" he asked. He then jumped in the air with his arms and legs spread out, mimicking his Masters leap.

Ideally, celebratory golf can serve as preparation for tournament golf. Mickelson, however, dismissed the notion that he had already begun to focus on the season's second major, the U.S. Open, which will be played in June at Shinnecock Hills Golf Club in Southampton, N.Y. He blushed and stammered when asked by a reporter if the Grand Slam was in his thoughts. (Answer: not yet.) But anybody who has watched Mickelson's game sharpen in 2004 senses that everything he does is aimed at producing a player-of-the-year season. To that end, he will prepare for the Open as he did at Augusta for the Masters, playing a couple of practice rounds at Shinnecock under the watchful eyes of Smith and short-game coach Dave Pelz.

In the meantime, all the 2004 Masters champion wanted from the Big Easy was confirmation that his game was where he had left it before he started pursuing his "opportunities." He got that confirmation on Thursday afternoon. Mickelson came out shooting at flags and made the turn in four-under-par 32. Unfortunately, English Turn Golf & Country Club was in the path of a series of thunderstorms and pelting rains that forced the Tour to extend a tournament to a Monday finish for the second straight week. Mickelson's round was interrupted after 14 holes and couldn't be resumed until early Saturday morning, when he finished with a five-under 67. His second round, begun after a short break, benefited from light winds, soft greens and a lift-clean-and-place rule, which allowed him to attack pins with impunity and shoot 65. "Phil showed no rust at all," said Matt Kuchar, his playing partner for both rounds. "He's riding a wave of confidence."

Not to mention a wave of public sentiment. One family of Phil fans at English Turn sought his autograph by having their little girl display a hand-decorated sign reading MICKIE IS LEFTY, PLEASE SIGN. A 12-year-old boy, refusing to leave the course with his friends because "I have to tell Phil something," waited a half hour for Mickelson to finish a practice session. When Mickelson finally came over, the boy said, "I wanted you to know that my mom cried when you won the Masters."

Nobody was going to cry if Mickelson won the HP Classic— except maybe Vijay Singh, whose rain suit was still wet from his victory in the Shell Houston Open, or Joe Ogilvie, the third-round leader. On Monday, Mickelson, apparently dazzled by a clear blue sky, missed three consecutive birdie putts on the back side and shot 66 to finish a shot behind Singh in a tie for second with Ogilvie. It was Mickelson's ninth top 10 finish in 10 starts this year.

Before he left New Orleans, the 2004 Masters champion landed yet another of those "opportunities" that have come to him of late—an invitation to be grand marshal of next February's Mardi Gras parade through the New Orleans suburb of Metairie. Asked if he would describe the parade as a major, famed New Orleans restaurateur Tommy Cvitanovich said, "On a bad day we get a half million or three quarters of a million people. On a good day, with someone like Phil Mickelson leading the parade, it's more like a million."

Mickelson, he didn't have to add, looked like a fellow who would be comfortable riding a float through a blizzard of streamers and confetti. And not simply because he's the 2004 Masters champion.

There, we said it again.

POSTSCRIPT: *Sportswriters can't resist an opportunity to knock an athlete for what he or she hasn't accomplished. Sam Snead, they point out, never won a U.S. Open. Arnold Palmer never won the PGA. And Tom Watson? Well, if he hadn't won the 2007 Outback Steakhouse Pro-Am, he'd be remembered for all time as "Best Player Never to Win in Florida."*

⁌

The Critic

FROM GOLF MAGAZINE

Once a plaid-panted gunslinger, Johnny Miller has reinvented
himself as the brutally honest voice, and conscience, of the game

I love hanging out in TV towers, so Golf Magazine *editor David Clarke
had no trouble talking me into writing this profile of Johnny Miller. It
was actually my third go at NBC's star analyst. My first effort, in 1994,
got spiked when the* SI *photo department couldn't persuade Miller to sit
for a portrait. ("If I'd known they were going to kill the story," he later
said, apologizing, "I would have cooperated.") The second try, a couple of
years later, went off without a hitch, and so did this one, although in both
instances I had to sit in a dark, cramped corner and keep my mouth shut
during lengthy telecasts.*

———————

THE DOOR TO THE BOOTH CRACKS OPEN, LETTING IN A SLICE
of sunlight. A man squeezes in, carrying a brown grocery sack.
He puts the sack on a table, just out of reach of Johnny Miller,
NBC's boyish-at-59 golf analyst. Miller glances at the sack, but
his eyes return to a flat-panel monitor, which has Tour player
Chad Campbell rolling a 24-foot putt down a slope, past the
hole and right off the green. "Didn't read it right and hit it the
wrong speed," Miller says into a microphone. "Besides that, it
was wonderful."

A commercial break gives Miller and his announcer partner Dan Hicks the opportunity to explore the sack. Miller tosses aside some Twizzlers and rummages through bags of pretzels and chips until he finds what he is looking for: a bag of Hershey's chocolate miniatures. Ripping open the bag, Miller dumps the chocolates on the table and starts sorting. The dark chocolate bars wind up in a little pile by his microphone. The milk chocolate, Mr. Goodbar and Krackle bars go back in the bag.

"How many tournaments is Faldo doing this year?" Miller says.

"Four thousand, seven hundred and twenty," says Hicks, returning to his chair. Miller snorts. Englishman Nick Faldo, the 49-year-old CBS and Golf Channel analyst, is Miller's only competition in the network golf-gab game. And since Golf Channel now carries the weekday rounds and some weekend play of every PGA Tour event, Miller sometimes has to slip into a chair still warm from Faldo's posterior. That's the case today at the Accenture Match Play, where Faldo and Golf Channel anchor Kelly Tilghman handed off to Miller and Hicks at noon.

"Johnny, how ya' doin', sport?" Faldo said during the change-over, stripping to his waist and slipping on a sweater. "Fifty-nine, are you really? Ten more than me?"

Miller took the needle good-naturedly, but now *he* is in the chair, the reigning king of commentary, and *he* has control of the snack bag that will be waiting for Faldo on Sunday morning. "We like each other," Miller insists, "but we steal each other's candy. We both like dark chocolate."

He pops one of the little bars into his mouth and chews contentedly. "Maybe I'll leave him one," he says.

"Five to air," says a woman who leans in from the shadows behind the camera. "Four . . . " The rest of her countdown is mute, signaled with three fingers, then two, then one.

Miller is still smiling when Hicks picks up the thread.

THE PHONE keeps ringing at Johnny Miller Enterprises in Napa, Calif. A reporter from Pittsburgh wants to talk to Johnny about the final-round 63. A cable network wants fresh audio from Johnny for a segment on the final-round 63. A mini-tour pro wants advice from Johnny on how to shoot a final-round 63. It's Miller time—always is when the U.S. Open returns to Oakmont. It was at Oakmont in 1973 that a willowy Miller shot a tournament-record final-round 63 for the most memorable win of his Hall of Fame career. You'll read so much about that final-round 63 between now and June 14—how a voice in Miller's head during warmup said, "Open your stance way up"; how he hit 18 irons into 18 greens, most of them no more than five feet off line; how Arnold Palmer, contending for the last time in a major, spotted Miller's name on a leader board and promptly folded; how Miller, coming down the stretch, stood over every iron shot thinking, "Don't shank it"—that you may end up remembering it better than he does.

The irony is that Miller is a star *now*, in the 21st century. Millions of his fans have never seen him hit a shot, and if you tell them that he was the first pro to shoot really low scores at Tour events, they'll shrug and turn up the volume on their iPods. Viewers don't love or hate Miller for his record. They love or hate him for saying "Verplunk!" when Scott Verplank hits one in the water at the 2006 Ryder Cup . . . for flaming Phil Mickelson from 72nd tee to 72nd green during last year's U.S. Open at Winged Foot . . . for suggesting that Ben Hogan, if forced to look at the ungainly swing of Australia's Craig Parry, "would have puked."

So with Miller returning to Oakmont for the third time as an announcer, perhaps it's time to reexamine his legacy as a gabber, to peer into the past to find out how he developed his practiced bluntness, caustic wit and preternatural ability to predict the outcome of a shot based solely on how it sounds through his headphones. Miller will tell you he already had two of those gifts in 1969, when he joined the Tour, a mop-topped bag of bones out of BYU. He remembers being on the practice range at one of his first Tour events when the great Lee Trevino stepped up to watch and then, as SuperMex was wont to do, heckle. "Lee thought I was this passive lamb," Miller says, smiling at the memory. "But I gave it right back to him. I seemed quiet on the surface, but if you got into it with me, I could hold my own."

Earlier, then. Johnny's businessman father, Larry Miller, in addition to being a low-handicap golfer, was an artist and songwriter. "He wrote both the melody and the lyrics," Miller recalls, "and he'd say amazing things. He was a total one-off thinker."

That's relevant, Miller says, because "my goal on the air is to say things you don't expect me to say."

But if you press him, Miller will say his on-air persona dates to the 1960s, his teen years, when fate (and a certain skill with golf clubs) delivered him to the rarefied precincts of San Francisco's Olympic Club. Miller, at 14, was Olympic's first *merit member*—the club's term for talented juniors given access to its courses and practice facilities—and the top player on its junior team. "We had a great group of guys," he says, "and we all had this *Animal House* mentality."

ANYONE WHO HAS been to the Olympic Club will raise a skeptical eyebrow at the frat-house reference. The clubhouse, on a landscaped escarpment overlooking the 18th green, is an Italianate pastiche of stucco walls, iron chandeliers and Oriental carpets, a place where a Medici might catch a few winks between poisonings. It's hard to imagine a foursome of 16-year-olds hitting bump-and-run shots down the hall while a jittery lookout covers the stairs to the porte cochere.

"The guy on the stairs was the flagger," Ron O'Connor says, giving a visitor a tour of the clubhouse. "He'd wave his arm if the coast was clear."

O'Connor, a real estate broker and longtime Olympic Club member, was the club's second-best junior golfer in Miller's day. (His friends call him Rocket—short for Rocket Man, a nickname Miller gave him.) The team captain, Steve Gregoire, was number four. More important, he was the son of the club member who put Miller up for membership.

Both boys caddied at the club, and Miller frequently looped for Leon Gregoire.

"My dad played with a bunch of guys who played five or six days a week, and they gambled pretty heavily," says Steve, who now owns an interior landscaping company. "Those guys would rib each other viciously and we all picked up on it. When we played, it was difficult to tee off on the 1st hole because the needle was going back and forth." Putting was no cakewalk either—not when Rocket Man assured you the line was a ball outside the hole, and Miller said, "Yeah, left edge," and you said, "Left edge? Or outside the hole?" and Rocket Man said, "Now that I look at it, it's dead straight."

"It toughened us up," Gregoire says with a smile. "Made us better."

Miller agrees. "The needling made me quick," he says, leaning on a rail outside the announcers' booth. "I'm not the smartest guy in the world, but I'm quick. I've immediately got something to say."

The ribbing desensitized Miller, too; it led him to assume that others shared his ability to handle criticism. "I'm brutally honest, to a fault, and some players don't like that." Oddly enough, it's the older pros—the guys Miller thinks should be thickskinned—who squawk the most when he politely points out that they're choking dogs. "The young players grew up listening to Johnny Miller, they've got that X Games mentality," Miller says. "They think I'm out there, sort of with it—not the old fuddyduddy, careful announcer."

In any event, Miller insists that his on-air jibes are not meant to sting: "When Mickelson has hit only one fairway in 13 holes, I'm like his caddie. I'm thinking, Don't hit the driver, Phil! Don't try to hit a low slice around the tree! I'm not trying to rip him. I'm using ESP. I'm trying to help him." And when he spots another player's swing flaw—say, a tendency to squat in the takeaway and then drive the left shoulder up through impact a la Tiger Woods—is Miller simply tweeting his coach's whistle?

He nods. "I'm trying to give the pro a free lesson. I'm hoping he'll watch it that night and say, 'Johnny's right, that's exactly what I'm doing wrong.'" His straight face begins to crack. "But that doesn't go over too well, I've found."

After all, who wants advice from a 16-year-old?

THE SECOND HOLE of the Olympic Club's *Animal House* course is an 85-yard par-7. You tee off from an alcove in the men's locker room and chip through a door and up some steps to a landing, where a well-played ricochet off the wall kicks your ball outside and across the sidewalk to a flower bed. That leaves you a delicate approach of 45 yards up a clubhouse-hugging, cliff-edge sidewalk to the practice putting green.

Miller honed his short game on this hole. He also practiced at the nearby Harding Park municipal course, where he played the flag game. The rules, set down by his father, were simple: Hit your ball within the length of the flagstick, roughly seven feet, on all 18 greens. Miller's friends remember how dejected

Johnny would get when his string of flags ended—usually around the 10th hole.

"Johnny's dad was his first coach," Gregoire says, "and as good a teacher as he was about the swing, he was twice that good between the ears."

It was Larry Miller's idea to turn the basement of his house on Ocean Avenue into a golf academy for Johnny. The basement had mirrors, mats, nets and instruction books by the likes of Ben Hogan and Cary Middlecoff. The basement also had a vibe—a very positive vibe, because Larry Miller believed you built a champion through encouragement and support, not bullying.

"His dad always called him Champ," Gregoire recalls. "There was never a negative word. If Johnny hit a bad shot, his dad would praise his setup or something. By the time he was 12, Johnny believed hook, line and sinker that he was going to be a champion."

By the time he was 17, Miller *was* a champion, winner of the 1964 U.S. Junior in Eugene, Ore.

"My dad was my turbocharger," Miller says. "That's what gave me the edge, his positive thinking and affirmation of greatness." The elder Miller also bequeathed his iconoclasm—the quality that makes established swing gurus puff up with rage when Miller claims, for instance, that he can wait until the moment of impact to put draw or fade spin on the ball. "Dad would give me crazy ideas," Miller says, "things that didn't work, but stuff I could learn from. I carried a left-handed five-iron. I hit balls out of iceplant and up against cactus, the craziest stuff you could imagine. So when I entered a tournament, it was a foregone conclusion that I was going to win."

Miller's friends are quick to point out that he had great parents, plural, which made the Miller home a haven for spirited kids with time to kill. "Mrs. Miller was an extraordinary cook," O'Connor recalls. "She'd bake blackberry and apple pies, and she'd say, 'If you can get here in 15 minutes, you can have a quarter of the pie.' " He shuts his eyes and smiles. "Her crust was killer crust."

ANOTHER KITCHEN scene. The year is 1993 and Johnny's wife Linda is fixing breakfast at the Miller's hilltop hacienda in Napa, Calif. "Mom, were you a hippie?" asks her 19-year-old daughter, Casie.

Linda, who has raised her six children without the benefit of liquor, tobacco, coffee, tea, soft drinks or profanity, is surprised by the question. "I was kind of straight back then," Linda replies.

"I would have gone to Woodstock," Casie says.

"Yeah, she would have," Linda says later. "She's more like her father. John is a gypsy and a horse trader."

Time has validated Linda's assessment of her husband, whose blend of Mormon devotion, bluntness and sass confounded observers in the '70s. Implicit in Casie's question, though, was the understanding that people—even parents—are influenced by historical forces, that today's Rush Limbaugh might be yesterday's Abbie Hoffman. There is a scene in *All the President's*

Men in which Robert Redford, as Bob Woodward, reads a note from Deep Throat while a radio drones: "In sports, in Muirfield, Scotland, Lee Trevino and Tony Jacklin share the lead in the British Open golf tournament, both at 141. Johnny Miller is . . . . "

And the scene shifts. We never learn what Johnny Miller is.

Today, his colleagues at NBC simply accept that Miller has his enigmatic side, that he will enliven their lives for three or four days and then disappear. "I've worked with the guy for 15 or 16 years, and I've probably had dinner with him twice," says course reporter Roger Maltbie, an unabashed Miller fan. Course reporter Gary Koch remembers the last time he played golf with Miller—the week of the 2003 U.S. Women's Open at Pumpkin Ridge—but adds, "Most of the time he doesn't even have his clubs with him."

Miller is the favorite uncle who brings toys but doesn't spend the night.

"I'm not the chummiest guy," he concedes. "I could hang around more, spend more time with players on the range." It's an anemic resolution, one he's been making for years.

His Olympic Club pals didn't consider Miller a loner; he was in and out of their homes all the time. "Then we had a little tournament here," says Gregoire, alluding to the 1966 U.S. Open, won by Billy Casper. "We all signed up to caddie—except for Johnny, 'cause that silly sucker qualified." Miller was 19 at the time, a loose-limbed sophomore from BYU, and he shook up the golf establishment by coming out of sectional qualifying to tie for eighth, low amateur by three strokes. "Johnny was upset," Gregoire recalls. "It was his home course. He thought he should have won."

The point is, Miller now had a new set of peers: Tour players.

"He didn't smoke and he didn't drink," O'Connor reminds us, and Miller certainly had no use for those pungent cigarettes that some players and caddies fired up back at the motel. "Johnny didn't condemn people if they had a drink, but they condemned him if he didn't. He had a different lifestyle. He wasn't in the group." Miller, a committed Mormon and family man, was swimming against the tide of the '70s.

That didn't bother him. What bothered him, his friends say, was the sight of Linda and the children in the driveway, the littlest one crying, when he'd drive off for two or three weeks of tournament golf. As the years went by, as he racked up an eight-win season (1974) and socked away a British Open title ('76), the divide between Tour time and family time became untenable, and Miller—an unsentimental man—simply drifted off the circuit.

MILLER, CARRYING his blue blazer on a hanger, walks through a desert wash toward the NBC compound. The setting sun reveals traces of the pancake makeup he applied before going on the air. ("Hey, look," Faldo had teased, "he's covering himself in makeup!") Miller doesn't seem to be in a hurry.

"I'm in a really good place right now," he says. "My family's doing well. I feel as if I'm in my prime as an announcer." He stops and looks back toward the clunky silhouette of the announcers' booth, a crate on stilts. "It's one of the rarest jobs in the universe, and now there's only two of us, two lead announcers," Miller says. "I consider it an honor."

This is a different Johnny Miller. Less driven. Unconflicted.

His friends see it. On a recent hunting trip, Miller sat with Gregoire in a fog-shrouded blind from dawn until afternoon, with only one dead duck between them. "Anybody who knows Johnny knows he can't sit still more than 15 minutes," Gregoire says afterward. "So for us to sit there in the fog with one duck for six hours and 45 minutes...."

Why the change? Gregoire shrugs. "He needed it. He's been burning the candle at both ends for 40 years." Oh, and Miller will soon turn 60, "and he's beginning to realize there's only so many shopping days till Christmas," Gregoire says.

"All my friends are shocked," Miller says, studying the sunny side of a giant saguaro cactus. "I've always been in a rush, trying to do everything at 85 miles an hour. I was too tight. The last two years, I've tried to slow down and not try to put too many things into one day."

Is a slowed-down Miller a gentler and kinder commentator?

"Maybe," he says. "I've made a resolution to not be quite as hard on the players. I don't know if NBC will like that idea, but I'm trying to be fair."

The catalyst for the change, he adds without irony, was CBS's decision not to rehire Lanny Wadkins as its lead analyst—the rap on Wadkins was that he was bland and too protective of players' feelings. "Lanny said when you get away from the game you forget how hard it is to hit good shots," Miller says. Then he nods, as if he's never heard this argument before. "I learned a good lesson from Lanny. I'll probably try to be a little kinder."

The cactus, looking down on Miller, is unconvinced.

So are his colleagues on the NBC golf team, which has built its whole pros-talking-on-the-couch coverage around Miller's astringent style. Says Maltbie, "We all have a filter that keeps us from cussing in front of our moms or the minister—not that Johnny would do that—but it's a filter he doesn't possess. If it's in his head, it's going to come out of his mouth." Dick Ebersol, chairman of NBC Universal Sports & Olympics, says Miller is just like television's other JMs, John McEnroe and Joe Morgan.

"None of them has a governor," Ebersol says. "You're getting them just the way they are."

Miller's colleagues might worry if they saw him pulling back on his preparation, but he still goes out early on broadcast days to take copious notes on the course setup. Before today's show, for instance, he drove out to the 1st green to see if an invisible pitch mark was really responsible for the four-foot putt Tiger Woods missed yesterday on the first playoff hole of his loss to Nick O'Hern.

"Tiger was right," Miller said upon his return. "The grass has grown up and been mowed level, but I felt around with my fingers and there was a crater nobody's ever fixed. You can't see it, but it'll cause a ball to veer, for sure." Asked why he had bothered to do what no other on-site journalist had—actually check Tiger's claim—Miller shrugged. "I thought I had to do it," he said.

Minutes later, after taking over from Faldo, Miller used the first commercial break to inform Hicks that he had searched for the pitch mark.

"What'd you see?"

Miller waved him off. "We've got to do it impromptu, on the air. I don't want to skew your thinking." Hicks nodded and the two men sat quietly, lost in thought.

"Five seconds . . . Four . . . "

Three fingers, two fingers, one.

POSTSCRIPT: *The reader mail that followed publication of this story was extreme, with half praising Miller for his sharp analysis and refreshing candor and half condemning him as petty, jealous and mean. A 2004 SI* Golf Plus *survey found that PGA Tour players were similarly split, with many picking Miller as their favorite analyst and even more naming him when asked the question, "Which TV commentator would you like to strangle?"*

༄

Bon Vivant Lite

Could the author, who doesn't drink, smoke, cuss, dance or eat mayonnaise, transform himself into the life of the Masters party?

Ask me about the 1999 Masters, and I'll give you a blank look. Who won it? Don't recall. Key shots? Haven't a clue. That's what happens when you spend more time on Fury's Ferry Road than you spend in Amen Corner.

"LIFE IS A HANGOUT. IF YOU DON'T HAVE ONE, YOU'RE LOST." My mentor, Frank Chirkinian, swirled the ice cubes in his Scotch and water and let me ponder his words. I was the student, he was the teacher, and we were embarked on a tutorial that I hope someday to develop into a book called *Tuesdays with Frank*. He sat on a bar stool with a window view of the Winn-Dixie parking lot. I sat on the other side of a tall cocktail table, my left elbow on the sill of an ice cart filled with gray oysters, pink shrimp and bright red crayfish.

I knew that Frank was testing me. I said, "When you say, 'If you don't have one,' "—and I lifted my gaze to the ceiling fans, spinning listlessly over the crowded dining room—"do you mean a hangout? Or a life?"

Frank didn't seem to hear the question. His eyes tracked a couple crossing the parking lot, a couple I recognized as CBS golf analyst and former Ryder Cupper Peter Oosterhuis and his wife, Ruthie.

"Nobody really parties anymore," Frank said over the din of the bar patrons. "Those days are gone."

By *nobody* Frank apparently meant no Tour players, media folk and celebrities—the colorful characters he chronicled for 38 years as producer of the Masters telecast on CBS. But on this Masters Tuesday, the French Market Grill (West) had its share of golf people, including former U.S. Open champ and CBS analyst Ken Venturi, seated with friends near the bar, and three-time Masters runner-up Greg Norman, trying to be inconspicuous in a corner booth. Joe Phillips, an accomplished saxophone player and longtime Tour rep for Wilson Sporting Goods, stopped by to tell Frank that Gene Sarazen's daughter was at a table. Frank said, "Joe, my man!"

I asked Frank if he behaved like a host when he was at the restaurant, which he co-owns with retired businessman Carl Swanson and restaurateur Chuck Baldwin, owner of the long-established French Market Grill on Berkman's Road, near Augusta National. "Like a host?" He looked almost as perplexed as he did in the movie *Tin Cup*, in which he played a television producer.

"Yeah," I said. "Greeting people at the door, going from table to table." Frank shook his leonine head and said, "I don't greet or mix with any of them." He then hurried off to welcome some friends who had just come in.

I didn't tell Frank the whole truth: that I had already decided to make his restaurant my Masters hangout, the place where print acolytes and other media chums will find me when I'm not hammering out stories on my old, battered laptop. I already had rejected several notable Augusta nightspots: the pricey Calvert's because it has white linen tablecloths; the Red Lion Pub because the music is too loud for conversation; Hooters because—well, I hadn't actually ruled out Hooters. The Partridge Inn and the Surrey Tavern, of course, are too closely identified with writer Dan Jenkins and the late golfer-TV commentator Dave Marr, who swapped stories and bar tabs in them for years.

Some of my colleagues made recommendations that were borderline facetious. Joe Posnanski, the columnist for my hometown *Kansas City Star*, mentioned the Sports Center, a downtown joint once favored by the staff of *The Augusta Chronicle*. "It's a biker-type place. A lot of tattoos," he said, "but really good hamburgers." Bill Lyon, sports columnist for *The Philadelphia Inquirer*, waxed nostalgic over an old roadhouse called the Rub It In Again Inn, where the sign outside once advertised AMATEUR JELL-O WRESTLING ON THURSDAY NIGHTS.

Back at the French Market Grill, Chirkinian made a distinction between the hangouts themselves—many of which were still around—and the characters who did the hanging out. "The kind of people who frequented those places are no longer with us," he said. "It was a harder-drinking group. They were iconoclastic, not trying to impress anybody. People today are more concerned with their images."

I wasn't sure that image consciousness explained the change, but I couldn't deny the change itself. My own reputation as a bon vivant suffers because I don't drink, smoke, cuss, dance or eat mayonnaise, onions or cooked tomatoes. I am not unlike most younger journalists—I'm 52—who drink tea, call home every night and wash their own shirts in the hotel's coin laundry. Lyon, who is 61, expressed my misgivings about this trend when he asked, "Where are the future reprobates coming from?"

Frank, whose eyes never quit scanning the room, suddenly stiffened. A TV camera crew had come in through the canopied entrance, followed by a nicely coiffed young woman with a microphone. "What's that? What's that?" He turned to me. "That's scary. We're always in bars with people we shouldn't be with." At Frank's insistence an employee hustled over to question the intruders and came back with the sobering news that they were from Channel 12—a CBS affiliate.

"Should I tell them to leave?" she asked.

Frank sighed. "No, they can stay."

A choice had to be made: Sit or stand. When Jenkins held court at the Partridge Inn, he usually stood by the island bar, his hands occupied with a drink and a cigarette. I thought I might be more comfortable with the head-of-the-table approach of SI's Ron Fimrite, the urbane San Franciscan who made Scottsdale's Pink Pony steak house an Arizona spring training landmark. Fimrite's table was actually three or four tables pushed together, and his regular guests included *New Yorker* writer Roger Angell, former National League president Chub Feeney, California Angels owner Gene Autry and the occasional Hall of Fame ballplayer. Fimrite, a man of great charm and warmth, liked the inclusive nature of the long table, which allowed more people to converse face-to-face.

Another choice: permanent or floating table? The FMG West already has a reserved nook called the Yacht Club, where a retired nuclear power plant worker named Yacht Mitchell hangs with his pals every afternoon. "How Yacht got his name," Swanson told me, "was his father was getting ready to buy a boat when Yacht's mother got pregnant. So his father said, 'There's my yacht.'"

Swanson, a big, Burl Ives sort of man with a beard and glasses, is retired from Club Car Corporation, the golf cart company he cofounded. Swanson said he got into the restaurant business because his old Augusta hangout, the American Diner, closed three years ago, "and Frank and I didn't have a place to drink." Unable to keep the place open any other way, they bought it and persuaded Baldwin to turn it into another French Market Grill.

"It's not my first restaurant," Frank told me. In 1986, the year he had the more recent of his two open-heart surgeries, Chirkinian opened a fast-food Italian place called Hello Pasta on Washington Road. "Three hundred thousand dollars later," Frank said, "Hello Pasta became *Arrivederci* Pasta." Length of run: six months.

Frank said, "I prove every day that impetuosity knows no age."

Thursday night was my maiden voyage. I invited a few veteran newspapermen, and they trickled into Frank's place between 8:30 and 9:30, detouring to the pay phone to see what their respective sports desks were doing to their first-round copy. We started with drinks at the bar, and Marino Parascenzo of the *Pittsburgh Post-Gazette* got us off to a Fimritian gallop by telling a Winston Churchill story and by asking a question with the word *cartilaginous* in it. Mike Kern of the *Philadelphia Daily News* then pulled us back to Jenkinsville by rhapsodizing over out-of-town meals past, a caloric litany of fried catfish, Philly cheese steak sandwiches and barbecue. He said, "That place you took us in Tulsa when the PGA was at Southern Hills [S&J Oyster House]—outstanding!"

On a signal from the reservationist, I led my entourage over to the assigned booth and ordered us a pound of boiled shrimp and assorted appetizers. The Oosterhuises were at a neighboring table, so I told our waitress that SPORTS ILLUSTRATED wanted to pick up their tab, as well. "Any players come in tonight?" I asked, ready to wave my corporate Amex at anyone's tab.

"Tom Lehman was here last night," a waitress replied.

"If he comes back," I said, "bring me his check."

Our booth was positioned for maximum visibility, close to the entrance and on the center aisle. That made it easy for recipients of my largesse to stop by to express their thanks. For ambience, however, I would have preferred a table along the east wall, under the mural depicting a New Orleans streetscape.

Not that ambience mattered, once the food began arriving. Dave Hackenburg of *The Toledo Blade* gave everybody a taste of his spicy jambalaya appetizer, and Joe Juliano of the *Inquirer* chewed thoughtfully on a marinated shrimp before proclaiming it, "Not hot, but very, very good." Our entrées included a stuffed trout, sesame-crusted tuna, steak and lobster, crab chop a la Charles and honey-pecan chicken, all of which received thumbs up from the scribes. I called our waitress over and said, "SPORTS ILLUSTRATED would like to buy drinks for"—I shrugged—"for the next table to buy drinks."

She said, "No matter who it is?"

I said, "Absolutely," and she went off laughing.

I was lost and now I'm found; that is to say, I finally have a Masters hangout. But when I told Frank that I would henceforth spend thousands of SI's entertainment dollars in his restaurant, his face expressed a certain ambivalence. I thought it was because our Tuesday tutorials on nightlife were about to end, but I later decided that he was simply worried that he might not have enough space for my boisterous entourage.

Frank said, "I'm the first guy to put a camera in a blimp, you know. Orange Bowl, 1960. Now they've got blimps at every f------ event you can think of—blimps at tennis matches, blimps at baseball games. They even have blimps above closed stadiums. They're taking pictures of a roof! At night! Does that make any f------ sense to you?"

I guess that was Frank's way of saying that the lessons were over and I was ready to go out on my own.

POSTSCRIPT: SI *suspended me from the nightlife beat after this story ran, probably at the insistence of the executive who monitors expense accounts. I made a triumphant return at the 2004 Masters, where I landed the plum assignment of writing about T-Bonz, a raucous steak house on Washington Road, and Mark Cummins, its Toots Shor–like co-owner. Since then, my newspaper pals and I have made a late Saturday dinner at T-Bonz the centerpiece of our week in Augusta. Cummins usually gives us a booth on the west wall, under a framed copy of my T-Bonz story and not far from the power table of Peter and Ruthie Oosterhuis.*

OCTOBER 1, 2001

Sacre Blues

Near Paris, an ambivalent European tour played on in the
wake of 9/11 despite an uncertain future

*A week or so after the Twin Towers fell, I boarded a half-empty jet in Atlanta
and flew to Europe to report on the cancellation of the Ryder Cup. To say
that my spirits were low would be an understatement. I couldn't get the
images of Ground Zero out of my mind. My brain locked up when I tried
to write. Then Bogie (not bogey) rescued me.*

———————————

THE PROBLEMS OF A FEW PROFESSIONAL GOLFERS DON'T
amount to a hill of beans in this crazy world, but no one in Europe
escaped the fear and confusion last week as war clouds gathered.
In Paris, where the leaves were beginning to turn crimson and
gold, players at the 32nd Trophée Lancôme struggled with their
emotions. The postponement of the Ryder Cup, scheduled to
be played this week in Sutton Coldfield, England, had shaken
their confidence and left them wondering if tournament golf,
as they know it, can continue. No loudspeakers on trucks were
announcing the imminent arrival of an occupying army, but a
notice on the doors of the empty party tent at Saint-Nom-La-
Bretéche Golf Club conveyed the impact of the terror attacks on
the U.S. Due to *les événements dramatiques*, the note explained, all
manifestations of a festive nature were *annulées*. Canceled.

To the players of the European tour, who live in a world in which the Scandinavian Masters follows the Dutch Open as surely as the 7th hole follows the 6th, the game suddenly seemed puerile, their efforts insignificant. "There's a lot less laughter," said Colin Montgomerie. "We are all quite flat, and it will take a number of weeks, months, years to get back to where we were." During the first round last Thursday, when a blast from an air horn signaled players to stop for a minute of silence, the golfers bowed their heads and stood motionless while it rained. Sergio García, who would win the tournament, said, "It was as if the sky was crying."

The funereal mood was not confined to France. At the Belfry in Sutton Coldfield, where organizers had been putting the finishing touches on the Ryder Cup site, work crews dismantled grandstands and hauled off acres of white cloth from the tented village. Forty thousand Ryder Cup–logoed Glenmuir polo shirts sat in boxes on the floor of the monster merchandise tent, destined for storage. Behind the sprawling brick Belfry Hotel, where the flags of seven nations flew at half-mast, a gardener snipped at a hedge with clippers, getting it just so. The unspoken message: There will always be an England.

Symbols had to do for expression, because officials of the European tour, the British PGA and the Belfry refused to discuss the impact of the postponement—the first disruption of the Ryder Cup since war wiped out the matches from 1939 until '47. One publication put the financial losses at $29 million, but that was speculation. "The Birmingham economy has been hit very hard," said a spokesman for De Vere Hotels, owner of The Belfry. "They were expecting thousands and thousands of people."

The emotional fallout was easier to gauge. Whereas in the months leading up to the Ryder Cup the match was characterized as a confrontation between bitter transatlantic rivals, tragedy produced an Anglo-American unity not seen since U.S. servicemen billeted with British civilians during World War II. "Everybody here has been overwhelming in their sympathy and support," said Jeff Erickson, a young American working in the golf shop at the Belfry. "People who hear my accent come over and say how sorry they are."

Only the chattering class, as some Brits call the media, defied the spirit of unity. There was criticism of Tiger Woods, whose withdrawal from the Trophée Lancôme and reluctance to travel to Europe were blamed for forcing the PGA of America to ask for a postponement. There was criticism of European captain Sam Torrance, who had said, "I don't think canceling or postponing is giving in to terrorism. Golf is nothing, nothing." There was criticism of U.S. stars Mark Calcavecchia and Phil Mickelson, whose manager, Steve Loy, had said, "A golf course would be an easy place to commit mass murder." Wrote a columnist in *The Mirror*, a British tabloid: "Someone needs to explain to these people they live in the real world. Someone needs to explain that we are all at risk, not just a few cosseted individuals who can't see anything beyond the end of their egos."

Fortunately, the finger-pointing lasted only as long as it took to count heads in Paris, where the players were every bit as concerned as their American counterparts—none of whom played in the Trophée Lancôme—for their personal safety. "I know a lot of guys are deciding to go home," said Adam Scott, whose mates from Australia and New Zealand were cutting short their European seasons. "I'm happy to go on, but only if things don't take a turn for the worse."

Jean Van de Velde, the suave Frenchman who blew a three-stroke lead on the last hole of the '99 British Open, speculated that a wartime European tour might consist solely of tournaments to which players could drive in their cars. "If we go to war, if something happens, what kind of security will we have?" Van de Velde said. "It's going to be hard."

European tour executive director Ken Schofield and his staff, had they been willing to break their public silence, might have accused Van de Velde of understatement. The first four months of the Euro tour, 14 tournaments in all, are played outside of Europe. It features a four-event swing through Australia and Malaysia, three weeks in South America, two weeks in South Africa and two stops in Arab countries and ends with a week in Rabat, Morocco. It's no trick at all to imagine the quick cancellation of the Dubai Desert Classic, the Qatar Masters and the Moroccan Open. Then, if the best players refuse to leave their homes in Europe, sponsors of overseas tournaments could claim breach of contract and withdraw their financial support. That would force tour officials to huddle over their map of Europe, changing dates and drawing new itineraries: Lisbon to Madrid, Madrid to Jerez, Jerez to Stockholm.

That was the sort of feverish thinking that prevailed as the players gathered in Paris. The tournament's co-owners, Lancôme, a perfume and toiletries company, and International Management Group, were in angry disagreement. Lancôme wanted to call off the tournament. IMG insisted that it be played, pointing out that 90,000 tickets—three times normal—had been sold in anticipation of Woods's appearance and that many of the spectators had traveled across Europe and were already in Paris. "For 31 years the Lancôme Trophy has been a big party," a statement from Lancôme said after a compromise was reached to hold the tournament but cancel the fete. "The tents and pavilions will not be used by Lancôme." The giant party pavilion behind the 18th green remained dark all week, and a banner on Lancôme's private grandstand testified to a larger emptiness felt by all: LE 11 SEPTEMBRE 2001—SOLIDARITÉ.

Golfers and spectators alike were conflicted, and it didn't help that heavy rains at midweek cast a palpable gloom over Saint-Nom-La-Bretéche, a picturesque complex a few miles west of the town of Versailles, where the armistice ending World War I was signed. "It is right that we are playing, and it is good that we are playing," said Montgomerie, one of four European Ryder Cuppers in the field (along with García, Niclas Fasth and Phillip Price). Montgomerie opened with a 75 and didn't survive the 36-hole cut, but his opinion held up. Saturday brought blue skies and the kind of gauzy autumn air that makes the French countryside irresistible.

Thousands of spectators, many of them blissfully unfamiliar with tournament etiquette, treated the course as a *bois*, wandering across fairways with children, walking onto greens to pat the grass and shaking apple trees to catch the sweet, reddening fruit. "We had a dog running around on the 9th tee, and there were enough telephones and crying babies to muck up a few shots," said U.S. Open champion Retief Goosen, the third-round leader, "but it was good. Everybody seems to be a bit happier now."

For a few hours, then, the distant horrors were put aside and future troubles willfully ignored. On Sunday, García and Goosen ran away from the field and staged what was, in essence, a brilliant singles match. Goosen made five straight birdies and led by four shots with four holes to play. García, undaunted, birdied holes 15 through 17 and won the championship when Goosen bogeyed 17 and 18. The win, worth $218,000, was García's third of the year.

"It meant a lot after what happened in America," said García, at 21 too young and full of life to grasp that it meant nothing at all after what had happened in America. An observer could only stand in García's jubilant orbit and share his dim understanding that whatever comes next, however dark and uncertain the future, he will always have Paris.

POSTSCRIPT: *When this story appeared, politicians were already covering their butts by saying, "Everything changed on 9/11." Time would prove them wrong. Americans kept shopping, golfers kept golfing, and the European tour announced that a new golf tournament, the world's richest, would debut in 2009 in—drum roll, please—Dubai.*

༈

All My Exes Wear Rolexes

WITH SETH DAVIS

The life (loony) and times (lately) of John Daly. Not a role model

John Daly crashes into my life at irregular intervals, but always with the fury and destructive power of a thunderstorm. I first laid eyes on him while covering the 1991 PGA Championship at Crooked Stick, which he won as the ninth alternate after an overnight drive from Memphis with his soon-to-be second wife, Bettye Fulford. I was on hand again three years later, at Firestone Country Club in Akron, when Daly got into a parking-lot brawl with the father of another player. John has never been dull.

The following story got its start when SI's Seth Davis, who moonlights as a golf writer when he isn't covering college basketball for SI.com and CBS, wandered into Daly's million-dollar RV at a typically turbulent time in the golfer's life. Seth and I joined forces to produce a piece that had to be rewritten several times before publication to keep up with Daly's manic turnarounds.

CLIENT: My wife has me between a rock and a hard place.
DIVORCE ATTORNEY: That's her job. You should respect that.
—*Intolerable Cruelty*

THE KNOT was tied two years ago in the wedding chapel at Bally's Hotel and Casino in Las Vegas. The bride wore white. John Daly, marrying for the fourth time, wore jeans and a sport coat. After the ceremony, the wedding party took an elevator up to Daly's suite and celebrated. The planets seemed to be aligned for the popular golfer, who had won $850,000 on slot machines the night before and was cresting on a comeback that had seen him rise from 506th to the top 50 in the World Ranking. "I really thought I'd found a woman who was a lot of fun, a lot of laughs," he said recently. "I really thought I'd found the right woman."

Stupid Cupid. When Daly returned to Vegas two weeks ago to tape a golf exhibition for Fox Sports, Sherrie Daly was just another verse of *All My Exes Wear Rolexes*, a country song that Daly wrote and recorded a couple of years ago. On Oct. 8, three days after the 37-year-old touring pro had flown to Seoul to play in the Korean Open, Daly had asked his attorney to file divorce papers in Memphis. In support of the petition, which would be governed by a pre-nuptial agreement the couple signed in 2001, Daly alleged that on various occasions he was physically and verbally abused by his wife in front of friends, family, other Tour players, the rock band Hootie and the Blowfish and, in one colorful incident, three strippers at a charity golf outing. He also claimed that his wife had failed to disclose to him that she and her parents were targets of a federal task force investigating drug smuggling and money laundering in six Southern states.

"It's cut and dried," a relaxed but subdued Daly said on the night of Oct. 13, sitting at the dining table in his suite at the Paris Hotel and Casino. "She gets 25 grand a year for two years—50 grand—and that's it." Asked if Sherrie knew he was leaving, Daly said, "I told her face to face in Memphis." He puffed on a cigarette and stared at a bowl of roses in the center of the table.

"I wanted to make it work. It's embarrassing to have to go through another divorce. There's two beautiful children involved." He shook his head.

"But I'm going to go insane if I don't get away from this woman."

TIM FINCHEM knows the feeling. He's the PGA Tour commissioner, and every time he takes a call at his Ponte Vedra Beach, Fla., headquarters there's a chance it's some tournament director complaining that John Daly has failed to show up for a pro-am or made a spectacle of himself at the local Hooters. The Tour, like an aggrieved spouse, would probably welcome a divorce from Daly—or, at minimum, a trial separation. Last week, the New Jersey wire service SportsTicker cited sources saying that Daly had entered an alcohol rehab clinic on orders from Finchem. That proved false, but on Oct. 5, the Tour's senior vice president and chief of operations, Henry Hughes, called the troubled golfer to express concerns over his recent behavior. Good thing, because any restriction of his playing privileges could be devastating to Daly, whose seven-figure income from corporate sponsorships, appearance fees and merchandise sales depends upon his ability to command an audience on golf's main stage.

It's a typically dire situation for Daly, who has lived a white-knuckle existence ever since he dropped out of the University of Arkansas in 1987. He won the 1991 PGA as a Tour rookie, causing eyes to pop with his hyper-extended swing, 320-yard drives and redneck flamboyance. Four years later he beat Costantino Rocca in a playoff to take the 1995 British Open. Only three weeks ago, while his friends back home worried that months of marital strife and binge drinking had left him suicidal, Daly shot a four-under-par 32 over the final nine holes to win the Korean Open by a stroke. "Your adrenaline gets pumping when you have a chance to win," he said upon his return to the States. "I was hitting my driver 30 or 40 yards farther than I normally do."

But there are pressures Daly can't handle, as evidenced by his history of hospitalizations, hotel-room tantrums, gambling sprees and tournament disqualifications. Since July—even as he tried to put a good face on his stormy marriage to the former Sherrie Miller of Collierville, Tenn.—Daly has been disqualified or has withdrawn from four of six PGA Tour events. Near Pittsburgh, during the 84 Lumber Classic, he started shaking uncontrollably and had to withdraw. At the Texas Open he raked in a missed putt while the ball was still moving and didn't report it to Tour officials until after he had signed his scorecard—an automatic DQ. Afterward, according to local reports, Daly trashed the interior of his $1.2 million motor home, breaking mirrors, windows and a plasma television.

"He's not really a golfer any longer," said a veteran pro. "More like a freak show."

A week later at the Southern Farm Bureau Classic, Daly six-putted a green, chasing after his ball and hockey-sticking it into the cup, tap-tap-tap-tap. On the next hole, after hacking a shot only a few feet out of deep rough, he slapped his ball onto the fairway with one hand. Southern Farm tournament director Robert

Morgan called Daly's ordeal a "sad situation" and added, "If he continues the way he is, the John Daly persona is not going to be an attraction any more."

As Daly's game and self-discipline spiraled downward, his inner circle shrank. Mick Peterson, his caddie, left him the week of the PGA Championship. Donnie Crabtree, his personal assistant and driver of 10 years and closest friend since the first grade, quit a week later. "It's hard watching somebody that you love self-destruct," Crabtree explains. "John can go weeks without drinking, but he's a binger. He'll drink and not eat, smoke three packs a day. He drinks Diet Cokes like they're going out of style. No rest, high stress, lots of caffeine, lots of nicotine. You add all those things together and you get what's happened over the last six or seven weeks." Asked if he thought Daly had become a danger to himself or others, Crabtree says he doesn't consider his friend "consciously suicidal," but cited the belief of people in 12-step programs that you have to hit rock bottom before you can come back. "My fear with John is that his rock bottom might be something you don't come back from."

Daly denies that he tore up his bus—he says a flying stone cracked the windshield on the way to San Antonio, and he insists the interior damage was caused by a fixture that had come loose—but he acknowledged in Las Vegas that everyone from Tour officials to musician friends have seen his despair and either shunned him or offered to help. "The sad thing is, everybody thinks something is wrong with me. Well, yeah, I'm mentally disturbed—because I have a wife I'm supporting and she's beating me and accusing me of all this crap."

Was he drinking again? "Yeah, I drink a little bit, but I haven't gotten drunk or anything. Hell, I don't have time."

He didn't deny that he was tired.

IN COLLIERVILLE, a small town a few miles southeast of Memphis, Sherrie Daly voices a similar mix of charges and denials. "People don't want us to stay married," she said recently, looking surprisingly chipper while pouring cereal for her four-year-old son Austin (from a previous relationship) and wiping the face of nine-week-old John Patrick Daly, her son with John. "John has the hangers-on, the sometimes friends, the exes. They all have their hands out. Everybody wants a piece of him." She sounded particularly bitter toward ex-wife number 3, Paulette Daly, who responded to the news of Sherrie's indictment by seeking a court order to restrict John's visitation rights with his daughter Sierra, eight, who lives with her mother in Palm Springs, Calif. "I thought me and Paulette were friends," Sherrie told SI. "And then she sends those papers to us in Reno, and I was like, 'What? Are you kidding me?' I cried for two days."

Those who were with John and Sherrie when they met weren't surprised that their marriage seemed to have ended in tears. The two were introduced by a mutual friend at the TPC of Southwind in Memphis as John passed the clubhouse during a round of the 2001 FedEx St. Jude Classic. Daly, who was engaged to another woman at the time, joked to his friend that he was going to marry Sherrie instead. "So I met John and went out with him that night," Sherrie recalls. "And the next day his girlfriend came into town and he broke up with her." Seven weeks later, to the accompaniment of slot-machine bells, John and Sherrie were wed at Bally's.

With the benefit of hindsight, John concedes that he didn't know Sherrie well enough to exchange Christmas cards with her, much less conceive a child with her. For her part, Sherrie says that they more or less caught each other on the rebound. "The only reason I met John is because I had kind of gotten over Austin's dad and gotten on my feet. I was dressed up and I had nowhere to go."

John probably wasn't looking behind her obvious attributes. At 27, Sherrie is a shapely, well-groomed blonde with a chatty air that can be disarming. She was a cheerleader at Collierville High and later studied at St. Joseph's School of Nursing, although she didn't get a degree. In recent years she has worked sporadically as a commissioned car salesperson, mostly at the Auto Center, a used-car dealership in Collierville owned by her father, Alvis Miller. "This is kind of how my deal worked with my dad," she says. "I would work for a little while, make a bit of money and then I would travel. Me and Austin would go to Disney World, we would go to the beach. We'd rent a condo at Sandestin. We'd hang out until we ran out of money, come back home and then I'd work."

The nature of her work is pertinent because Alvis and his wife of 39 years, Billie, have been indicted by a federal grand jury on charges that Alvis, through a series of cash transactions involving used cars and real estate, laundered illegal drug profits for three members of a domestic drug ring, all of whom pled guilty. The case focuses on 47 cash deposits ranging from $2,000 to $9,500—just under the $10,000 level that must be reported to federal authorities—made by the Miller family over 33 months, all of them at two Collierville banks. Four of the deposits were made by Sherrie, which is why, unless she or her parents make a deal with prosecutors before their scheduled trial date of Nov. 17, she faces penalties ranging from probation to 20 years in prison if convicted.

"The whole thing is a joke," Sherrie said recently. "I borrowed money from my dad because my checking account was overdrawn . . . and because I had bought too much inventory [for the dealership]. Yes, I made a $9,500 deposit, but this lady at the bank, she was a little old lady, she was like, 'Oh, you don't want to deposit all that cash. You need to keep it under $10,000 or we'll have to fill out all those forms.'" Sherrie added, "Now, this lady that told me that is 80-something years old, and I don't think she remembers it. [But] from then on, that's what they told my dad, too. He didn't know any other way to do it."

Sherrie's lawyer, Kemper Durand, says his client may have made the deposits, "but our take is that she was just a flunky doing what she was told by her father." The indictments of Billie and Sherrie, says Durand, are the government's way of pressuring Alvis to plead guilty. "This is what we call Southern gentlemen justice. They're hoping the man will take the hit so his wife and daughter will get dismissed."

That approach may not work with Alvis, a voluble man of 60 with the blocklike physique and belligerent outlook of his son-in-law, John Daly. "I'm not scared," Alvis said two weeks ago, leaning back in his office chair at the Auto Center. "I'm not giving in to anybody, because I didn't do anything I thought was wrong. If we laundered any money, we certainly didn't know it." Miller characterized his business dealings with three of the drug-ring principals as favors for lifelong friends, and said he had no idea they were involved in drug trafficking. "This has ruined my business," he complains. "I haven't sold a car in two months. People aren't going to buy a car from me. They think I'm a drug dealer."

While they wait for the scales of justice to tip one way or the other, the Millers—and, at times, Sherrie, Austin and baby John—live in a spacious four-bedroom house with swimming pool and gazebo on 35 acres of farmland at the edge of Collierville. The house, decorated with flagstone floors, Mediterranean furniture and a framed print of Clark Gable embracing Vivian Leigh, will be forfeited to the federal government if the Millers are convicted. The feds have also put liens on the Miller's bank accounts and used cars.

John Daly "is not in any way implicated," according to a highly-placed government source. Nevertheless, it is Daly who has behaved like the beleaguered suspect, losing sleep, chain-smoking and confounding his nervous system with alcohol and caffeine. The loss of his beloved mother Lou, who died last year of cancer, clearly contributed to his personal and professional decline. His refusal to take anti-depressant medicines prescribed by doctors probably has made things worse.

"He has more pressure," Sherrie told SI. "Every month, before he can take a breath or miss a cut, he has to pay $20,000 [in child support and alimony]. When you're not making any money, that comes pretty quick." In passing, Sherrie took another dig at ex-wives numbers 2 and 3, who seem to rank ahead of the feds on her don't-like list. "They live in Rancho Mirage and Orlando in very, very fine homes. Tile roof, the whole bit. They live large, and they don't even have to go to the mailbox to get their check. We wire it. All they have to do is spend it."

Daly, on the other hand, says the principle cause of his recent distress is wife number 4, who clearly brought some baggage to the marriage that didn't have Louis Vuitton's initials on it. Among other things, John claims that Sherrie kept him in the dark about her legal troubles and then dismissed them as trivial when they emerged. "I had to find out from the newspaper," he says of the part of the federal indictment that involved the laundering of drug money. "I saw it in the Memphis newspaper, and that hurt me more than anything."

Crabtree supports Daly's claim that he was shocked. "His jaw dropped. His face was in his hands. Because the headline, if I remember right, [called her] JOHN DALY'S WIFE. His name was the one that was up there."

In recent weeks, however, Daly has repeatedly defended the Millers. "I believe they're not guilty, and I'm standing 100% behind them," he told SI in late September, adding, "Granted, if Sherrie is going to prison for 20 years, I'll have to divorce her." On his return from Korea he stood up for his wife again ("I believe she's been honest about that case"); praised her parents ("I love Alvis and Billie, they've been great to me"); praised her parental skills ("She's always been a good mother"); and insisted that he wasn't divorcing her because of the charges.

So . . . why?

"I couldn't deal with it any more," Daly said in Las Vegas, tapping another cigarette out of his pack. "The things that she's done to me in front of people. I have let her beat the living s--- out of me . . . just poundin' on me with her fists." In Fayetteville, Ark., Daly said, he was schmoozing with singer Darius Rucker and other members of Hootie and the Blowfish on his bus when an angry Sherrie pushed him so hard that he fell into a counter and injured his right shoulder. Another time, during a locker-room card game in Texas, she smacked his head repeatedly with the buckle on a cap because he had autographed it for a female fan with the words "You were great last night!" The worst abuse? "When she about choked me in Ontario [Canada]. She'd had too much to drink and she just lost it, took it out on me."

Allegations of abuse are common in divorce cases, and Daly himself was accused of throwing his second wife, Bettye Fulford, against a wall during a drunken rampage in Castle Rock, Colo., in 1992. (Both Daly and Fulford later denied this had happened. "I've never hit a woman in my life," Daly says. "I don't even spank my kids.") Witnesses, however, support Daly's claims. Brian Van Der Riet, a former teaching pro who is president of John Daly Enterprises, says Daly called him at two in the morning the week of the Bell Canadian Open. "John said, 'You better come to the bus quickly, this woman is going to kill me.' So I high-tailed over and he was outside the bus and she was inside. [John said] she had tried to strangle him with his gold chain and snapped the big lion head off. John was out by his courtesy car looking for the gold chain, and we eventually found it on the ground." The couple argued through the night, Van Der Riet says, and Daly withdrew from the tournament after a first-round 75. "You can't play golf with 45 minutes or two hours' sleep, I don't care who you are."

Crabtree cites another example from another Ontario. In January, at a sports bar in Ontario, Calif., Daly, Crabtree and caddie Mick Peterson were watching a live women's boxing match. "They had these girls with big blown-up gloves on their hands," Crabtree recalls. "They're not naked, they're not anything. Sherrie came up behind John and hit him on the back of the head, absolutely as hard as she could. His head snapped forward, like he had been in a car accident. She started screaming, 'If you want to see women fight, you pick any woman in this club and I'll go beat her right now!'"

Sherrie, while confirming some details of the incidents, says it was John, not she, who had the alcoholic rages. The choking incident? "He's lying about that." The Texas bus bashing? "He started slamming the cabinet, then he ripped it off the wall and started banging it into all the mirrors and breaking everything." The boxing match? She had been told it would involve huge men, not college-age girls "wearing thonglike shorts and bikini tops." The story that she attacked three strippers last spring at a charity golf outing in Little Rock? "I did try to choke one of the girls, but she shouldn't have been naked in front of me like that."

Had she ever physically abused her 230-pound husband? "Oh my god, no. Well, one time, but he was yelling in my face so bad." She adds, "Look at the size of him and look at me. Does that make any sense?"

The constant bickering, those close to Daly say, goes a long way toward explaining why he has had only one top-25 finish in 2003 and is 169th on the PGA Tour money list. "The boy had no peace," says Arkansas jeweler Blake Allison, who has worked for Daly in various capacities for 20 years, most recently as operator of a merchandise trailer that Daly tows to tournaments. "If he would go somewhere, she'd sneak up on him or hide across the parking lot. It was a brutal situation." Van Der Riet says, "I'll tell you what I said to the PGA Tour—that as far as I'm concerned, 95% of this has nothing to do with alcohol. At the John Deere Classic she wasn't there. At the Buick in Flint she wasn't there. Those two weeks John didn't drink a drop of alcohol. He missed the Deere cut by one or two, but he hit it great." In Korea, Daly's friends all point out, he had only his caddie for company. "That win in Korea might not be a big win in the world of golf," Crabtree says, "but in the world of John Daly it is a big deal. As bad as things have been for him, I think the future could be that good."

Daly, looking out his Vegas hotel window at the lights of the Strip, shared Crabtree's optimism about his playing ability. ("I wouldn't be out here if I didn't think I could still win.") His PGA Tour career, though, had hit a new low, and his personal life had slipped even further into the abyss of honky-tonk heartache.

"It saddens me that it has to go this way," he said. "The hardest thing for me is losing Austin. I know he's my stepson, but he's four years old and he's been calling me Daddy for almost three years. Little John is going to be fine, I'm always going to take care of Little John, but Austin, snuggling up to me in bed and stuff . . . . "

Daly's eyes teared up and he swallowed hard.

Here's how the song goes:

Momma Lou makes chocolate gravy; she's so nice
Poppa Jim set me aside and gave me some advice
Quit spending all your money on all those skanks
Put some in your pocket, put some in the bank

On the day that Daly flew back from South Korea, Sherrie was waiting for him at a private airport in Las Vegas. Austin was at her side, restless. Little John wriggled in his stroller.

"I thought John would be happy to see us," Sherrie said when she got back to Collierville. "He just acted really ugly. We rode with him from the airport to Bally's. I said, 'If you're going to divorce me, we need to do this in a civilized manner.' He wouldn't even talk to me. He just got us settled into a room. He called [later] and said, 'I'll come see you in the morning,' and he never showed up. I haven't talked to him since. He never saw the kids.

"I'm in shock that John has turned on me like this. I think he has gone really nuts. I think he has drank himself to where his mind's not even right.

"I mean, honestly, I thought I knew him."

POSTSCRIPT: *Three years after this story ran (and after Sherrie had served a five-month sentence in a minimum security prison), John showed up for the second round of the Stanford St. Jude Championship with scratches on his face. He claimed his wife had attacked him with a steak knife while he was sleeping and had run off with the kids, etc., etc., etc.*

As this book went to press, John and Sherrie were still married.

ॐ

The Accidental Tourist

Arriving in Scotland without an itinerary or a tee time, the author discovers the 'wee secret' of the natives and plays 10 courses in 10 days

The idea for this story came from Matthew Harris, the British golf photographer. His motives were transparent—he wanted to photograph some of the quirky little town courses that are scattered across Scotland—but SI golf editor Jim Herre took the bait. Coincidentally, I had just received in the mail a couple of glossy brochures for high-end golf tours of Scotland and Ireland.

TO: *Thistle, Tartan & Tweed Tours*

SUBJECT: *Open Championship Travel Packages*

THANK YOU FOR THE BROCHURE DETAILING YOUR THREE-day, five-day, 11-day and 33-day Scottish golf vacations. I wish I could afford your Gleneagles from Dawn to Dusk package, including motor-coach transportation to and from Scotland's most expensive golf resort. Ditto your Firths of Fife excursion, which includes rounds at St. Andrews Old Course, New Course, Jubilee Course and Duke's Course, plus complimentary golf towel and ball marker as well as welcoming remarks by the motor-coach driver.

As it happens, I just got back from a Scottish golf trip. Nothing like what you folks offer, I hasten to add—no motor coach, no guides, no 5 a.m. wake-up calls, no "cocktails with the hotel manager." My wife and I simply rented a car and cruised the lowlands. She visited cathedrals and crystal factories, and I played golf. Ten courses in 10 days, none of them famous, none of them "championship," none of them costing more than £15 to play. In fact, and this isn't meant as a criticism of your tours, my greens fees for the whole trip came to £105. That's less than the cost of a single round and a caddie at the Old Course. Anyway, I thought you might get a laugh out of my self-styled travel package, which I call Town Courses of Scotland.

First off, my wife and I saved a few quid by flying separately, I on a full-fare ticket to Glasgow, she on a frequent-flyer coupon to Manchester, England, via Laredo, Texas, and Kuala Lumpur. (She missed my airline's in-flight film about Scottish golf, narrated by a Texan.) Once settled into our downtown Glasgow hotel, I warmed up with a quick nine at the King's Park municipal course, a rudimentary layout with pleasing views of the city and a pleasing price: gratis. "The Council shut it down on April 1," a trolley-pulling Scot explained, "but they keep mowing it, so we keep playing it." There were no flagsticks, but there was a metal cup on every green; and I only lost four balls in the matted rough. You might consider adding an abandoned golf course to your tours.

Our trip began in earnest the next day, when we drove down Scotland's west coast into the district of Ayrshire, artfully dodging the golfing shrines of Royal Troon, Prestwick and Turnberry. I played instead at rustic Maybole—at £8.50 the cheapest of 43 courses listed by the Ayrshire and Arran Tourist Board—and then at Girvan, where the fee was £12.50 and the view of brooding Ailsa Craig as good as that from Turnberry. Girvan was designed around 1903 by five-time British Open champion James Braid and consists of eight wind-lashed seaside holes and 10 pastoral inland holes. (To get from the 8th green to the 9th tee, players must march through town, dodging traffic and resisting the lure of pubs and chandleries.) The course is challenging enough, with its parade of drivable par-4s and unreachable par-3s. Par is 64, so Girvan is down the list of future Open sites, but as the head starter, Marion Brown, told me, "The majority of people here are not interested in championship courses. We're interested in having a good time."

Girvan, like most Scottish courses, has names for its holes. The 8th, a 243-yard par-3, is called Right Scunner (something you're fed up with). Haggerty's Loup (Scottish for leap) got its name when a club member stepped behind his ball on the 9th tee, backed up for a better view and fell into the River Girvan. "Come back when the wind is blowing," said Brown. "I've seen tee shots fly backward into the car park."

The next day, on the recommendation of an innkeeper in Ayr, I played at Ballochmyle Golf Club, on the A76 outside Mauchline. Ballochmyle is not as inviting as Girvan: Eight of the parking spaces are reserved for club officials, while signs define seven UNACCEPTABLE MODES OF DRESS. Fortunately, the arch tone was offset by a cow grazing at the 1st tee—I like to play in close proximity to livestock—and by the Gents Locker Room, which features wooden lockers painted in birdhouse colors. After my round, my wife and I sat in the lounge under a portrait of the poet Robert Burns, who lived and farmed nearby. Also on the wall was this poem by a lesser Scottish bard:

> *In ev'ry glen the mavis sang*
> *All nature list'ning seem'd the while*
> *Except where greenwood echoes rang,*
> *Amang the braes o' Ballochmyle.*

I mention the poetry because your tours seem heavy on golf and light on culture. My golf courses offered a Pictish burial site (St. Michael's Golf Club, outside Leuchars), a Stonehenge-like ruin (in the 2nd fairway at the Lundin Ladies Golf Club in Lower Largo) and an active lawn-bowling club (Maybole). At the Glencorse Golf Club, south of Edinburgh, I even got an art lesson. It came on the 16th tee, atop a high bluff, when a club member introduced me to a new way to take in the landscape, what he called the picture frame. "Just bend over and look backward through your legs," he said. Warily—and only because he did it first—I bent over and got rewarded with a significantly more sublime view, though inverted, of the lovely Pentland Hills.

Speaking of poetry, the 12th at Ballochmyle is called Aft Agley. This allusion to Burns's "best laid plans" came to mind on day 5, when we scaled the legendary Braid Hills in central

Edinburgh. Bliss! Blue sky, rocky crags, great golden swatches of whin and a view of the city so vast that dark Edinburgh Castle, on its citadel rock, looked as small as a toy.

Every Scot we'd talked to about affordable golf had said, "Ye have to play the Braids!" Three holes into my solitary round I was winded and dubious. The layout did not correspond to my scorecard map and seemed to have been constructed as an alpine mystery. Nine of the first 10 holes required a blind tee shot. The greens, too, were hidden from me and from the two other golfers I spied staggering among the rocks. It was only when I neared the end of my round that I looked downhill and noticed a slew of more attractive holes. The truth dawned: I was on the wrong course.

A young clerk at the clubhouse confirmed that I had played the par-65 Braids 2 course and not the par-70 Braids 1. "There's not much difference between the two," he said. "One is a bit longer and a bit flatter and a bit better maintained, and there aren't as many blind shots." You might want to hire this fellow.

By this time we were happily ensconced at the Dalmahoy Hotel and Country Club in Edinburgh, site of the 1992 Solheim Cup. I didn't play either of the 18-hole layouts, of course. Not at up to £50 a round. The day after I played Braids, I drove to nearby Penicuik to explore Glencorse, the home club of two-time Walker Cup captain George MacGregor. "I daresay someday they will name a hole for George," the head pro, Cliffe Jones, told me. "Probably when he's dead."

Glencorse is a par-64 with no par-5s, but it has some of the best par-3s in Scotland. The 5th hole, Forrester's Rest, made me gasp. From the medal tee, on a pinnacle above the rooftops of town, the hole tumbles down a wooded slope to a meandering brook and a shady green. Two hundred thirty-seven yards, pretty as a postcard and strong as any hole in Europe.

After playing, I spoke with 75-year-old Jim Stewart, a former club captain who was a finalist in the 1939 British Boys Championship. I asked if he knew the origin of any of the Glencorse hole names, such as Auchindinny or Hills O' Home.

Stewart cleared his throat and began, "Robert Louis Stevenson lay dying in Samoa. . . . " We were off on a historical and literary ramble that wrapped up, a minute or so later, with the old golfer quoting the writer's expiring words: "No more will I see my beloved hills o' home and the Glencorse Burn." I wiped away a tear and mentally scratched theater off my list of things to do in Edinburgh.

Day 7. We crossed the Forth River Bridge and drove east into Fife, checking into the Lundin Links Hotel, 30 minutes south of St. Andrews. To this point, the weather had been splendid, but isobars were piling up in the Irish Sea, and I only got in nine holes over the next 48 hours. (I can imagine the stress you fellows feel when a force four gale blows in on the day your tourists are supposed to play the Old Course. Having no schedule to follow, we experienced no such disappointment. My wife and I simply retired to our room, turned on the telly and drank tea and hot chocolate while watching *Dunstun Checks In*.)

After two restful days, we drove to St. Andrews and checked into Rufflets Country House, renowned for its food and formal gardens. (No motor coaches in the parking lot.) In a light rain we drove back down to the Firth of Forth so I could play Kinghorn, designed in 1887 by Old Tom Morris. "Points of view unsurpassed among the golfing grounds of Scotland," raved an old book about golf in Fife. I can't confirm that. As I teed off on No. 1, clouds and rain covered the treeless hills and the estuary.

But what holes! The 3rd, Loup Ower, is a picturesque par-3 from a highland tee to a valley green, guarded in front by an old stone wall. ("You don't want to be leavin' it short," a helpful Scot told me.) The 18th, Cryin' Hill, is the longest 196-yard hole in the world. The blind tee shot is straight over a vertical cliff face and can be lofted sufficiently only because the tee is canted upward like a ski jump.

When I finished, I found my wife, who had gone off to explore indoor activities, waiting in the car in the rain in an otherwise empty car park. She couldn't reconcile my drowned-rat state with my broad grin.

For my last day of golf I wanted something special. On the advice of David Joy, the playwright-actor who plays Old Tom Morris in videos, I set out for Cupar (pronounced with three *r*'s at the end) to play another of Fife's venerable layouts, a nine-holer built on the side of a big hill. "Oh, it's torture," Joy said. "You wind up with one leg longer than the other."

I parked outside the Cupar Cemetery and walked uphill past stone walls and headstones to the clubhouse, where I gave £12 to a lonely barmaid. She looked out the window and said, "Are you sure?" The great hill was shrouded in clouds and mist.

The 1st hole is a flat par-3. Then the climb begins: a 259-yard uphill par-4, three more par-4s back and forth like ramps on the sidehill, a wooded par-3, still climbing, and then the final scamper up to the 7th tee. How can I describe the view? The rain had fled on a freshening breeze, leaving deep blue holes in the clouds. Far below, sunlight fell on the rooftops and steeples of the Eden River valley.

After my round I shared my satisfaction with the greenkeeper, Trevor Harris, who was cleaning equipment in his shed behind the 9th green. I told him I had played nine courses in 10 days with no itinerary, no tee times, no pulling of strings and no asking of favors. I told him I had never waited to tee off. I told him I had mingled with hospitable Scots and tasted the fruit of poets. I told him I had enjoyed wondrous scenery and saved enough money to start a college fund for my grandchildren. Harris smiled knowingly. "It's our wee secret," he said.

So there you have it. Granted, only a head case like me could enjoy 10 unhurried days of golf on quaint layouts like these. You folks know what sells, and it's not Town Courses of Scotland.

Funny thing, though. After my round at Cupar, I drove back to St. Andrews, made a U-turn by the Old Course Hotel and pulled into the golf parking lot. The sun was still high in the sky and the wind was starting to whistle. I fancied a few more holes before dinner.

The Old Course was out, and the New, Jubilee and Eden Courses didn't suit my mood. I grabbed my bag and walked instead to the par-30 Balgove Course, a flat piece of grassland enclosed by an old stone wall. "This course," my guidebook told me, "appeals to the beginner, the schoolboy, the happy family and the golfer when in a lazy mood."

I plunked down £7—"You can go 'round twice for that," the cheerful clerk told me—and went out to play a short, featureless track with nothing to recommend it but golden sunshine, a bracing wind and the feel of genuine linksland underfoot. Even so, I barely looked up when a motor coach full of tourists rumbled by on its way out of town.

Best wishes,

JOHN GARRITY

P.S. Almost forgot why I wrote! Please take me off your mailing list.

POSTSCRIPT: *Once or twice a year some stranger approaches me at a tournament and says, "I read the story about your Scottish golf tour, and two years later I followed in your footsteps. Girvan! Kinghorn! It was the best vacation of my life." The tour operators, however, were unmoved by my prose. I'm still on their mailing lists.*

ϲ

A Giant in Japan

In his homeland Jumbo Ozaki is the undisputed king of golf.
So why can't he get respect anywhere else?

*I'm 6' 7", so I smiled when I read the title my editors chose for this profile.
I obviously stood out like a sore Yank in Japan, but the Japanese are very
polite; I rarely caught them staring at me.*

JUMBO'S LEGS ARE WRAPPED IN GREEN BAIZE. HIS TAILOR
must have stripped a pool table for the cloth. Jumbo's sweater
comes to Kyushu by way of Las Vegas. Swirls of aqua and silver on
black cashmere suggest peacock feathers against a night sky.

Jumbo's gallery is two or three thousand strong, lining the fairway
and treading on pine needles, a silent army in the trees. Jumbo's ball
rests on a white tee, a good four inches off the sweet green turf.

Jumbo's cigarette touches his lips. When he exhales, smoke
plumes past his bold sideburns and unblinking eyes. Jumbo's
caddie stands by, holding a leather pouch of sand. He will douse
the cigarette when Jumbo is ready. Jumbo's tight-lipped smile
suggests boredom. Or menace.

Here, in Japan, Jumbo is huge. He is the rising sun on the
white flag. His feet leave permanent footprints. His muttered
jokes bring smiles to spectators 400 yards away, as if transmitted
over the gallery ropes. He is *ichiban*. No. 1. Here, in Japan.

OUT THERE, it's different. The golfer from Australia, the so-called Shark, thinks Ozaki-san is a cheat. Players in Europe whisper that Jumbo uses illegal equipment. The Americans sneer at his World Ranking, which is 10th despite his age, 51, and at his reluctance to play much outside Asia. Visitors to Japan eat up rumors that Jumbo is a member or fellow traveler of the *yakuza*, the Japanese mafia.

"If I can get my hands on one of his golf balls, I bet I can sell it back to him for a bundle," says an American caddie. "Everybody knows he uses a hot ball."

"What's he ever won?" asks an American sportswriter. "The Osaka Seaweed Invitational?"

"No way is Jumbo better than Mark O'Meara or Steve Elkington . . . or . . . *me!*" says an American pro fighting to keep his PGA Tour card.

Have they actually seen him play? Not exactly. A swing or two at the Masters. On the range at the British Open. What matters is the record, and the record shows that Jumbo Ozaki has never won a major. Never even threatened. But here, in Japan. . . .

You don't finish the thought. It's like arguing that a koi—one of the colorful carp in the hotel garden pool—could devour a shark.

HIS REAL NAME is Masashi Ozaki, and he's the eldest of three brothers from Tokushima prefecture, in southwestern Japan. In his teens he was the star pitcher for the spring national champion Kainan High team, which in Japan bestows status comparable to that of the quarterback of a U.S. national champion college football team. He was introduced to golf by the manager of the Nishitetsu Lions pro baseball club, the team Ozaki signed with in 1967.

"There's a Jumbo, and there's a Masashi," Ozaki says, making a distinction between the showman and the inner man. Jumbo emerged about 30 years ago while Ozaki was teaching himself the game, and burst full-blown on the scene when he gave up baseball for tournament golf at age 22. "From the beginning I wanted to look good, to wear good clothes, to be in the spotlight." To behave, in other words, in a distinctly un-Japanese manner. Jumbo's hair—a shag cut that spills down his neck—sets him apart. You see such hair behind the wheel of a flashy car after midnight in one of Tokyo's bawdy soapland districts.

Masashi, on the other hand, lives outside Tokyo with his wife, Yoshiko, and their three children. His walled estate—a palace by Japanese standards—has a backyard driving range and a garage for his collection of classic cars.

When Jumbo goes abroad, he travels with an entourage, what the Japanese call a *kobun*. At the Masters he rents a large house and flies in a sushi chef from New York. "He is the Arnold Palmer of Japan," says Sadao Iwata, the country's best-known television golf commentator. "Golfers here dress like him, buy the equipment he plays, smoke the same brand of cigarettes."

Westerners don't get it. Jumbo has finished no better than a tie for eighth in the Masters. He has missed the cut seven times, missed the entire tournament from '80 through '86, and has shot several rounds of 78 and higher. His best showings in the other majors are equally drab: a 47th in the '94 PGA, a tie for sixth in the '89 U.S. Open and a 14th in the '78 British Open.

It's startling, then, to talk with Americans who play the Japanese tour—golfers who see a different Ozaki. "He's unbelievable, a big hitter with a fantastic short game," says Todd Hamilton, who was a star at Oklahoma. "Guys from the States wonder why he's ranked so high, but you don't see many of the famous players beating him when they play here. He makes the putts Nicklaus used to make, the ones to keep a round going."

Peter Teravainen, the Harvard graduate who joined the Japanese tour in 1996 after 14 years on the European tour, practically erupts when it is suggested that Ozaki isn't as good as his ranking. "I get so pissed off at the golf magazines in the U.S. and Europe that say Jumbo is no good. They never get off their butts and come here to see him play."

Ozaki fans can point to more than testimonial evidence. When he won the Dunlop Phoenix Invitational in 1996, beating the cream of Asian golfers and a score of top international players, it was Jumbo's 100th pro victory. Last year, when he could have been playing Senior golf, Ozaki won five more Japanese tour events (one by 12 shots), won the Peugeot Open de France, finished seventh on the European tour's Order of Merit and led the Japanese money list for the 11th time. "Anytime you win a hundred tournaments, you can flat play," says five-time British Open champ Tom Watson.

Even when he fails to win, Ozaki produces shots that linger in memory. Last November he trailed Ryder Cupper Lee Westwood by three strokes in the final round of the Taiheiyo

Masters. Needing eagle on the par-5 18th hole, Ozaki spanked a long-iron second shot over water to a pin placement no larger than a tatami mat. He then holed the putt. Westwood, playing in the final pairing, heard the crowd roar and knew his cushion had been yanked away.

"I'm glad I didn't actually see that shot," the young Englishman said after sealing his one-shot victory. "I might have been silly enough to try to match it."

SKEPTICS ASK: Is Jumbo honestly that good? Answer: Yes.

Cynics ask: Is Jumbo that good *honestly*? Answer: Depends on whom you ask.

Greg Norman, for one, thinks Japanese officials need to crack down on Ozaki. Four years ago, in a tournament at Japan's Tomei Country Club, Norman accused Jumbo of improving his lie in the rough by pressing down the grass behind his ball with a club head. The local rules committee did nothing. Last year in the Crowns tournament at Nagoya Country Club, Norman claimed he again saw Ozaki use his driver to improve a bad lie before switching to another club for the shot.

"Norman was very angry," says a Japanese journalist who witnessed the event. But again, no official action was taken, and Norman's accusations got delicate treatment in the national press. "In Japan cheating is not tolerated," says Kazuhiko Muto, an editor at the *Hochi Shimbun*. "But as a whole Japanese sportsmen have a more shallow knowledge of the rules." His explanation for the JPGA's inaction?

"There is a saying in Japan: 'You place a lid over a smelling pot.' "

Norman's charges aside, suspicion of Ozaki is rampant among golf's moral majority, the professional tour caddies. "I've got a friend who says when Jumbo marks his ball it looks like he's playing Chinese checkers," said Jerry Higginbotham, Mark O'Meara's caddie, during a swing through Japan. "I'm going to be watching him like a hawk." Other caddies swear that Ozaki, a nonconformist, plays with a nonconforming golf ball—that is, a ball that flies long when Jumbo hits it and curves right or left at his command. "He's the only one who plays that ball," says another American looper, referring to the custom-made Bridgestone Precept Ozaki uses in competition.

Ozaki's defenders scoff at the equipment claim. Jumbo, they note, lent prototypes of his J's Professional Weapon driver to Jack Nicklaus and Ray Floyd at the 1990 Masters. The Americans hit long drives with the clubs, touching off a sales run for Bridgestone, but research later revealed that the drivers were essentially stainless-steel knockoffs of the persimmon MacGregor club Nicklaus had used for most of his career. "I think it's sour grapes to say he's playing with illegal stuff," says Teravainen. "I'm longer than Jumbo, and nobody's ever accused me of playing a doctored ball."

Even O'Meara's caddie has a different take on the cheating allegations now that he has watched Ozaki play. "If he's pulled anything, I've missed it," says Higginbotham, watching Ozaki hit balls on the range after another low-scoring round. "And I'm amazed at how good he is. He can really play."

Back at the hotel, you study the biggest koi in the pool, the fat gold one, and you decide he might be a match for an eel or even a barracuda.

Jumbo's response to criticism is the sound of one hand clapping. He rarely acknowledges it. Typically, he strolls into the interview room after a tournament round, takes a seat behind a microphone, and fires up a cigarette. (In a smokes-mad country, Jumbo stands out as a compulsive puffer.) The reporters are deferential, and Jumbo answers their questions with a smile that often devolves to a smirk. He looks very cool, a Japanese Brando. He makes the reporters laugh with his wry asides, and then he rises abruptly and walks out the door, followed by his minions. "Jumbo likes to be in control," says a Japanese journalist.

Requests for private interviews are usually deflected to Bridgestone, to his own company, Jumbo Ozaki Enterprises, or to World One Company Ltd., the new equipment company that recently signed him to a multimillion-dollar endorsement deal. Those companies, after a dignified delay of several days—or weeks—usually report that Jumbo is unavailable.

Persistence is a form of flattery, however, and after two months of haggling, Ozaki agrees to a rare, one-on-one interview. He insists that the interview be conducted away from his home, that it not involve his wife, who runs Jumbo Ozaki Enterprises for him, and that an interpreter be provided. "Jumbo understands English, but he speaks it with hesitation," says a Japanese golf writer who has visited his house. "He does not do something in public if he is not perfect."

The interview takes place in November during a pro-am party at the Taiheyo Club in Gotemba. Ozaki, followed by a couple of *kobun*, enters the clubhouse in his playing outfit—shimmering velour pants and a sweater with colorful geometric shapes—and selects a private room on the second floor. There he sinks into an armchair and lights a cigarette. Outside, afternoon clouds mute the fall foliage and cover Mt. Fuji. Inside, clouds of smoke veil the world's most enigmatic golfer.

You begin: "You are a man of many interests. . . " because, as you understand it, Ozaki-san is something of a Renaissance man. He reads travel books. He collects cars. He plays guitar, sings, collects instruments and hit the pop charts in Japan with three singles in the late '80s. Ozaki is the antipode of his rival, Isao Aoki, Japan's other great touring pro. Aoki knows only golf.

But your information is outdated. Ozaki says that his cars—a Ferrari, a Lamborghini, a Maserati, three Rolls-Royces—are garaged. That hobby is *"finito."* So, too, is his music. He says, "I think the guitar is in the attic and food for mice." The interpreter, a young woman, smiles at the translation. Ozaki rewards her with a thin smile of his own.

What, you ask, are his current interests? Wine and bonsai, he replies. His wine collection consists of "about a thousand bottles" of French wines of good vintage, which he buys by the case, drinking one bottle and saving the rest. More involving, because it requires patience and the hands and soul of an artist, is bonsai—a traditional Japanese discipline in which a gardener shapes dwarf plants to idealized forms.

"Aoki-san looks at golf as his hobby *and* his work," Ozaki says. "I envy him, in a way, but I know I cannot do that. I need to get away." He crushes his cigarette in an ashtray and lights another. "I have used up a lot of time and money on hobbies."

His interests, then, explain why Ozaki does not move to the U.S. and play the rich Senior tour. He would be giving up his culture, his life, for a succession of hotel rooms. Ozaki nods and continues: "Also, in my generation to be Number 1 in Japan was the major goal. You didn't have [Hideki] Nomo going to the major leagues when I was young. It's unfortunate because I've seen the American tour, the enthusiasm of the galleries and the level of play. It's too bad I wasn't born there so I could feel that same fire in me."

Ozaki sums up. "The Japanese golf world needs me." Needs . . . Masashi?

He smiles indulgently. No. Japan needs *Jumbo*—his speed-tribe melding of Elvis, James Dean and Liberace. "The tournament site is a stage for me. I want to be the sort of person that the fans want me to be."

A Bridgestone rep enters the room and whispers in Ozaki's ear. He is needed at the pro-am party. Bows must be taken, egos massaged. Ozaki puts out his cigarette and rises. "If you need more time," he says, "I will come right back."

THERE'S A QUESTION still to be asked, but the interview will end if you so much as utter the word *yakuza*.

"There have always been rumors about Jumbo," says a Japanese newspaperman. "Similar to your Frank Sinatra." According to one story, Ozaki played with a *yakuza* in a private event. When he was admonished by the Japanese tour, he said, "How was I supposed to know? The guy was wearing a golf glove." (Amputated fingers are a *yakuza* trademark.)

Hard facts are few. In 1987 Japan's biggest newspaper, *Yomiuri Shimbun*, obtained photographs of Ozaki in a dinner jacket at a birthday party for Susumu Ishii, the alleged leader of Inagawa-kai, one of Japan's biggest criminal enterprises. *Yomiuri* reported that Ozaki had met Chihiro Inagawa, eldest son of the gang's founder, in the late '70s at the Hawaiian Open. The paper said Jumbo was subsequently entertained by Inagawa-kai's top executives, played golf with them at a resort outside Tokyo and even gave them golf lessons. Inagawa reportedly displayed in his house a framed photograph of himself with Ozaki and showed it proudly to guests. Four days after the *Yomiuri* article appeared, the Japanese tour officially warned Ozaki.

Since then journalists have shown little interest in following up. Ozaki punishes *Yomiuri* by refusing to talk to its reporters. "It's still a delicate subject," says a *Yomiuri* business writer. "You don't ask whose money is behind Jumbo or World One."

Bridgestone, for one, would like to know. The Japanese golf equipment company dominates its home market, thanks largely to a long relationship with Ozaki. Last November, however, Jumbo signed an equipment deal with little-known World One, an entertainment company that started 10 years ago as a pipsqueak outfit renting karaoke machines. The payoff for

Ozaki—estimated to be as high as $200 million over five years and no lower than $20 million—invited speculation that the deal was designed to funnel cash to the golfer, who is believed to have lost millions in real estate investments in the early '90s. Bridgestone, meanwhile, was left with a ball deal.

So you have this business question for Jumbo. When he returns, you ask if he has been hurt by the popping of Japan's so-called bubble economy. Jumbo lights another cigarette and frowns. "I don't have any particular interest in money," he says. "If I produce wins, the business side goes well." His eyes wander to the window, then to the floor. He waits for the next question.

THE 17TH HOLE at Kyushu's Phoenix Country Club is fronted by a pond, and in the pond is a small fountain. In 1994 Jumbo hit his approach shot on the final day of the Dunlop Phoenix onto this birdbathlike perch, three feet above the water. "I still think he should have played it," says Australian golf writer Graeme Agars, studying a picture in a display case of the stranded ball.

You're in Jumbo's Corner, a museum of Ozaki memorabilia on the second floor of Phoenix's luxurious clubhouse. Here's a photo of Jumbo in '71, as skinny as Tiger Woods and wearing wild-striped pants. Here are the clubs he used to win his 100th tournament, and here is a document, on rice parchment, executed in precise, elegant calligraphy, lovely enough to frame. It's a letter to the club from Jumbo, in his own hand.

You've seen other evidence of his perfectionism. A photographer wanted Jumbo to pose beside a bonsai. Jumbo winced, smiled, leaned back in his chair. Finally, he shook his head. "I don't want to get my picture taken next to a cheap bonsai," he said. "If you buy a $10,000 bonsai, I don't mind."

IT OCCURS TO YOU that Jumbo is a funny nickname for a man who is not large, even by Japanese standards. "They say he's a shy person," says David Ishii, the touring pro from Hawaii. "I find that amazing because he doesn't act like it in a crowd."

Jumbo walks on stage for a major press conference at Tokyo's Akasaka Prince Hotel. He wears a stylish gray suit, a crisp white shirt, and a striking gray and white tie. He sits down to applause and the popping of camera flashes. He speaks, and laughter fills the ballroom. "He's a very funny guy," says a Japanese reporter. "Maybe after professional golf he can be a TV personality."

Shy he may be, but Jumbo is not reclusive. In his backyard, by the practice facility, he has built motel-style housing for members of his *gundan*, the 20 or so golf apprentices who look to him for instruction and career guidance. Every January the *gundan* moves to tropical Okinawa or Kyushu for Jumbo's spring camp, a sort of Grapefruit League for golfers. There Jumbo leads calisthenics and prepares his charges for the rigors of international golf. The irony, of course, is that Jumbo has chosen the most parochial of career paths. His biggest win outside his home country is the 1972 New Zealand PGA Championship.

Why is he a lesser golfer when he leaves Japan? His detractors say it's because he can't stretch the rules outside Asia. Others point out that Ozaki has never made a concerted assault on the majors. He doesn't play for a few weeks in Scotland or the U.S. to get comfortable with local conditions. He doesn't use caddies familiar with the courses. He doesn't even allow for jet lag; he just wings in and tees up.

A more intriguing theory—and one that mirrors a common complaint of many Japanese women about their husbands—is offered by Ayako Okamoto, the Japanese pro who won 17 tournaments on the LPGA tour. Ozaki and the other men can't win abroad, she says, because they are victims of the "doting mother syndrome" prevalent in Japan. That is, they are so spoiled they can't function on their own. Or as she puts it, "They can't make it without their Cup Noodles." Ozaki has his own nonexplanation: "When I get in that atmosphere, I don't get the urge to win as strongly."

It is interesting, then, to hear that he still dreams of winning the Masters, which will welcome him next week for the 17th time. "The Masters, to me, is the ultimate in sports, showing golf in its best form," he says. "To win the Masters would be the glory of my career."

But *can* he win it? He has finished no better than 23rd in this decade. He missed the cut in '94 and '96. Suddenly energized, he leans forward in his armchair at the Taiheyo Club. He waves his cigarette, making smoke trails. "Five years from now I will still have the power and the length and the physical skills to win it. I don't think anybody else, at the same age, would have that energy."

But with Woods now in the picture. . .

"Tiger is young," he interrupts, "and purposeful and has that enthusiasm to win. But to win at a ripe age, that's something I feel is very difficult to achieve. There's only one condition for that. You have to win like a young player. It doesn't mean anything if you just win with technical skills. You have to win like a young player."

The interpreter catches your eye. "It is difficult to translate. Ozaki-san asks if you understand what it means, 'To win like a young man.' " You assure her and Ozaki-san that you understand perfectly.

In truth he has probably offered you a $10,000 bonsai, and you have taken it for a $30 Kmart ficus.

"WHAT DID Ozaki have to say?" someone asks you later.

"Oh, a little of this and a little of that."

You go to the garden pool one last time to study the swarming koi. The fat gold one is missing. Sleeping maybe, or lurking in the shadows near the stone lantern, or gone?

You wonder how a certain fish might fare in deeper waters.

POSTSCRIPT: *The "hot" golf ball that Jumbo was playing turned out to be a solid-core Bridgestone ball that any golfer could buy off the shelf. Two years after this story ran, Tiger Woods switched to a similar ball and promptly swept all four major championships. No one accused him of cheating.*

❧

Of Straitjackets, COFs and Mystical Clarity

If you want to become a better golfer, don't go to golf school, or at least don't go to more than one

I kicked the golf habit from 1965 to '80. Didn't touch a club. Didn't set foot on a course. When I took up the game again in my mid-30s, I drove out to the Kansas City Country Club for a few lessons with Stan Thirsk, who was Tom Watson's teacher. Stan got me pointed in the right direction, and I was soon shooting in the low 80s. I was happy with that.

But then SI's golf-mad managing editor, Mark Mulvoy, handed me a dream assignment. "We're sending you to golf school," he said over the phone. "Go to a couple of schools, sharpen your game and fill up your notebook. And if they show you something that works, share it with me."

A few months later I turned in the cheery prose that follows. But if I were writing the story today, I'd title it: How to Lose Your Swing and Your Mind in Five Easy Lessons.

Please fill out questionnaire so your pro will know your goals.
NAME: *John Garrity* AGE: *43*

HANDICAP: *14 (My best round was a 78 on a course that had only four trees but was otherwise a true test of golf.)*

WOULD YOU DESCRIBE YOURSELF AS A BIG HITTER OR A SHORT HITTER? *Big hitter but not too accurate. Maintain that long-driving contests should be staged from the center of concentric circles, like frog-jumping contests, with trophy given to contestant who reaches most distant ring, never mind direction.*

WHAT, IN YOUR OPINION, IS THE WEAKEST PART OF YOUR GAME? *Explaining 14 handicap after driving ball 300 yards off the 1st tee.*

WHAT, IN YOUR OPINION, IS THE STRONGEST PART OF YOUR GAME? *Explaining why I have to wait for players to leave the green 250 yards away just before topping a four-wood.*

WHAT MADE YOU DECIDE TO ATTEND A GOLF SCHOOL? *Haven't had a good night's sleep since I learned there's something Dan Quayle does better than I do.*

DO YOU HAVE ANY DISABILITIES, CHARACTERISTICS, ETC., THAT YOUR PRO SHOULD KNOW ABOUT? *I'm 6' 7" and have short arms, so I play with extralong clubs. They're just long enough to affect the balance of my Sunday bag, and sometimes they spill out. I've been dealing with this problem by carrying more balls in the pockets as a counterweight. Sometimes I overcompensate, creating too much torque and a tendency for the bag to twist around my pelvis and for the towels to get tangled in my legs. These difficulties have added 15 to 20 minutes to my rounds.*

WHAT DO YOU HOPE TO GAIN FROM YOUR STAY AT OUR GOLF SCHOOL? *A single-digit handicap, mystical clarity and a sense of oneness with the universe.*

IT SEEMS LIKE an uneven exchange. A young woman at a steel desk gives me a plastic bag tag with my name on it, a blue folder full of schedules and a 19-cent spiral notebook. In return, I write her a check for $1,540, made out to "Ben Sutton Golf Schools."

"Happy hour is at 5:45, dinner is at 6:30," she says, sweeping the check out of view with the deftness of a three-card monte dealer. "You'll meet your pro at dinner. Do you know who you have?"

I do not, so she runs her finger down the roster. When she finds my name, she snorts. "You've got Toby Lyons. He's a crazy old fart."

It figures. The palm-lined streets outside are choked with COFs driving golf carts. On the way from the Tampa airport I had passed this billboard: SUN CITY CENTER—AMERICA'S RETIRE-MENT TOWN. I even spotted the classic COF bumper sticker: A BALD HEAD IS A SOLAR PANEL FOR A SEX MACHINE.

I smile gamely and wander off to look for my room. The Sun City Center Inn is more early Travelodge than the El Dorado it appears to be in the promotional video. A brisk breeze has picked up and a citadel of thunderheads is about to overwhelm the afternoon sun.

An hour later, it begins to rain. The wind howls. Water rises in the rock garden between the units and laps at my doorsill.

I call my wife, Pat, in Kansas City. "I'm homesick."

She says, "I don't want to hear about it."

Thus comforted, I go to dinner.

The welcome dinner is in a warm and cozy private room at the inn. There are seven or eight tables, segregated by sex, each presided over by a teaching pro. The introductions are quick and cordial. My group of 14-to-24 handicappers consists of a Penn-sylvania glass merchant-sculptor, a corporate executive from Taiwan, a college history professor, a West Coast businessman, a Sun City Center retiree and a retired Air Force One pilot.

All these are pale characters compared with Toby Lyons, our pro. I cheer up the minute I meet him: a gruff 75-year-old with a big-featured, leathery face and thin gray hair raked straight back over his skull.

"Ready to learn some golf, boys?" he asks, mauling a dinner roll. He answers his own question: "You bet you are."

In a matter of minutes, we coax the essentials out of him. He spends his summers teaching at the Niagara Falls Country Club, but his reputation is based on lessons given long ago to Yogi Berra, Joe Louis, Bing Crosby and Bob Hope. He played in 15 U.S. Opens in the '40s and early '50s. The names of contemporaries fall freely from his lips: Sarazen, Snead, Nelson. "At one time I was probably the best putter in the world," he says, "but I could never hit the ball very far." He reaches for another roll. "It's a grand game, boys. It'll carry you through life."

Someone asks if Ben Sutton, the school founder, was ever a touring pro. "Oh, no, no, no!" Lyons looks shocked. Sutton is no golfer, he says. Sutton is a former engineer for the Hoover vacuum cleaner company.

Just then someone taps a glass at the head table, and the ceremonies begin. Sutton, a cheerful, cherubic 82-year-old, rises to say a few words. Welcome, he says, to the 485th Ben Sutton Golf School. He knows we will have a great time, and if we apply ourselves diligently, we will receive our diplomas on Saturday. He is sure of this, he says, because so far 40,000 students have enrolled in the school and only one has failed to graduate.

Sutton looks around the room, beaming. "His check bounced."

Oh, swell, I think. Another COF.

A MONTH LATER, I am on the practice tee at the Mission Hills Resort in Rancho Mirage, Calif., where a swing doctor and his assistant, Igor, are fitting me for a straitjacket. Igor pulls a black strap across my chest and secures it with Velcro so tightly that I can barely breathe. The doctor gleefully binds my upper arms to my rib cage with more straps and rings. When Igor and the doctor finish, I can flap my forearms and walk like an emperor penguin, but if a bee lands on my nose it can camp there.

The doctor, in his Georgia drawl, says, "O.K., John, try hitting one." Igor hands me a five-iron and tees up a ball for me.

I want to scream out, "No, you fools! I'm a graduate of the Ben Sutton Golf School!" But I don't want to anger the swing doctor. Besides, this is a three-day Golf Digest Instruction School, and my Ben Sutton diploma doesn't carry much weight here.

So I grip the club, take my stance and try swatting the ball . . . and I blade it about 50 yards.

Igor tees up another ball, and I try again: a toe hook, maybe 70 yards. I swear under my breath. I try a third time—don't ask me what kind of swing I put on it—and the ball jumps off the club face, rises majestically, draws back toward the target, and lands in the green valley below, 200 yards away. Igor whoops and spins like a dervish.

I turn to the swing doctor and say, "Can this thing be worn under a sweater, does it come with a warranty, and how long can I leave it on before gangrene sets in?"

A NORMAL PERSON, you say, doesn't go to two different golf schools in a month's time.

A normal person, I respond, doesn't go to a golf school at all.

When I told friends that I planned to attend a couple of golf schools for a magazine story, half of them (golfers) said they envied me. The other half (nongolfers) gave me patronizing looks, as if I had announced my intention to matriculate at the Klip 'n' Kurl School of Hairdressing.

I remember a night in a hotel room a year or so ago. Three a.m. Can't sleep. A golf instruction video comes on the tube: the Jimmy Ballard Golf Connection. Ninety minutes with Jimmy Ballard, "the professional who teaches the professionals, the leading edge of golf pedagogy in the world today." A bunch of golfers sitting obediently in chairs on a fairway at the Doral Resort in Miami. Ballard, wild with Rasputin eyes, lecturing, cajoling, slashing at straw men: "It's physically impossible . . . there's no way . . . never in the history of golf has there ever been . . . ." The golfers, motionless in their chairs—dead maybe. Words pour from Ballard, thousands of words without a breath, and when the video is over I have retained just this one nugget of instruction: "You curl your toes up in your shoes."

So don't talk to me about normal.

Take Toby Lyons. If he has a golf theory, it is "Mama don't 'low no pedagogy 'round here." His first objective, always, is to demystify a technique.

"It's the easiest shot in golf, boys," Lyons said on Day 2 of the Sutton school. He then dropped a ball in a sand bunker, dug in his feet and splashed the ball out with a swing no longer than a summer sausage. The ball stopped a foot from the pin.

He threw down another ball. "Don't open the blade. Just hit behind the ball." He chipped out another; it slid a foot past the pin. He threw down another ball, stepped on it, kicked some sand over it. "Fried egg lie. Gotta close the club face." He planted his feet, swung, and the ball stopped two feet from the pin. "That's all there is to it, boys. Go to work."

A minute later, sand was flying, grown men were grunting and Lyons's three shots sat in isolated splendor near the hole. "No, no, no!" he roared. I looked up. He was staring at me with an anguished look, as if he had caught me spray-painting graffiti on his car. "Not like *that*. Like *this*!" He made an abbreviated flick with the club. I tried to imitate his swing and left the ball in the trap again.

"No, no, no," he said—softly this time. He grabbed the shaft of my sand wedge and yanked it back and through while I held the grip. "Do *this*." Instead, I did something else.

"No," he shouted. "Can't you do this?"

"Apparently not," I said.

"Your swing is too big," he muttered. He moved on.

A minute later, I heard him scolding Lyle the pilot, whose claim to self-esteem was that he had once been entrusted with 800 tons of Boeing 707 and the lives of the sad-eyed leader of the free world and his beagles. "You're doing *this* . . . I'm doing *this*!" Pause. Sound of sand splashing and ball landing softly on green. "Why can't you do what I do?"

That, of course, was the question we had paid $1,540 to have answered.

"Toby," Bob the professor asked on Day 3, "has any student ever killed one of the pros around here?"

"No, no," Lyons said placidly.

GOLF SCHOOL, you say, must be physically and mentally taxing.

It is. At the Ben Sutton school, some of the students skipped lunch to take naps. Others complained of blisters, insomnia, hemorrhoids and out-of-body experiences.

I was not immune. On Night 4, I dreamed the history of golf schools in America. It was a short dream. U.S. golf schools are a fairly recent phenomenon. "In America, private instruction used to be the thing," says Shelby Futch, president of the John Jacobs Practical Golf Schools in Scottsdale, Ariz. "Americans thought if you shared a lesson with somebody it was because you couldn't afford to pay for it yourself."

That began to change in 1968, when Sutton, after 31 years with the Hoover Company, put aside his upholstery attachments and approached other retirees with a novel idea: "Why don't 35 of us COFs get together and pay five golf pros to go down South and vacation with us for a week?" Close on Sutton's heels came the Craft-Zavichas Golf School in Pueblo, Colo., which still bills itself as "the nation's second-oldest golf school."

The next significant player in the golf school game was Bob Toski, a runty touring pro who retired from tournament golf not long after winning George May's 1954 World Championship at Tam O'Shanter in Niles, Ill. Toski, who was critical of the instruction the average golfer was getting at the country-club level, went to *Golf Digest* editor Dick Aultman in '70 with his idea for a permanent floating golf school for highly motivated amateurs. Aultman bought the idea, and within a few years Toski had put together a stable of top teaching pros, including Jim Flick, Davis Love, Paul Runyan, Peter Kostis and John Jacobs. Jacobs bolted in '76 to put together a school for a rival magazine, *Golf.* That school failed, but Jacobs then teamed up with Futch, and the Jacobs schools are now second only to *Golf Digest* schools in the number of sites and students.

The golf boom of the late '80s spawned a number of new schools with different approaches and philosophies. It also led to dramatic expansion among the established schools. *Golf Digest*'s '90 schedule lists about 250 sessions at 16 different clubs and resorts. Sutton's school is open every week of the year, employs 28 pros and treats about 2,300 patients a year. Says *Golf Digest*'s Flick, "I don't think any of us thought the golf school business would grow like it has. Last year I did 46 schools, and 96 percent of the spots were taken."

Naturally, this growth has encouraged the development of rival theories about the golf swing. Jimmy Ballard teaches "connection." Toski teaches "the free arm swing." Dave Pelz teaches the "3 × 4 system."

Isn't it confusing, I am asked, to attend golf schools with different philosophies? Not at all, I reply. As in medicine, a second opinion is always valuable.

On our first day at the Ben Sutton school, Lyons led us out behind the bag room for videotaping and diagnosis. One by one, we stood in front of a wall marked out with grid lines and hit balls for the camera. Then Lyons took us into the viewing room and analyzed our swings. He found major fault with every swing but mine, finding much to admire in my high hands at the top and my driving leg action. "Boy, I bet you can bust it a mile," he said.

I admitted that this was so. Then we went out to range station 4, where I took my seven-iron and pounded balls 175 yards with ease, all landing in a tight pattern about 70 yards wide.

"Attaboy," Lyons said.

At the *Golf Digest* school, the cameras caught a different Garrity. Teachers Jack Lumpkin and John Elliott looked at my X-rays and saw something terminal. Said Lumpkin, "Your hands are too far inside on the takeaway, and the club isn't parallel to the target line when your hands reach your waist. You don't have enough connection between your upper arms and body, so you tend to block the shot and leave the ball to the right instead of rotating through the ball. I'd like to see your back a little straighter. Your angle of attack is too steep, which is why you catch some shots fat or thin. That's also what makes your trajectory so high, instead of producing a lower shot that bores through the wind. . . ."

I'm thinking: One thumbs-up, one thumbs-down. Should I go to the Craft-Zavichas school to break the tie?

To be fair, the learning ambience varies with the school. Ben Sutton students, I found, came for the social activities as much as the lessons—the cocktail parties, the Thursday night Hawaiian luau, the shadowy liaisons by the pool. My *Golf Digest* classmates, on the other hand, while congenial, gave the impression that they were slightly more committed to improvement, that they would, in fact, sell their mates into slavery if it would cut two strokes off their handicaps.

DOES THE STUDENT see instant improvement at a golf school?

Not necessarily.

By Day 3, we had all begun to suspect that Lyons was on a different page from the other Ben Sutton pros. At dinner, we compared notes. "How does your pro teach the pitch shot?" I asked a young woman from California.

She demonstrated with a salad fork and an olive. "Ball in the middle of the stance, club face square, follow-through as long as the backswing. . . . Isn't that what you're learning?"

It was not. Lyons was teaching us *his* pitch shot: ball off the right foot, weight over left foot, club face open, hands low, a short, descending lefthand blow with lots of leg action and no follow-through. "Toby uses his legs on all his shots," muttered Abe, the glass man. "Including his putts."

Abe was clearly undergoing a crisis of faith. "He's got me shanking," he said gloomily. "I've never shanked."

I, too, was beginning to have doubts. I had expected Lyons to suggest that I hit shots with handkerchiefs tucked under each arm, that being all the rage in the golf magazines.

"I even brought a couple of handkerchiefs," I told Abe.

"Nothing's as bad as a shank," Abe said.

But by Day 7, our swing changes no longer felt so strange, and Lyons could stop watching his back.

The point is, most golf schools warn you that you'll probably leave them hitting the ball worse than you've ever hit it in your life. This is normal, maybe even desirable. The *Golf Digest* pros even told us how long it would take us to get comfortable with our swing changes: 21 days. That's 21 practice days, not 21 calendar days; and if you got mixed up and started practicing the wrong thing, that meant 21 more days.

Back home in Kansas City, it's Day 98, and I keep getting asked what I have to show for my time and dollars. I pull out my Ben Sutton "checklist and graph check analysis" with the eight-frame sequential photographs of my swing; the *Golf Digest* video of my swing; my Ben Sutton golf balls; my *Golf Digest* visor and tote bag; the golf ball decanter of whisky I won in the Ben Sutton scramble tournament. . . .

No, I am interrupted, what did you *learn*?

Oh. From Toby Lyons I learned that nifty little finesse pitch—a great shot off tight lies and from wooded areas where there's no room for a follow-through.

From the *Golf Digest* school I learned a dependable greenside lob for hitting over a bunker, a consistent bunker shot (sorry, Toby) and a preshot routine that eliminates mishit chips.

I also learned that I'm going to be working on my full swing for the rest of my life.

DEAR GRADUATE,

IN WHAT WAY(S) DID OUR SCHOOL MEET OR EXCEED YOUR EXPECTATIONS? *Short game instruction was exceptional. Learned why I was skying my putts.*

IN WHAT WAY(S) DID OUR SCHOOL FAIL TO MEET YOUR EXPECTATIONS? *Achieved only one of preschool goals—mystical clarity.*

WOULD YOU RECOMMEND ANY CHANGES TO IMPROVE THE QUALITY OF INSTRUCTION? *Two words: house calls.*

POSTSCRIPT: *That final crack about "house calls" wasn't a throwaway line. My golf school swing quickly deteriorated, and before long I couldn't break 100. I still hit some quality shots, but in the middle of a round I'd start topping balls with my driver or chunking my wedges. I'd hit push-slices so high and long that the ball would disappear over houses and then reappear on the first bounce as a distant dot against the clouds. My dream of becoming a single-digit handicapper was shattered. Or so I thought.*

The following spring I picked up my annual USGA handicap card, which reflected the scores I had posted before going to the golf schools.

I was an 8.

Not a Bad Life

Amy Alcott proves that a successful golfer cannot be defined by
numbers alone—especially one particular number

*For years, LPGA players and officials have complained that the media
doesn't give them a fair shake. "Why don't you write about Annika? Why
don't you write about Karrie? Why don't you write about Paula?" My
answer is usually short: "Because they won't give us the time of day." The
following piece, about a golfer/pond diver from L.A., shows how simple it
is to get good press. You simply open your front door.*

HERE'S WHAT WE'RE GOING TO DO. WE'RE GOING TO FOLLOW
Amy Alcott from the ground floor to the roof of her house in
Santa Monica Canyon, near Los Angeles, and we're going to do
it without ever bringing up the word *thirty*.

This will be difficult because if you tell Amy you're thirsty, she
sighs and says that she no longer gives the LPGA Hall of Fame
a thought. Look at your fingernails and say they're dirty, and
Amy replies that 29 tour wins, including five major championships, should get you into anybody's Hall of Fame. Murmur that
the orange sun dropping over that ridge sure looks pretty, and
Amy insists that she's not concerned that four years and seven
months have gone by since she has won. The number 30 flutters
around Alcott like bluebirds around Snow White.

Sad, that. To view Amy Alcott as a 39-year-old golfer chasing a missing integer is to blind oneself to her other gifts. She lives, bless her, not in a fairway condo but in a tall, white stucco house halfway up a ridge of crowded cliff houses and small gardens. "Living my whole life in California, I'm convinced it is the land of fruits and nuts," she says. Perfect, in other words, for Amy Alcott. Sun spills across the threshold of her open front door as one of her two Scottish terriers snuffles contentedly around the legs of a visitor. The living room is sparsely decorated—white walls and hardwood floors with techno furniture and a few pieces of contemporary art. But the conversation starts outside, by a long, narrow swimming pool that gets even narrower at its shaded end, finishing at a modern sculpture called *Vertebrae Man*, which moves in the wind.

"I have two different sides," Alcott says, growing relaxed in her pool chair. "One is the Pisces, this fish who likes the cool water, the peace, the freedom. The fish becomes immersed in things and doesn't like loud noises and overly boisterous people. That's the side that has made me the great concentrator, the course manager—the side that can focus on one thing and focus on it really well."

Alcott clings to memories of a childhood spent as "a loner and an outcast." Teased by other children for her tomboy tendencies, she spent countless hours in private communion with her golf clubs. Since then, she has spent as many hours educating herself. It is this self-sufficient Alcott who, when she's on the road, often enjoys going solo in search of an out-of-the-way diner.

"Then there's the other side," she says, "the gregarious show person." This Alcott is the extrovert who dived into a pond to celebrate two of her three Nabisco Dinah Shore victories; the would-be actress who delights sportswriters with her dead-on impression of Edith Bunker singing *Those Were the Days*; the flaky celebrity who used to spend her off days baking and selling pastries to customers at Santa Monica's Butterfly Bakery. She's the mischievous golfer who, when asked what she would do with her winnings from a tour event sponsored by the Archdiocese of Trenton, joked that she would give the money to the United Jewish Appeal.

"That side has come out more as I've grown successful as a golfer," Alcott says. "My mother instilled it in me. She'd say, 'Just go out this week and let the world enjoy you.'"

Linda Giaciolli, Alcott's agent of 15 years, deals mostly with the gregarious show person. "Amy doesn't actually come to my office," says Giaciolli. "She honks her horn in the street, four floors down. Like a hillbilly." Susan Hunt, who next spring will cohost with Alcott a television show about women's golf, describes her partner as "a pretty eclectic personality." Eclectic, as in willing to try almost anything. A friend told Hunt, "The two of you will be like Lucy and Ethel."

But here's Alcott by the pool, her head buried in the newspaper, and you know you've caught the fish again. "Cineplex Odeon, that's down to 2," she says. "I bought it at 4 and sold it at 3. Ashworth and Callaway Golf, I never invested in those . . . . Syntex! I think that's a great stock. It's a uniform company, 38¾." Her eyes roam the business pages. "I don't own a lot of stocks, but sometimes something will jump out at me. One night I had a dream about being in line at a Sizzler steakhouse." She looks up. "I can be really crazy. I had this dream and I bought some Sizzler, and it went down five points. So I don't necessarily pick winners. But I've had some good ones and I think they equal out. I do it strictly for fun."

A quick tour of the ground floor reveals Alcott's other enthusiasms. In her kitchen, ensconced like a shrine, is a gleaming, six-burner Garland professional range with broiler and griddle—the sort of unit upon which a restaurant chef can prepare 10, 20, maybe 29 omelets at a time. "The cooking I do when I'm calm," Alcott says, proudly running her hand over the chrome molding. "I love preparation the most because it gets your mind off everything. Chopping onions, chopping carrots, chopping anchovies, chopping salami, chopping cheese. I like that. And I love the presentation. I look at myself more as an artist than as a golfer."

When she mentions her artistic side, Alcott usually mentions her mother in the same breath. Alcott's father, an orthodontist, encouraged her creativity, but it was her mother who convinced her that anything could be art—conversation, clothing, food, even golf. As a teenage golf prodigy, Alcott was granted rare playing privileges at exclusive Riviera Country Club. She spent hours on the club's secluded practice hole, learning to shape golf shots the way a sculptor shapes clay. It is no coincidence, friends say, that Alcott's game lost its luster when her mother died four years ago. Amy's father had died in 1981, and Alcott suddenly realized that she had been "steamrolling professional golf for 17 years" and that maybe she was tired and "a little burnt out," and maybe she should have gone to college instead of turning pro at 19, and . . . .

But her canvases tell it better. Several are hung on the walls, unframed. Others clutter the floor of an upstairs hallway. The work consists of great violent splashes of color with objects glued on: Q-tips, paint tubes, golf tees, dried pasta. "I tend to paint when I'm angry about something," Alcott says, taking a canvas from the floor and turning it several ways as an act of assessment. "I go to a local paint store and buy premixed house paint that nobody's picked up. Then I go up on my roof and literally throw things around.

"I think I was upset or confused about something," she says of the work she's holding, "and my unconscious self knew that I was only going to feel like this for a little while, and then I was probably going to be back to my spirited self. I needed to do this to get it out of my system."

How long, one asks, has she been painting?

Alcott stares at the canvas. "About four years."

Reconciling the golfer with the abstract expressionist would take more than an afternoon. Tournament golf has been at the center of Alcott's existence since she was nine, and it is a life of practice routines, travel itineraries and tee times. The golf swing itself is a miracle of precision and minute tolerances. At her best—when winning the 1980 U.S. Women's Open by nine strokes or when winning the Dinah in '91 for victory number 29—Alcott has been able to visit that place where conscious thought bails out and the subconscious starts playing. "And that is a very healthy place," she says, "but it's also extremely structured."

Climbing another flight of stairs, Alcott throws open a door and steps into sunshine. Her rooftop is a flat rectangle—a stage?—from which she can look down on other rooftops and upon which the gazes of residents higher up the ridge fall unobstructed. The roof is where she throws her paint, although on this day there are no cans of paint, no canvases—just a rubber doggy toy that she predicts will end up on some future work.

"I think this is the nicest place in the house," she says, watching a car glide past her front walk. "A friend was going to give me a hundred bucks to come up here and paint nude."

And?

"I said, 'I'll do it!'"

(Later Alcott says, "I want to come back in my next life as a *Solid Gold* dancer. Remember that show?" One is reminded how much her facetiousness has contributed to women's golf and how joyless her quest for the LPGA Hall of Fame has been made by the requirement that a player with two or more major championships must also win more than 29 tournaments for automatic inclusion. This year the closest that Alcott has come to winning was a tie for fifth in March at the Ping/Welch's Championship in Tucson.)

The view from Alcott's rooftop, of course, may be part of her problem. By simply turning around, she can see into many windows and gardens, each suggesting alternatives for her own life. "Sometimes I think the focus I need as a golfer kind of keeps me in a cocoon," she says. "The longer you do it, the more single-minded you become. The thing that bothers me most. . . ." She hesitates. "I'm interested in a lot of things, but I wonder if I'll ever have that passion again, the all-consuming passion I've had for golf."

With a last look around the canyon and a wave to *Vertebrae Man*, the gregarious show person leaves her sunny perch and takes the stairs back down to the cloistered realm of the fish. It's a tall house, a lot of steps. If you're compulsive, you find yourself counting: . . . 27, 28, 29. . . .

But not out loud.

POSTSCRIPT: *Amy never got win number 30, but the LPGA eventually changed its Hall of Fame criteria to a points system, awarding one point for every LPGA victory, two points for major championships and one point for each Vare Trophy or Player of the Year Award. Alcott qualified easily under the new rules and entered the Hall in 1999. The new magic number, if you're interested, is 27.*

꙰

The Jones Boys

Despite a prickly relationship, different styles and professional rivalry,
Robert Trent Jones and his sons thrive in the course design business

Golf architects are the most interesting people in golf. They tend to be
bright, curious people with wide-ranging interests. They know how to oper-
ate construction and farm equipment, but they also have an artistic bent
and, in some cases, a philosophical bent (to go along with their creeping
bent). They are employers, salesmen and marketers. They are poets. They
are world travelers. They are great talkers.

They are also, to a greater or lesser degree, crazy.

"GOD IS THE BEST ARCHITECT," ROBERT TRENT JONES LIKES
to say. But he says it in a way that makes one suspect he's simply
feigning modesty.

Jones, most everyone agrees, is a 600-yard par-5 with bunkers on both sides and an elephant buried in the middle of the
green. Among older golfers the name alone causes pupils to
dilate. Jack Nicklaus, asked for his appraisal of the 86-year-old
dean of golf-course architects—known as Trent—stammers,
hesitates and finally declines to comment. Arnold Palmer,
standing with a drink in his hand by a swimming pool in
Hawaii, squints as if the name barely registers, and he's only
minutes from Mauna Kea, one of the old man's signature
courses. Another pro, a winner of several major champion-

ships, refuses to be quoted by name but bitterly resurrects some unflattering comments made about him by Jones some years ago. "You ask about his golf courses," the pro says, "but golf courses are not that important."

The tale is oft repeated: Ben Hogan had just shot seven over par over 72 holes to win the 1951 U.S. Open, at Oakland Hills (remodeled by Trent Jones in his prime), in Birmingham, Mich., when he wearily said, "I am glad to have brought this monster to its knees." The famous quip made Jones's reputation and ushered in the era of the high-profile golf architect. It also altered forever the relationship between the golfer and the golf course. Henceforth the land would speak to the golfer through a malevolent interpreter—the demon architect.

"I'm not a fiend. I don't hate golfers," insists Jones, who also designed Baltusrol Golf Club, in Springfield, N.J., site of the 1993 U.S. Open, which will be played next month. Before architect Pete Dye made target golf the bane of the Tour, though, the touring pros thought otherwise. They incessantly groused that Jones's courses were too long, his greens too contoured, his penalties too severe. Lee Trevino once played a round at Spyglass Hill, in Pebble Beach, Calif., another one of Jones's many great works of art, and said, "They ought to hang the man who designed this course. Ray Charles could have done better."

"Golfers complain a lot," Jones observed.

In 1970 Nicklaus griped about too many blind shots at Hazeltine, in Chaska, Minn., site of that year's Open.

"Maybe Nicklaus is blind," Jones replied.

Back home, in Montclair, N.J., Jones's sons, Bobby and Rees, would often read about the attacks on their father. "It made me angry," Bobby said recently. "Made me upset. I said, 'Dad, we've got to answer them!' "

Rees read the same unflattering remarks and shrugged. "I was on Dad's side, but I guess I'm more accepting of different people's views," he says. "And I understood that Dad stirred up a lot of the controversy himself, to gain publicity."

The Jones boys grew up with this background of professional contentiousness, to which was later added a patina of familial tension. Trent Jones was usually away from home—he claims to have flown 12 million miles during his life, more than the average pilot flies in a career—and when he *was* home, his boys competed for his attention and approval. "He was away so much, the values we derived were mostly from my mother," Rees recalls.

The boys grew up: Bobby went to Yale and Stanford Law School; Rees to Yale, California and Harvard School of Design. Both young men joined their father's firm, known as Robert Trent Jones Inc., learned the business and—particularly Bobby—battled with the old man. Bobby, now 53, split off in 1973, opening an office in Palo Alto, Calif., under the imposing shingle ROBERT TRENT JONES II. Rees, 51, started his own design firm one year later, based in Montclair, to brother Bobby's dismay. The older brother claimed all business west of the Mississippi, the younger brother worked the East and the Middle Atlantic states, and the father went after the clients of both. Praise among the men, when proffered at all, was so patronizing it approached insult.

"It was a Freudian psychodrama," says a writer who followed the Jones family saga for some years. "You had these three very intelligent, very talented men acting like children."

"A dysfunctional family," echoes a famous touring pro.

With time the hurtful impulses weakened; the three men reconciled. Jones Sr. and Bobby now describe their relationship as close, and they have resumed working on golf courses together. Bobby and Rees commend each other's work, if not as effusively as one would expect from brothers. The three are seen together at major venues, such as the U.S. Open and the Masters, and at meetings of the American Society of Golf Course Architects: the aged man and his two aging sons, all short, plump and sad-eyed and wearing short-brimmed caps.

"TOGETHER," says course designer Michael Poellot, "the Joneses would be the IBM of golf."

It was a better quote before IBM's stock went south, but the point holds. The three Jones design firms have altered the landscape of every continent but Antarctica; they have shaped dunes on the shores of every ocean and most minor seas; and they have introduced golf to several archipelagoes.

Nature can't sneeze without getting in the face of a Jones. When Hurricane Andrew struck Florida last August, it destroyed 200 trees at Coral Ridge Country Club (Trent), downed more trees at Inverrary Country Club (Rees) and brushed past the new Weston Hills Country Club (Bobby). Then, after bursting into the Gulf of Mexico and landing again near New Iberia, La., the storm inflicted major damage on Le Triomphe Golf Club (Bobby). Two weeks later Hurricane Iniki plowed into the Hawaiian island of Kauai and tore up four more of Bobby's courses: The Prince at Princeville and Makai, the Kiahuna Plantation Golf Club and the Poipu Bay Resort.

"Storms happen," Bobby says.

If you're a Jones, golf courses happen.

The actual number of Jones courses is unclear. Bobby has asked his dad to stop claiming that he has built 500 by himself, because "somebody's liable to count." But 700 seems a reasonable guess for the family output. Rees is the laggard, focusing his fine eye for detail on no more than five or six projects a year. His father, although reduced to shuffling around with a five-wood cane (a gift from Rees), started 20 courses in 1992 and recently signed a contract to build seven courses for the state of Alabama before '94. Collectively, the courses will be called the Robert Trent Jones Golf Trail. And nobody is busier than Bobby, who has four associate architects supervising work at dozens of sites around the world.

Predictably, their relative output is a bone of contention. "I'm astounded by architects selling themselves by the number of jobs they do," Rees says. "If you build too many golf courses, you can't control their destinies." The typical Rees Jones layout is an exclusive private club or destination resort—Atlantic Golf Club, in Bridgehampton, N.Y., and Haig Point Golf Club, at Daufuskie Island, S.C., for example—where the land can be massaged with money and intellect until near perfection is achieved.

Bobby, who tires of reading that Rees is the best of the Joneses, counters by describing his brother as a "gentleman architect, part of the East Coast establishment." His own mission, Bobby says, is to democratize the game and make it more accessible to the masses, which is why he builds more daily-fee and housing-tract courses and why he follows his father's example by taking golf to foreign countries. When Bobby does take on a high-profile project, the results are often praiseworthy, e.g., The Prince, a course once described by golf writer Dan Jenkins as "the most enthralling that I, for one, have ever seen."

The brothers also go their own ways on design philosophy. Rees, the apostle of definition in course design, positions his fairway mounds and hazards to clearly delineate the hole for the golfer. "His philosophy," says Bobby, "is that you should have a specific line of sight for any shot. And that probably comes from his more conservative view of what a golf shot should be." Bobby, in contrast, puts more deception into his designs and is not afraid to taunt the golfer with blind shots or camouflaged slopes.

To those who know both sons, the interesting thing is not that they differ, but that they put so much weight on their differences. Golf writers are used to Bobby's practice of answering a question with one of his own: "How did Rees answer that?" Gratuitous asides seem part of a lifelong debate between the siblings, as when Rees says, "When I'm through with a job, I want my clients to think they have a limited edition."

Bobby claims the differences are exaggerated. "In terms of our careers, we're probably Siamese twins," he says. "By that I mean Rees's success and failure reflects upon me, and vice versa. People say it's uncanny the way we speak, the way we sound alike on the telephone."

MEANWHILE the father carries on. Robert Trent Jones used to winter in Florida and summer in New Jersey, but now he spends the whole year in his Fort Lauderdale high-rise apartment, straddling the blues of the Atlantic and the Intracoastal Waterway. The decor, unchanged since the death of his wife, Ione, in 1987, is a surprising onslaught of still more blues—royal blue, powder blue, sky blue, diabolical-water-hazard blue. An exercise bicycle sits in the living room, a therapeutic tool for his back, injured a few years ago in a golf cart accident.

Most days his driver, George, gets out the white Cadillac and drives Trent to his headquarters, just off the 17th fairway of Coral Ridge Country Club, which Jones owns with his sons. The offices are modern and functional; computers inhabit the design rooms. "Mr. Jones is still an innovator," says his chief operating officer, Alan Blake Davis. "He's on the cutting edge."

That's surprising, considering that Jones grew up imitating the swings of turn-of-the-century champion Harry Vardon and that other Bobby Jones (Robert Tyre), with whom he is sometimes confused, though there is no relation. His first courses were built not with computers but with horses pulling slip scrapers. "When I was a boy in Rochester, New York," he recalls with a smile, "we went out twice a year to cut rough with sickle bars. When you lost a ball, the caddies would roll on the ground to find it."

Asked for memories of his sons as children, he hesitates. "When they didn't want to go to bed, I'd take them to the driving range," he says. "But Ione really raised the boys. I wasn't home much." The boys noticed.

"My earliest memories," Bobby says, "are of World War II, when we'd turn off the lights and go downstairs and hide under the tables during air raid drills. My mother would tell stories. She graduated first in her class at Wells College (in Aurora, N.Y.), a Phi Beta Kappa. She met my father while he was nearby at Cornell. She came from that very Puritan background: strict individualism, self-confidence through knowledge, but with deeply humanitarian instincts. On the other side, you had my father, a free spirit. My mother loved that, but it drove her crazy sometimes. He'd come home and say, 'Dear, I just made a wonderful deal—we're going to *buy* the golf course!' And she'd say, 'We can't buy dinner!' "

The Joneses lived in Montclair, a collection of comfortable homes on a bluff affording a dramatic view of the Manhattan skyline. Jones Sr. had a small office in the city, but he often worked at home, littering the house with drafting materials and sketches of golf holes. Golf came visiting in the person of clients like the fabled Bobby Jones (with whom Trent built Peachtree Golf Club, in Atlanta) or famous writers like Herbert Warren Wind. "Our vacations," Rees recalls, "were at Myrtle Beach (S.C.) or

Pinehurst (N.C.), someplace where Dad was building a course."

Bobby played competitive golf from the age of 14 and led Montclair High to the state title in 1957. Rees played baseball, basketball and golf. One summer to earn money for flying lessons Bobby ran a bulldozer for his dad at Wilmington (Del.) Country Club, sharing a double bunk with his supervisor and getting up at five each morning. "In about two weeks," he remembers, "I had shaped a bunker and another tee somewhere. My father came out to see what I had done, and he said, 'Hey, this looks pretty good.' Then I told him it had taken me two weeks. He said, 'Go back to playing golf. You're going to break me!' "

Bobby did return to competitive golf. He won his sole match against Scotland as a member of the 1956 U.S. Junior golf team, took lessons from famed golfer and teacher Tommy Armour and helped Yale win the Eastern Intercollegiate championship. But never, he insists, did he or anyone else in his family project a playing career for him. "My mother would say, lightheartedly, 'Your father's a genius, a dreamer, and there's only room for one in the family.' " Bobby worked one summer as an intern for Missouri senator Stuart Symington. He then entered Stanford Law, hoping, he says, "to learn the secret language of government." Instead he learned that he didn't want to be a lawyer. He pulled out after a year and talked his father into opening a West Coast office—headed by himself.

If Bobby knew nothing about course architecture, he didn't lack for exciting training grounds. Among his early assignments as his father's dogsbody were Spyglass Hill Golf Club, in

Monterey's Del Monte Forest, and the Mauna Kea Beach Hotel Golf Club, on the lava-strewn Kawaihae Coast of Hawaii. "Dad was lonely and needed company, and I wanted to learn," says Bobby. "But it was hard because he'd undercut any idea I had. Just destroy it." At Mauna Kea, Bobby walked the site with his father, in search of hole routes. At Spyglass he learned about the economics of construction. "We didn't think about moving the land; there wasn't enough money," he says. "Spyglass was built for under $500,000—half the fee Nicklaus charges now for his design alone."

At times the father and son argued openly over shot values, aesthetics, business matters. "He'd have these hourlong fights with his dad over the phone," recalls a former Jones staffer. "Bobby wanted to be 'Mr. Jones.' He wanted the attention, the staff and the chauffeured car, and he didn't understand that his father had worked 30 years for those things."

The first time Bobby was principal designer of a course— Silverado Country Club, in Napa, Calif.—he provoked a clash by violating Trent Jones's mantra of "longer, tougher, harder."

"You have to remember, my father didn't play a lot of golf after he got to 55," Bobby says. "I was out there playing in this stuff, and I couldn't reach his par-4s in two. So I shortened Silverado, and my father disagreed with me violently. He let me have it in front of Ed Westgate, the owner, and Westgate said, 'Trent, I agree with your son. I can't play Spyglass Hill. I love it, it's beautiful, but I can't play it.' "

Bobby smiles. "My father didn't like that at all."

Another conflict involved the redesign of the Mauna Kea greens—a job that Jones Sr. gave Bobby only after developer Laurance Rockefeller threatened to give it to rival architect George Fazio. "Mauna Kea was, and is, a piece of art," Bobby says, "and my father didn't think there was room for refinement. But it's a resort course, and it was rejecting the ball." The problem was a prevailing wind that lengthened the course and made the crowned greens unassailable. "That's my brother's and father's style," says Bobby. "Their greens tend to be aircraft carriers on which to land the ball, surrounded by a sea of trouble."

Bobby took the severity out of the troublesome greens, making them lower and more concave, and changed some bunkering patterns—all to his father's chagrin. "He'd call me at four in the morning and say, 'What are you doing to my 3rd green, Bobby?' I'd rub my eyes and say, 'I'm not doing *anything* right now, Dad.' "

Bobby eventually struck out on his own, setting up the Palo Alto office in a storefront. Today his headquarters is a three-story house on the edge of the downtown shopping district. It houses four architects, a staff of eight, a library and boardroom and mementos from three decades of course construction. Along with the expected paintings of golf holes, one finds photographs of Bobby with world leaders, such as former president Jimmy Carter, former Philippine president Corazon Aquino and industrialist-statesman Armand Hammer. "I'm sort of a nut about world humanity through sport," says Bobby, who was appointed by President Carter as a delegate to the Helsinki Accords. The *new* president, he is quick to add, plays out of Chenal Country Club in Little Rock, another of his courses.

The experience Bobby gained from politics, according to the firm's senior architect, Don Knott, is what gives him his preternatural persistence, which is reflected in his 18-year effort to build a course in Moscow and his 11-year struggle to persuade environmentalists to stop fighting a resort course in Olympic Valley, Calif. "He likes power struggles and confrontations," says Knott, "the sort of political ground where you go in there and battle it out." Another architect, a rival, credits Bobby for his intelligence and awareness: "He's one of the few golf architects you'll find who reads *The New York Times* every day."

The whole package, some say, makes Bobby as transparently manipulative as a Chicago alderman. When Desert Dunes Golf Club, in Palm Springs, Calif., installed a rock garden and a colonnade of saguaro cacti around its 17th green a couple of years ago, he flew down there to argue for restoration of his original design. "This is a very natural course," he told the owner, smoothing his way into an explanation of how the cacti and rocks just might conflict with the harmony of line he had established between the course's contours and the mountain backgrounds.

"I understand his feelings," Bobby said afterward of the owner, who is Japanese. "His tradition is Zen gardening, in which sand and rock are used to create a meditation piece."

Allusions to Zen or to Renaissance art come easily to Bobby, who speaks the languages of spirituality, commerce and environmentalism with equal facility. Golf Plan architect Ron

Fream says, "When a prospective client asks me if I go out on the site and wait for the spirit of the land to infuse my being, I say, 'Ah! He's been talking to Jones II!' "

Above all, Bobby is relentless. Golf architect Tom Fazio characterizes him merely as "professionally aggressive," but other architects paint a picture of a man willing to go to almost any lengths to win a contract—including backstabbing and misrepresentation of his rivals' work. "I don't like his ethics," says Tom Weiskopf, the former tournament player who now designs courses with architect Jay Morrish. Another rival says, "He's vindictive when he loses." Much of the ill will dates from the mid-'70s, when business was slow and competition keen among the architects, but Bobby is still regarded as his father's son when it comes to bad-mouthing competitors. "Players used to rip a Robert Trent Jones course because they didn't like the man," says one Jones associate. "Bobby's work gets put down for the same reason. Actually, he's every bit as good as his father now, and maybe better."

Surprisingly, Bobby's grandiosity does not extend to his golf courses. More than any other marquee-name architect, with the possible exception of Tom Fazio, Bobby builds courses the way players say they want them built—not too hard, not too long and not too tricked-up. His greens are open in front and rarely elevated, allowing short hitters to run the ball to the hole. He usually resists the impulse to decorate the landscape with exotic flora and improbable waterfalls. There is, as a matter of fact, no identifiable Jones II style. "I don't try to impose a signature," he says, "except on the check from the client, of course."

And that check need not be exorbitant. When Tom Fazio was collecting raves for Shadow Creek, in North Las Vegas, a $37 million gem commissioned by casino owner Steve Wynn, Bobby reminded everyone, "You can get 10 of my courses for what Wynn paid." The inherent value judgment didn't seem to bother him at all.

It *would* bother Bobby, though, if you could buy 10 of his courses for one of Rees's.

"I DON'T have Dad's name," Rees says.

In stating the obvious, he puts his finger on a continuing source of tension with his older brother. Not that he concedes there *is* tension. "I think it worked out well for Bobby to have Dad's name," says Rees, "because he wanted to travel the world. It's worked out well for me because I want to have my own identity." Rees says this while sitting on a stool in the kitchen of his Montclair headquarters—an old house strikingly similar to the one Bobby operates out of in Palo Alto.

This form of flattery, however sincere, used to get under Bobby's skin. "Whatever I did, he followed," Bobby once told *The New York Times.* "I was in the Boy Scouts, he went to the Boy Scouts. I went to Montclair High and Yale. He went to Montclair and Yale. I went to California. Rees went to California. It's a little strange."

Rees, asked about the old quote, says, "I don't know where that came from. When I went into business for myself, in 1974, I went to a little room and waited for the phone to ring. The first job I had was for such a low fee I don't even want to talk about it. I didn't have Dad's name."

Rees *did* have the experience gained running his father's East Coast office, and he gives most of the credit for his development to two of his father's longtime employees, construction super-intendent Bill Baldwin—"my second father"—and Baldwin's No. 2, Austin Gibson. Having taken design courses at Yale and landscape architecture at Harvard, Rees also had the formal training Bobby lacked.

But without the name, Rees had to scramble. His early work was mostly remodeling existing courses, a task that expanded his design vocabulary beyond the Jones vernacular. When he got to build on his own, he got good reviews for courses like Inverrary Country Club, in Lauderhill, Fla.; Arcadian Shores, in Myrtle Beach; and Miami's Turnberry Isle Country Club. And just as the remodeling of U.S. Open courses had made his father's reputation, the redesign of The Country Club, in Brookline, Mass., for the 1988 Open made Rees's. The players liked the way he used mounding to turn holes visually, the way he gave the golfer the sense of always being a little elevated and able to see the available shot options. "I knew when I got Brookline, that was going to turn the corner for me," says Rees, who visited the course 17 times in the summer of '85. "That put me in the upper echelon, where I could truly express myself, because I would have clients with great sites and good budgets."

Indeed, since 1985 Jones has designed a number of acclaimed courses, including Haig Point, Pinehurst No. 7 and the recently opened Atlantic Golf Club. He has also inherited his father's title as "the Open Doctor" for his makeovers of Hazeltine, site of the '91 Open, and of the Congressional Country Club, in Bethesda, Md., which will host the event in '97. Some jokingly refer to Rees as the popular Jones, and even Weiskopf will interrupt a flow of anti-Jones invective to throw in a bit of praise for Rees's work.

"See, I like Tom Weiskopf," Rees says on a spring afternoon, driving his Jaguar from Montclair to Long Island. "And he likes me. I think it's that simple. The real problem in this profession is that nobody wants to concede that anybody else is doing good work."

Bobby acknowledges that Rees is more popular: "I think I'm much more of a risk taker and take a higher profile and am therefore attacked more easily than Rees is. But I also think I've probably had more fun and more rewards in life. My mother used to say Rees was an 'old soul.' By that, she meant he could be taciturn." Taciturn or not, Rees was elected president of the ASGCA in 1978, at the age of 36. Bobby's peers didn't grant him the same recognition until '89, when he was 50. (Trent, an ASGCA founder, was elected president in '51.)

THE RECOGNITION both men crave most, of course, comes from the man in the blue rooms high above the Fort Lauderdale strand. In his elegant coffee-table book, *Golf's Magnificent Challenge,* Jones Sr. wrote: "Without sounding too much like a proud father, which I am, I'd say the two best architects today are my sons, Robert Trent Jr. and Rees."

In person, though, he says, "Tom Fazio is the best."

At such moments the Joneses seem locked in an endless trip on which the boys elbow each other in the backseat while Dad is cranky at the wheel. "I do know that I love them," the old man wrote, "and I am proud of them, as individuals and masters of their profession."

And maybe that's exactly how it is. All three of them insist that they have put aside their differences since Ione's death. Bobby, in particular, is credited with pulling his father out of a period of despondency and inactivity. "Bobby's got his dad involved again," says a Jones insider. "He's put the fire back in his eyes."

Last year Bobby and his dad worked on a course together for the first time since the '70s. The site was in France, north of St. Tropez, in a forest of parasol pines. Father and son walked the hills, Bobby making sketches for the front nine, Trent making sketches for the back. Bobby's nine, predictably, had open-entrance greens and soft, flowing contours. His father's nine was 150 meters longer, had stronger contours and forced the golfer to play to the greens over cut-off bunkers. But neither man went to the mat over the differences, and both express satisfaction with the results. "It wasn't creative tension, like it was when I was growing up," Bobby says. "It was creative dialogue, and it was fun."

Not that there weren't disagreements. There was a tree in the middle of the 18th fairway, between the landing area and the green. Bobby thought the tree should stay. His father thought it should go.

"The tree is still there," Bobby said recently. "We've decided to let God choose whether the tree should or shouldn't live."

If He knows what's good for Him, God will stay out of it.

POSTSCRIPT: *Robert Trent Jones died in 2000, but his sons continued to feud. Rees sued Bobby in 2005 over proceeds from their mother's estate and licensing fees for the use of their father's name. ("It's my name too," Bobby shot back.) Bobby then countersued over Rees's appropriation of the term "the Open Doctor," which had previously attached to RTJ Sr. After a round of depositions, the brothers settled and retired to their respective corners.*

Neither Rees nor Bobby expressed any animus toward me after the story appeared. Rees admitted he was taken aback by my description of him as "plump," but he said it motivated him to go on a weight-reduction program. Bobby was equally sanguine about the piece, calling me up from time to time to provide updates on the family situation. Both men have helped me with subsequent stories, providing pertinent quotes and solid analysis. The only thing they haven't offered—and I haven't asked for one—is a joint interview.

๛

A World Apart

On the far-flung South American tour, pros quickly
learn that only the game is the same

*"You've written a lot of stories," people tell me. "What's your favorite?"
At the time I'm asked, a peculiar amnesia envelops me, and I find myself
stammering, "Oh, 'College of Cardinals' was pretty good . . . and Billy
Scripture, he was a baseball coach and champion trap shooter . . . and I
once wrote a long piece about ballpark bugs. . . ." But if you ask me who
my favorite character is, I'll throw you a big sweeping curve and say, "A
golfer you never heard of, a guy who won nothing. And if he called today
and told me he was promoting a mink-ranching scheme in Malaysia, I'd
probably catch the next flight to Kuala Lumpur."*

His friends call him Cookie.

––––––––––––––

I believe that something like that could be true.

—Steve Cook, executive director of the South American tour

FOR INSTANCE, THIS COULD BE TRUE. IT'S A STORY ABOUT
Pedro Martínez, the Paraguayan golfer, that was told in Argentina in late October on the shuttle bus between the Presidente
Hotel and the Rosario Golf Club. "I've heard that Pedro showed
up for his first tournament in a T-shirt and jeans," says a North
American from behind a seat piled high with golf bags. "He
was so poor he had to sleep in a sand trap."

At the course, the story is repeated for Cook, a plump, im-
perturbable man facing middle age with a laptop computer

and a bulging passport. "I can check that," he says, the corners of his mouth turning up. "I believe that something like that could be true."

Five minutes later he returns with Martínez, who after four tournaments leads the South American tour's money list with $33,846.67. "This is going to sound like the circus tour," Cook says with a grin. "Pedro never slept in a bunker, but he says he fished for food and hunted birds with a slingshot. Plucked them and cooked them himself." In halting Spanish, Cook presses Martínez for more details of his remarkable life—his childhood in a rural village, his life as a caddie in Asunción, his improbable tournament career. "He broke Sam Snead's 72-hole record at Sao Paulo Country Club," Cook says. "But one time he missed the cut here in Argentina and had to sell his clubs to get home."

Another for instance. Two players in the backseat of a Volvo speeding down the floodlit channel of the Paseo de la República in Lima, Peru, are comparing what they've heard about the city's rainfall. One says it hasn't rained in Lima since 1948. Another says it rained in '78, causing roofs to collapse and pigs to float down streets. As the car turns onto a frontage road, the city itself seems to testify: block after block of roofless buildings with bundles of rebar poking out of half-built walls. Cook, at the wheel, says, "We can ask Humberto about that."

Humberto Berger, a prosperous dentist, is president of the South American Golf Federation and one of the founding fathers of the six-year-old South American tour. He answers the rainfall question at dinner, while watching a Chinese chef in red tunic, gold epaulets and a guardsman's hat carve up a Peking duck. "We live on a coastal desert," says Berger, his English more than respectable. "The year that it rained was 1971. It rained for three or four hours, and the city was devastated. We have no sewers. There was no place for the water to go."

A related for instance. Antonio Barcellos, a young golfer from Porto Alegre, Brazil, whose swing is replicated on 5,000 MasterCards in his country, insists that until this year the fairways of Lima's Los Inkas Country Club were flooded every Monday. "The water passed through a poultry plant on its way to the golf course," he says, "so during our practice rounds the course would be covered with feathers. They would drift like snow, and when you hit the ball, feathers would fly."

IS IT ALSO TRUE, what I've heard? That in a village called Macondo, all the people caught a virus that robbed them of their memories? That no one could remember what things were called, so village officials had to put labels on everything: *Cama* for bed, *pared* for wall, *cabra* for goat? Is this true?

No, says a voice on the bus. That's from a novel by Gabriel García Márquez, the magic realist. The story of the South American tour is being written by Cook, the *comic* realist. "Cookie," as most of the players call him, appreciates novelty. He fields folly like a Venezuelan shortstop. His smile proclaims, "What a privilege to witness such lunacy!" Of course, this may be the only posture to assume if you're the brains behind the world's most overlooked and charming golf tour. Launched in 1991, the

South American tour began as a five-tournament dash across a continent consumed in political and economic turmoil. Six years later the tour has grown to 10 tournaments, played from October to December, and seems poised to develop into a Latin American tour of 15 or more televised events linking Mexico to Patagonia. "South America is golf's great hidden secret," Cook says.

For now, though, Cook's tour is a menagerie: 90 or so South American pros, some of them unable to read or write; six light-haired Swedes; a Namibian who plays out of St. Louis; a vacationing PGA Tour player; a Belgian who was once a professional clown; a Canadian who signed up, French Foreign Legion–style, when his fiancée gave back the ring; a gaggle of young Americans cramming for Q school; and a Japanese player learning to swear in English.

Any resemblance to the PGA Tour is coincidental. On a Monday morning in Guayaquil, Ecuador, Cook lets a man in a business suit into room 422 of the Oro Verde Hotel. The man hands Cook a paper bag containing $101,000 in U.S. currency, and while Cook counts the cash, Rafael Miranda Roca, the president of Guayaquil Country Club, lights up a cigar. "This kind of money is meant for smoke-filled rooms," Cook says approvingly.

Thirty minutes later players begin rapping at Cook's door. When Cook says, "Next victim," Corina Bronger, the tour's administrative assistant, lets one in. The biggest bundle of cash, $18,000, is set aside for Argentina's Gustavo Rojas because the winner of the Ecuadorian Open is already winging toward Peru, the tour's next stop. The second-biggest bundle, $11,140, is picked up by Jeff (Game Show) Schmid, a tall, thin Minnesotan with wispy red chin whiskers and a perpetual air of wariness. Schmid counts his money twice before signing for it. "We would rather not pay the players in cash," Cook says, "but banking in South America presents some difficulties."

Some players don't have bank accounts, for one. For another, local currencies are not fairly or readily exchanged between countries. That leaves the U.S. dollar as the only dependable medium and the money belt as the most trustworthy depository. Jeff Peck, a young pro from Carrollton, Texas, won a few thousand dollars his first season and walked around hugging his wealth as obsessively as Midas. "It was all the money I had in the world," he says. "I put it in this toy room safe, but I couldn't sleep at night, and when I got to the golf course I couldn't keep my mind on my game." To save his sanity, Peck finally wired his money home—at a cost of $200.

"It's the largest diamond in the world!" says a character in *One Hundred Years of Solitude.*

"No," responds a gypsy. "It's ice."

ECUADOR IS NOT a golfing country, but Guayaquil Country Club is 53 years old. The first course was a nine-holer and as recently as 1958 the greens were sand. That year, for the first time, Ecuador sent its best golfers to the South American Amateur Championship, played entirely on grass. "They were good players," says Miranda, "but they three-putted or four-putted every green."

Grass greens were subsequently installed, but the club continued for many years with stone-walled tees topped with dirt and asphalt. "You teed off with cutoff tees because you couldn't sink a long tee into the asphalt," Miranda says. An engineer educated in the U.S., Miranda now presides over a club with a modern stone clubhouse, two swimming pools, a tennis club and an equestrian center. The lush 18-hole golf course may be the least of the club's attractions. The whole of Ecuador has four 18-hole courses and perhaps a thousand players, counting caddies. "The waiters play golf on Mondays," Miranda says. "They count!"

Only at the IMG-cosponsored Argentina Open, the continent's oldest and most prestigious tournament, are tickets sold to the general public. The spectators at other tour events are club members, sponsors and invited guests who wander the fairways unrestrained, if they wander at all. (The average South American tour player could teach the novelist a thing or two about solitude.) There are no leader boards, no concession stands and no portable toilets.

There are mosquitoes. "We'll need to keep moving," Cook says, spraying his arms and hands with insect repellent during the final round of the Ecuadorian Open. "In the low areas the insects tend to swarm." Steering his golf cart around hibiscus hedges, up and down hills, over crunchy pepper pods and under canopies of *guaya pelliblanco*, Cook keeps an eye out for rules infractions and slow play. "A lot of the South American players slow down on Sundays," he says. "It's sort of a stare-down, macho thing."

Cook's slow-play warnings are gentle—and companionable: "I need to ask you to play faster," he says. Some golfers react defensively; others simply nod. One player, a gringo, high-steps down the fairway like a drum major, waving at Cook. "You see the fear I inspire," Cook says dryly.

Out of curiosity, Cook looks for the Argentine golfer, Rafael Gomez, who reportedly fired his caddie an hour into his round. (In the middle of the first fairway, the caddie handed Gomez his putter. On the first green, the caddie proffered a 7-iron.)

"There he is," says Cook, steering toward a striped-shirted player climbing a hill. "*Mejor* caddie?" Cook calls out, pointing to the substitute looper.

"Yes," Gomez replies with a smile. "The other one was drunk."

Later in the day Schmid visits the tournament office to mildly protest the slow-play warning that he and his partners in the last group received at the turn. "They never time the last group at the Masters," Schmid argues. "Fred Couples can be four holes behind and they don't time him." To this Cook cocks his head and smiles blissfully, as if to say, Did one of my players just compare this operation with the *Masters*?

Schmid leaves, but comes back 10 minutes later to borrow $100. "Cookie, how much is five percent of $11,140?"

"That would probably be 570 dollars," Cook says, handing Schmid a crisp Franklin.

Three to six percent of one's winnings is a typical caddie fee, but Schmid reacts to the $570 figure as if someone has pinched his windpipe. "Get your camera," Cook urges a bystander. "Take a picture of this: American Skinflint."

"That isn't it," Schmid sputters. "It's just that his five percent is worth more in his country than my 95 percent is worth in mine!"

Schmid finally decides to give his caddie 480 U.S. dollars plus 100,000 Ecuadorian *sucres*, worth about $30. "I'm sure he'll be very happy with that," he says, going out the door.

Cook, standing behind a desk, just grins.

SCHMID, ONE DISCOVERS, is the canary in the coal mine, the squeaky wheel, the five-page, single-spaced, typewritten letter in the suggestion box. He's a natural quizmaster—hence his nickname. "I'd see him in the morning and he'd start with the questions," Cook says of Schmid in his rookie season. "They'd spill out so fast I couldn't answer them. He totally baffled me."

Some questions, you see, are unanswerable. Why is Inka Cola yellow? Why is Bogotá, Colombia, the pothole and mad-driver capital of the world? Or the one every player asks, sooner or later, usually while gazing stubble-faced into a hotel mirror: *What am I doing here?* The tour's orientation booklet provides hints: You finished in the top 60 on last year's South American money list or are a former tournament winner or hold a card from either the PGA Tour or the European tour or paid a $390 fee and played for a spot at a qualifying tournament.

But the booklet ducks the truth: that some players are *destined* to play in South America. How else to explain Blair Piercy, the young Canadian who decided that a change of latitude was the best medicine for a broken heart? Or John Rudolph, the 19-year-old college dropout from San Diego whose poignant answer to the mirror query is, "There was really nothing else I could do."

Not that South America is much clearer about its own destiny. In the equatorial countries, rifle-bearing guards in bulletproof vests greet downtown shoppers. In Buenos Aires the mothers of Plaza de Mayo stand vigil for their children, Argentina's thousands of "disappeared." Peru, with its history of political instability and Shining Path terrorism, is traditionally the most menacing stop. "Three years ago they were revising the constitution while we were here, and there were 10,000 demonstrators outside the hotel door," says tour veteran Ted Gleason. "The police were all lined up with their shields and helmets and truncheons."

In ambiguous circumstances, hedonism flourishes. Some players succumb to the Latin diet, gorging on *seviche* (delicious seafood cocktails marinated in lime juice), fried plantains with hot salsa, grilled steaks and sausages—washed down, perhaps, with a longneck bottle of Nevada *cerveza*. Others give in to the young women in tight jeans and platform shoes who follow the tour. ("That's a par-5 there," says a Brazilian player, watching a six-foot blonde carry a plate of toast across a dining room in Guayaquil.) At 4 a.m. the golfers playing cards in the hotel lobby don't even look up as incoming players tango toward the elevators. "This is a late-night tour," Cook says, "and South American nightlife is extreme."

NOW YOU'RE laughing. This tour is some kind of joke, right? A place where disappointed golfers go to keep the dream alive? Tell that to Philip Jonas as he stands over his tee shot on the final hole of the Peru Open.

Pressure doesn't need a sound track, but a windblown stand of bamboo creaks and moans behind him. Jonas is a warm and modest South African who lives in British Columbia with his teaching-pro wife, Pat. He hasn't won a tournament in six years, but here he is with an *un golpe* lead over Pedro Martínez. If Jonas can draw his tee shot along the drip line of the big trees lining the right side of this dogleg par-4 and not snap-hook it over the white out-of-bounds stakes in the trees to the left, he will probably claim the $27,000 first prize and mock-silver trophy that goes to Peru's *número uno*. And if he's human, he's thinking of the Sarazen. The winner of the Peru Open gets a pass into the $1.9 million Sarazen World Championship held every fall in Braselton, Ga.

Does the example of David Ogrin make his heart beat faster? Ogrin, one of golf's nomads and, since 1983, a persistent plodder on the PGA Tour, won the Peru Open in '88 and '94. Recently, in San Antonio, Ogrin won his first Tour event, withstanding a charge by Tiger Woods. His wins in Peru, Ogrin said, had kept the fire alive and hardened him to final-round pressures.

Don't think. Hit. Jonas swings and launches a shot at the right tree line. "Hook!" he yells. "Hook!" And like a trained hawk, the ball slides left and drops obediently to the fairway. Ten minutes later Jonas holes the winning putt and thrusts his arms into the air. "His nickname for a couple of years was Rain

Man," fifth-place finisher Scott Dunlap says afterward, watching his friend cuddle the trophy on a clubhouse sofa. "There was always a cloud over his head. Now he's afraid they'll cancel the Sarazen on him."

The drawback to Jonas's victory is that few people in the English-speaking world will ever hear of it. Cook is working on a TV contract that will make South American tour highlights available around the globe in 1997; for now, tour news moves by the player grapevine and via GolfWeb, a data-cluttered tributary of the Internet. "Television is the key for us," Cook says, shifting unexpectedly into nonironic mode. "International and local TV rights will provide income for the tournament committees and allow us to sell tourwide sponsorships." Television could also fuel expansion to Central America, the Caribbean and Mexico, realizing Cook's dream of an eight-month-long, 25-tournament Latin American tour.

What Cook has to overcome is the perception of South American golf as peasants in ponchos playing on dung-covered courses. In reality the tour's courses tend to be well-maintained layouts like the Club de Golf del Uruguay, which Alister Mackenzie designed around the time he was building Augusta National. One country, Argentina, supports a European-style golf culture with perhaps 70,000 players, 250 courses and an infrastructure of golf shops and lighted driving ranges. Colombia, with 18,000 players and about 100 courses, is also golfer-friendly, although the country's touring pros have not had much success.

But how does one explain Paraguay? With three courses and perhaps 350 golfers, Paraguay is home to Martínez and four other players who, between them, have won 30 international championships. Carlos Franco got his start when he was five and was given coins for mimicking golfers' swings on the 6th hole of the Asunción Golf Club. In 1993 Franco qualified for the Asian tour by topping the South American money list. In '94 he led the Asian tour, qualifying him for the Japanese tour. Since then Franco has won four Japanese tournaments and more than $1.3 million. Two of Franco's six golfing brothers, Ramón and Angel, have won in South America, and country-man Raúl Fretes has been national champion of four countries—Peru, Uruguay, Chile and China. "I can't explain why we have such good players," says Fretes, who at 31 dreams of playing in the U.S. "Golf is not that popular in Paraguay, and most of us have never had lessons." In fact, so tepid is the support for golf in Fretes's homeland that Cook had to cancel this year's Paraguay Open.

THEN THERE are those moments that play like the third reel of an anxiety nightmare. The two charter buses are pulling out of the Buenos Aires airport when someone spots a golfer inside the terminal, running along the glass wall and waving frantically. "Cookie, stop the bus!" a player yells. "Mayday!" shouts another, tickled by the sight of the player pressed against the glass, arms outstretched, like a fly caught in an ice cube.

The bus shudders to a halt, and the driver hops off to retrieve the castaway and his bags. Schmid, watching from his recliner seat, says, "You should fine this guy, Cookie. Slow play!"

These are the times when the South American tour seems like just that—a tour. Most of the players take the same flights between cities, with Cook and Bronger supervising baggage handling and distributing boarding passes. Buses move the players between airports and hotels. Buses carry golfers to and from the courses. "That's a big reason for the great camaraderie on this tour," says Dunlap, who joined the group in Peru two days after missing the cut at the Disney Classic in Orlando. "You share the experience with so many guys."

Sometimes the system breaks down. Two years ago an airline overbooked a flight from Montevideo to Asunción, and Cook had to charter a bus for 30 stranded golfers. The trip, which lasted 25½ hours, took the travelers into Argentina, then Brazil, Argentina again, Brazil again and finally into Paraguay, with customs and immigration at each crossing. The players shivered in the mountains and sweltered on the plains, and everything meltable in the luggage melted. "We had a born-again Christian player with us, a fellow who literally carried his Bible everywhere," Cook recalls. "The movie *Philadelphia* was running at the front of the bus, and this guy kept preaching that AIDS was God's revenge for homosexuals. Sitting in front of him was the girlfriend of a player, and she finally turned on him and screamed that she had lost a family member to AIDS. They got into quite a fluff-up."

Tonight's trip, a four-hour drive up the Parana River to Rosario, promises to be less stressful: a four-lane tollway, a landscape as flat as Kansas, dinner at a roadside McDonald's.

"What's the movie?" someone asks.

"I hope it's not *Philadelphia*," Cook murmurs, slumping into his window seat and closing his eyes.

ROSARIO AT 1 a.m. still has a pulse. Late diners linger over checkered tablecloths. Neon *helados* signs glow in ice-cream shops. Lovers embrace in the shadows of sprawling fig trees. However, the buses stop on a dark street with shuttered storefronts. The lobby and bar of the Presidente Hotel are posh enough, but—how to put it?—slender. "It's the narrowest hotel I ever stayed at," Cook has warned the players, but they are not prepared for elevators the size of phone booths and rooms as cozy as cupboards. "I'm not staying here," Schmid says, spinning in the lobby like a cornered cat. "This is a joke."

For once, Cook has no answers. The Presidente is a last-minute substitute for the roomier Riviera Palace, which canceled the Tour's reservations without notice. Now the players are grousing, a journalist is stuck in an elevator on the sixth floor, and the phone call Cook takes at the front desk is from a South American player at a budget hotel across town, who says that he is about to head-butt the hotel manager over his refusal to let eight golfers share a room.

Cook handles the crisis like a juggler whose Indian clubs have all crashed to the floor. He smiles beatifically and simply takes in the chaos. "Have you ever noticed," Jonas observes from a barstool, "that no matter how small the room is down here, they always find space for a bidet?"

Clearly Cook's casual authority wears well on the players. He is their guide and portent and, in a way, their inspiration—living proof that a lifetime of letdowns can add up to something grand. Cook is divorced and has a B.A. in English from Long Beach State. He played on the African and the European tours in 1972 but failed to win his card at the '73 PGA Tour Q school. Afterward, a shoulder injury nudged him into the real estate game. "It took me a year to forgive golf," Cook says, "but when I got the interest back, I decided to play tournaments for the travel. I realized early on that I wasn't going to be a world-beater."

Unless, of course, he could wear the world out. Cook has had three passports in 24 years, one of which maxed out at more than 100 pages. He has played in 33 different national championships, including one British Open. An infrequent winner—the 1978 South Australia PGA Championship is his biggest prize—Cook began to dabble in tour administration in the '80s, assisting Asian tour director John Benda. "I never felt that just playing was enough," Cook says—a sentiment heartily endorsed by those who have seen him play.

Cook's path and South America's crossed in 1990 when Dr. Berger contacted Benda for help in establishing the Peru Open and other regional events as something more than tournaments staged by a few friends. Benda advised the Peruvians and the other South American golf committees to schedule their tournaments on consecutive weeks, establish common rules and regulations, negotiate lower room rates with hotels and put the money earmarked for appearance fees into bigger purses. In other words, establish a tour.

The South Americans complied and brought in Benda as coordinator. The first event, the 1991 Venezuela Open, attracted 50 players, including Benda and Cook. "In the beginning the guys came down more as a vacation than as a serious attempt to play golf," Cook says. "We used to have guys who would shoot 82. Me, for example."

These days the fields are stronger (45 pros broke par for 72 holes at the La Sabana Open in Bogotá in October), and the South American tour operates independently of Benda and the Asian tour. "I'm thinking of moving our headquarters to Miami," Cook says. "A move like that might make the sponsors more comfortable." Two part-time employees, meanwhile, conduct some of the tour's business from Cook's home office in Seal Beach, Calif.

> *Time was ruled by caprice; in half an hour I could make six*
> *trips around the globe, and a moonbeam in the patio would*
> *fill my thoughts for a week.*
>
> —ISABEL ALLENDE

PLAYERS KEEP peeking into the room, trying to catch a glimpse of the old golfer. He sits in a comfortable armchair. Everything in the clubhouse seems to complement his calm dignity: the polished plank-and-peg floorboards, the stucco walls, the framed clippings showing him with pleated pants and dark, slicked-back hair. His first tournament win came here, at the Rosario Golf Club, in 1942. He was also the club pro for two years in the '40s. "I come here because I like the golf," says Roberto DeVicenzo, the famous warmth still evident. "No pay. These people are friends."

Someone mentions the Masters. Not the famous mishap of 1968, in which DeVicenzo forfeited a possible victory by carelessly signing for a higher score than he had shot—but the tournament of today. Will he ever return? Might he one day grace the dawn at Augusta and smack a ceremonial drive with Byron Nelson, Gene Sarazen and Snead?

DeVicenzo shakes his head. To visit again with old friends, old players, he would like that . . . but to be in the clubhouse and not on the course . . . impossible. "I want to play the way I *used* to play," he says. "I don't want to show my game in public."

Today is different. Today, in the pro-am of the Litoral Open, the 1967 British Open champion will play to support the new tour. "This one is really a South American tour," he says, comparing Cook's operation to the handful of winter events that attracted stars such as Arnold Palmer and Jack Nicklaus in the '60s. "The other one was a Caribbean tour—Jamaica, Puerto Rico, Panama. The prize money was just $10,000 or $12,000."

Someone mentions the South American tour's purses—as little as $80,000 in Colombia and Uruguay, as much as $310,000 for the Argentine Open and $200,000 for the season-ending

Volvo Masters in Brazil. "Is that enough?" he is asked. "Will players continue to come?"

DeVicenzo nods. "They come here to get the money, but also to get the *power*." He thumps his chest. "Inside. To win!"

An hour later, in bright sunshine, the old golfer shows what he means by the power. On the 2nd hole Dunlap, the designated pro in his fivesome, smacks a 285-yard drive. DeVicenzo, 73, answers with a perfect draw up Dunlap's tailpipe, about 280. "Is that unbelievable?" asks Phillip Hatchett, one of a half-dozen tour players in the gallery. At the green Jonas asks DeVicenzo for his autograph. The great man complies, and Jonas carefully covers his treasure with plastic.

On the next hole DeVicenzo rifles a long iron over the flag, a shot that has the young golfers rubbing their eyes. "If I could hit like that," Jonas whispers, "I'd turn pro." On the 4th DeVicenzo wedges to four feet and makes birdie. "That's tempo at its best," says another player.

But the golfer who seems most elevated by DeVicenzo's play is Dunlap. "I'm not trying to outdrive him," the 33-year-old says with a grin. "I'm trying real hard to *beat* him." Whatever his aim, Dunlap looks like a man who has bitten into magic fruit. His drives whistle, as they must have in 1995 when he won the Canadian Masters by 10 strokes. His iron shots shape themselves to wind and terrain. Dunlap is five under par at the turn, and when he stops in the clubhouse for a soft drink, he practically glows. It's as if someone from memory-impaired Macondo has taken a soft brush and written across him: WINNER.

FIVE DAYS later the results crawl out of a fax machine. Scott Dunlap, with a 17-under-par 267, has won the 62nd Campeonato Abierto Regional del Litoral. This must be true, but it merits a late-night phone call to Cook in Uruguay.

"Yes, that happened," he says from his room in the Balmoral Plaza Hotel. "But the really interesting thing that happened was. . . ." And Cook tells this story about a club member at the Rosario barbecue who hacked at his meat with a gaucho knife yanked from a sheath behind his back.

It's a funny story—not at all implausible—and it ends with Jeff Schmid counting his money twice.

POSTSCRIPT: *I keep track of the players I met on the South American Tour. Scott Dunlap has had a couple of brushes with fame, most notably at the 2000 PGA Championship, where he finished ninth after trailing Tiger Woods by a stroke through three rounds. Ian Leggatt won the 2002 Tucson Open. Jeff (Game Show) Schmid settled down and became a club professional in Florida.*

Steve Cook served as SAT commissioner for another year or so, but his life took an unexpected turn when a band of Bolivian rebels kidnapped him and ransomed him for a one-quarter share of a discotheque in Santiago, Chile.

That's what I heard, anyway.

❧

Muscled Out
Of the Masters

Half a century after getting run out of the tournament,
Frank Stranahan is still going strong

*I never saw Frank Stranahan play, but my father used to talk about him.
"Heir to a fortune," Dad would say. "Played golf for a hobby. Lifted a lot
of weights and got all muscle-bound."*

And now, as radio's Paul Harvey likes to say . . . the rest of the story.

———————

CLIFFORD ROBERTS IS DEAD, AND FRANK STRANAHAN HAS
long been mute on the subject. So who's to say if we've got a
50-year-old sex scandal here? The safe and sensible thing to do
is to simply slide our copy of the book across Stranahan's desk.
He can read the bookmarked pages for himself.

The 75-year-old market player puts his copy of *Investor's Business Daily* on top of a pile of securities reports. He slips on his
reading glasses and studies the book's title: *The Masters: Golf,
Money and Power in Augusta, Georgia* by Curt Sampson. He
looks up. "What's this?"

*(Note to editor: I know space is limited, but I think this descrip-
tion of Stranahan is misleading. He isn't a Smith Barney type. He
answered the door to his Florida fairway home in a green sweater
and a pair of skintight trunks exposing some very pale legs. The*

desk in his cluttered kitchen was covered with cardboard boxes, newspapers, stacks of envelopes and a copy of Muscle and Fitness *magazine. All the vertical blinds in the house were closed.)*

Hearing my explanation—that the book is an unauthorized history of the major golf championship created by Roberts and the sainted Bobby Jones, and that he, Stranahan, is a key character in Chapter 4—he opens the book to the first bookmark. "I remember," he says. "Fellow came here and asked a bunch of questions."

(Note to editor: In his book Sampson describes Stranahan's house. "Except for a bed and a tiny kitchen table, his house contains no furniture. An assortment of 50-year-old free weights and a lifting bench preside in the nominal living and dining rooms. No pictures or mementos adorn the white walls. Scrapbooks in boxes and framed black-and-white photographs lean together in casual disarray on the floor." I could add a detail or two—the sun visors hanging from the weight rack, the milk cartons full of bodybuilding trophies—but everything seems to be as it was when Sampson visited. Minimalism is a Stranahan trademark. When he lived at Seagull Cottage, next to the Breakers Hotel in Palm Beach, Fla., he installed a golf practice cage in the living room.)

Stranahan begins to read. Or at least he looks at the pages. His deep-set eyes have long had a haunted look, and it's hard to tell what he's thinking.

The first marked passage introduces him as Frankie, the headstrong 17-year-old son of Robert A. Stranahan, the Champion Spark Plug millionaire from Toledo. At Inverness Country Club in the early '40s, the reader learns, young Frankie took lessons from Masters and U.S. Open champion Byron Nelson. When not hitting balls compulsively on the practice range, Frankie bulked up his ballroom dancer's body with barbells. "And Frank was such a handsome devil," Sampson writes, "that young women pressed their phone numbers into his hand." This may be the passage Stranahan is reading when he snorts with amusement.

(Note to editor: Stranahan himself has never been an easy read. My sister met him by chance in the 1970s, when she sat next to him in the first-class section of a flight from New York City to West Palm Beach. Shortly after takeoff the intense-looking gentleman opened a leather case, revealing a long, sharp knife. Those were the days of frequent hijackings, so my sister was alarmed, as was the flight attendant who spotted the weapon from the galley. Hypnotized by the big blade, the two women watched as Stranahan lowered his tray table and spread out a sheet of plastic. It was only when he pared an apple and started chopping stalks of celery that they correctly pegged him as a health nut.)

Stranahan turns the pages. He's now up to the part in which he's a postwar sports celebrity . . . the best amateur golfer since Jones . . . the crowd-pleasing ladies' man who won the 1948 Fort Worth Invitational "against Hogan and Nelson, on the course they'd grown up on as caddies." There is, of course, the obligatory retelling of the classic Stranahan gag: how he used to ask bellboys to carry his bags up to his room, and how the bellboys would stagger and grunt over the barbell-filled suitcases.

(Note to editor: My father used to tell me golf stories at bedtime, and several were about Stranahan. Collectively, they constituted

the Parable of the Spoiled Rich Kid and the Old Pros, in which a
young man of privilege joins the Tour and is shunned by those who
toil at golf for a living. Herbert Warren Wind, writing more than
40 years ago, concurred that "the boy flew off the handle on several
occasions," such as the time, in a British Amateur match, when
Stranahan accused his caddie of purposely giving him the wrong
line to the hole. Or the time at Carnoustie when the Ohio strongman
shocked his opponent, a Scotsman, by claiming victory on a hole he
had actually halved with a conceded putt. But Wind concluded that
"Frank was essentially a likable young man, warm in his affection for
the people he liked, if a little too inexperienced in handling unusual
situations properly." I recently asked Nelson about Stranahan, and
the gracious Texan replied that his former pupil was well-liked by
his peers. Nelson said, "The only comment I heard was, 'If I had his
father's money, I'd play for fun too.' " Another old Stranahan friend
says the pros ribbed him good-naturedly about his barbells and about
his birdseed diet, and they sometimes set off a smoke bomb in his
Cadillac convertible, "which Frank didn't find so amusing.")

Stranahan's eyes stop for a moment. He's reached that 1947 passage from *Collier's*, the one describing him as "Golf's Bad Boy . . . the most egocentric, monomaniacal character who ever swung a niblick."

He stares at the passage. "The writer came to our house once and asked me and Dad a lot of questions. He promised to let us see the article, but that was a lie." He smiles. "Dad canceled $300,000 worth of advertising in the magazine."

(Note to editor: At this point Stranahan said some negative things

about journalists. He fixed me with a stare and said, "Writers act like they care. Like you. You're pretending to be interested, but you just want me to say something I'm not about to say." When I lied that that was certainly not my intention, he smiled placidly and resumed reading.)

Now he's at the pertinent section, the pages covering the 1947 and '48 Masters. This is where the book relates how Stranahan, an amateur playing in his second Masters, shocked the sports world by finishing second in '47, tied with Nelson, two shots behind the colorful Jimmy Demaret. "I never really had a chance to win," Stranahan says. "I shot 68 or something in the final round. Made it look close."

(Note to editor: My brother, a onetime touring pro, has a vivid memory of Stranahan's golf swing. "It was not graceful or natural," he says, "but more like someone following a checklist of muscle movements. He took the club outside until his hands were eight or 10 inches in front of his right shoulder. Then he brought his hands back level with the ground until they were behind his shoulder. Then he came down to the ball. He hit it very well, but he was truly a mechanical man.")

I straighten a bit in my chair because now Stranahan has reached the shocking events of 1948, which saw him pulled off Augusta National during a practice round and kicked out of the Masters. To my amazement Stranahan gives this material the briefest glance, riffles the remaining pages and puts the book down.

Well? What does he think? He shrugs. "I didn't read it very closely," he says, "but it looks like he got every word I said."

(Note to editor: Stranahan seemed uninterested. He left the kitchen and came back with a couple of recent magazine articles that mention him in connection with Tiger Woods. Both pieces were about weightlifting—Tiger lifts, too—and one pictured Frank as winner of the over-70 division at the 1997 National Physique Committee Gold Cup Classic bodybuilding competition. Flexing in a photo, his body covered with oil and gleaming under stage lights, he looked bigger than he does in person. That may be due to his paleness. He leads a vampirelike existence, getting up at 3 a.m. to lift, often running five or six miles before daybreak (he's a former marathoner) and working out under artificial light at a commercial gym. One old friend claims that Stranahan's vegetarianism is not absolute. "I've seen him eat half a beef roast," she says, but allows that Stranahan's binges are offset by his 10-day fasts, which leave him weak and emaciated. "It would scare you to death," she says, "if you ever caught him on the ninth day.")

I ask to hear the story of the expulsion in his own words, and Stranahan obliges. It was April 1948, he begins. Masters week. He arrived at Augusta National for a practice round and found a rumor nursery instead. "They told me in the golf shop that they were out to get me," Stranahan says. "The pro told me they would do anything to get me out of the tournament."

The pro, Ed Dudley, was also the president of the PGA, and he warned Stranahan not to hit a second ball to any of the greens during practice rounds, which the amateur had done in '47, breaking a tournament rule. Stranahan took in the warnings and then went out by himself with a caddie—playing, he insists, just the one ball. He dropped additional balls on the greens and putted to spots, a practice permitted then as now.

Suddenly the course superintendent, Marion Luke, was in his face. "He said, 'You can't do that!' " Stranahan says, mimicking Luke's angry face. "'You're hitting a bunch of balls to the green!' I told him I wasn't, but he gave me a hard time."

Luke left, but two holes later he was back. This time tempers flared. The two men swore at each other, and Luke said, "I'm going in to report you." Stranahan sighs. "I said, 'You're ridiculous.' "

Ridiculous or not, a delegation of club members met the Ohio amateur at the 8th green. They told him that his invitation had been revoked and he had to leave the grounds immediately.

(Note to editor: That last bit is from Sampson's book. Stranahan told me he was bounced by the tournament chairman himself, the overbearing Roberts.)

"So I bought a ticket [to the tournament]," Stranahan continues, "and I stayed there."

Not sure how to proceed, Stranahan called his father and then phoned the Silver Scot, former British and U.S. Open champion Tommy Armour. Both men counseled him to appeal his case to the club's president, Jones. "They said Jones was one of the premier sportsmen in the country," Stranahan says. "He would certainly listen to me and give me a fair trial." But Jones dodged Stranahan for two days, and when they finally met, on Wednesday, the great man threw up his hands. Sorry, Frank. Cliff runs the tournament. "I never had a chance to give my side of the story," Stranahan says. "I never had much respect for Bobby Jones after that."

Or for Roberts. Stranahan admits he shed no tears, 29 years later, when the tournament chairman went out one night on the par-3 course and fatally shot himself by Ike's Pond.

(Note to editor: Stranahan's actual words were, "I wish I'd been there when he committed suicide. I would have rolled the son of a bitch into the water.")

Of course, the question we want answered, the question that has never been answered satisfactorily, is *why*? Why was the club "out to get" Stranahan?

Curt Sampson quotes a 1948 magazine article to the effect that Stranahan had dated a blonde "who was palsy with a club member," and that the club member had retaliated by getting Stranahan in trouble at Augusta National. "The rumor within the rumor," Sampson writes, "was that the affronted member was Himself, Clifford Roberts, and that the blonde was his secretary."

In the book Stranahan says, "I don't want to go into that." To me he says, "I've heard a lot of stories, but I'm not going to tell you those."

(Note to editor: I didn't push for an answer, but a former female acquaintance of Stranahan's told me that she found the story of the blonde plausible. "In those days," she said with a laugh, "Frank would grab everything but the third rail." Neither did I challenge Stranahan when he voiced no resentment toward the Tour players who would not stand up for him in 1948, or the golf writers who were afraid to cross Roberts and Jones, or the officials of the PGA and USGA, who studied their own fingernails. "I'm sure the players were jealous," Stranahan told me. "They had every right

to be. My dad was bankrolling me, and I could play every week without worrying." Nelson has always assumed that Stranahan did hit extra balls onto the greens. "Frankie's probably forgotten," Nelson told me. But he added that Stranahan impressed everyone by staying the week and acting like a gentleman. "Most of these kids today would say, 'Cram it,' and leave town.")

Stranahan does have one curious bit to add to Sampson's account. The year after his banishment, he says, he returned to the Masters and drew a large bid in the club's Calcutta auction. His buyer? None other than Cliff Roberts. "But I didn't finish very well," Stranahan says.

(Note to editor: I don't want to leave the impression that Stranahan was a one-tournament wonder. He won two British Amateurs, finished second to Ben Hogan in the 1953 British Open and finally turned pro in '54, winning two Tour events before retiring around 1960. I worry, too, about not having the space to get into his personal history. Cancer took his wife, Ann, when she was 45, and killed his son Frank Jr. at age 11. Another son, Jimmy, quarreled with his father and painted his bedroom black before dying of a drug overdose at 19. Then Stranahan, a full-time stock trader after studying at the Wharton School of Economics, lost much of his inherited fortune in the Wall Street crash of October 1987. Understandably, he tries to control his fate and that of his loved ones. He started his youngest son on barbells when he was five, and Lance grew up to be a good junior golfer, a karate black belt and a Teenage Mr. West Palm Beach bodybuilder. In 1993, when a promoter asked father and son to "guest pose" at a competition, Lance choreographed a routine

straight out of vaudeville. His father, playing a decrepit codger, limped on stage with a cane. Enter the sexy nurse, who "injected" the old man with an oversized hypodermic needle. Voilá—the suddenly virile Stranahan stripped off his shawls and flexed, revealing a sleek, delineated torso. "Anytime my father goes into something, it's with total dedication," says Lance, who is 35, engaged to be married, and selling real estate in South Florida.)

Stranahan pushes the book away. He would rather talk about the swell party that he attended the other night, the one at Ballen Isles Country Club. Sam Snead was there. Gene Sarazen. Perry Como couldn't make it, but the old comic from Fort Lauderdale, Woody Woodbury, had 'em in stitches. An old guy sang. Stranahan frowns. "Who was the old guy who sang?" he asks.

Vic Damone? (It was in the paper.) "Not Vic. He's a young guy." He catches himself. "Well, yeah, he's old too. No, the old guy, sings real loud. Those great old songs." Stranahan gives up. "I'll think of it before your car is out of the driveway."

(Note to editor: Stranahan is not always so comfortable at social events. "I'll go to a party," he told me, "and someone says, 'I hear you're a golfer.' I say, 'Well, I was the best amateur in the world.' And they say, 'Did you ever meet anybody famous?' " He snorted. "They don't know what the hell's happening. They don't even read the newspaper." On the other hand, he still enjoys a spin around the dance floor. Stranahan recently went out dancing with a widow of long acquaintance and came back raving about how good she looked. He said, "I told her one of my interests is longevity, and she seems to have found the secret!")

He seems distracted now. Apparently, 50-year-old memories of green grass and sunshine are no longer compelling. He has survived Jones. He has survived Roberts. Through exercise and the use of the powders and pills that fill his refrigerator, he hopes to reset his cellular clocks to a life span of 100 or 120 or even 150 years—surviving us all. He has changed games.

(Note to editor: A friend gave me this Stranahan quote from the '70s: "Golf is a waste of time.")

I've overstayed my welcome, and if there's a scandal here, it has cooled considerably over half a century. I pick up the book, thank Stranahan for his time and move toward the door. "I'll remember that name," he says. Then I'm outside, blinking in the blinding sun.

An hour later I call my answering machine. "It's Frank," says a now familiar voice. "The old guy who sang was Don Cornell."

POSTSCRIPT: *Stranahan called me after the story ran to ask for a few dozen copies of the magazine. He said the photos of him were great—photographer Ben van Hook had posed him in his shorts and Gold's Gym tank top—and the article was "all right, I guess—except for all the stuff you got wrong."*

"What was wrong?" I asked, wondering what could have gotten past SI's fact checkers.

Stranahan's reply: "All those things that people said about me."

I relaxed. "You mean the quotes?"

"Yeah, the quotes."

"Well," I said, "they're accurate quotes."

Stranahan's reply: "If you say so."

❧

Point of View

Tom Watson remains a hero on the course, but his way of looking at the world and his penchant for speaking out have made him a heavy off it

I'm only two years older than Tom Watson. We both grew up in Kansas City, Mo. We both wound up at Stanford during the student-protest years of the late '60s. (I was a protester; he was not.) I went on to become a golf writer, and Tom went on to become a Hall of Fame golfer.

You would expect, then, that our respective careers would be closely intertwined. But, in fact, I have written about Watson only a handful of times. We have never shared dinner or played a round of golf together.

It's a pity really. I'm sure he'd find me as fascinating as I find him.

YOU *COULD* LOSE A PAINTING AT THE KANSAS CITY COUNTRY club. The main hall of the clubhouse passes room after room filled with portraits in gilded frames—characters in pantaloons and ruffled collars who probably never lipped out a putt. But a certain portrait was not visible last week, and nobody at the club seemed to know anything about it. A painting of a champion golfer—late 20th century. A sometime member, in fact. Used to hang in the Tap Room.

"It might be up in the attic somewhere," said a young staff member, frowning with concentration.

"I haven't been here that long," said another with an apologetic smile.

Understandable. The portrait came down five years ago amid controversy. Touchy subject, really; the member resigned, the national press got its nose across the threshold, voices were raised. . . .

History. By now, you thought, the portrait would be restored to its position of prominence. After all, the member was back in the fold, officially, as of June 27.

"Check in the golf building," suggested a young man in coat and tie. "I'm sure it's not in the clubhouse."

No matter, you assured him. You only wanted to see if the portrait was still a reasonable likeness.

TOM WATSON was never a liberal. He may have *looked* like a liberal when he joined the PGA Tour in 1971, fresh from the glass-strewn and tear-gas-polluted quadrangles of Stanford. But a mustache and longish hair were not particularly bold statements in those times, and it was not unusual to see young men with longer hair than Watson's boarding the buses that left San Jose every week for the Oakland Induction Center. Even at Silverado Country Club, an hour up the road from the notorious University of California at Berkeley, facial hair and wind wings on a golfer hardly warranted a second look.

Lanny Wadkins, who would one day succeed Watson as captain of the U.S. Ryder Cup team, has a clear memory of his friend's pro debut, at Silverado, and it's not the long-since-discarded mustache that stands out, nor Watson's views on world issues. It's the fact that Watson had gotten his playing card at the PGA

Tour Qualifying School just the weekend before in Florida, had caught a plane for San Francisco on Sunday, had qualified to play at Silverado on Monday and had opened his pro career on Thursday and Friday with consecutive 68s. "Everybody noticed that," Wadkins says, speaking for his Tour peers. "Tom busted his butt to get there."

The Tom Watson who appeared that week at Silverado was a typical young golf professional, in the sense that ambition and resolve circumscribed his outlook. It's his own view that he entered a tunnel in 1971 and emerged sometime in the '80s, blinking and looking around in wonder at a world larger than the one he had come to dominate. He probably overstates his detachment—Watson is an avid newspaper reader and a man with strong opinions—but until his commitment to tournament golf waned, he struck observers as a gap-toothed huckleberry, the sort of Midwesterner you pictured, as golf historian Herbert Warren Wind put it, "sucking on a stem of grass as he heads for the fishing hole with a pole over his shoulder."

Universally admired for his sportsmanship and good manners, Watson steered around controversy with one hand on the wheel and one on the roof. He won five British Open championships between 1975 and '83 without publicly weighing in on Thatcherism. He put on the green jacket of the Masters champion in '77 and '81, and if he wanted to chide the host club for its restrictive membership policies, he held his tongue. He won the '82 U.S. Open on California's Monterey Peninsula and somehow accepted his trophy without declaiming on the fate of the humpback whale.

Civility is a fragile flower. These days, *Los Angeles Times* columnist Larry Stewart calls Watson a "backstabber," while Jonathan Rand of the hometown *Kansas City Star* settles for "stuffed shirt." Golf writers, in his corner for two decades, edge away in print. A tabloid in England, where Watson was a hero until he declined to autograph a dinner menu for an opponent at a 1993 Ryder Cup banquet, ran the screaming banner, YOU'RE A DISGRACE, WATSON. And the mail! In '90, when he captured headlines by resigning from the Kansas City Country Club over its blackballing of a prospective Jewish member, the mail to Watson's office in Westwood, Kans., was heavy and, in the words of his business manager, "99 percent positive." Now, for writing a pair of confidential notes that may have cost a cheeky television commentator a week's work, Watson receives mail that is, at best, mixed—much of it condemning him as humorless and meddlesome.

The backlash stings. "It bothers me," Watson admits. "I don't have the thick skin of a politician."

The nature of Watson's hide may be pertinent. He likes to quote Winston Churchill, who said, "If you are not a liberal when you are 18, you have no heart; if you are not a conservative when you are 38, you have no brain." So some now ask: What has become of Watson's heart? His staunch advocacy of tradition and traditional values, once so praiseworthy, now strikes many as merely trendy. ("I'll be glad when he's over his Rush Limbaugh phase," says an acquaintance jokingly.) Oddest of all, there is a growing sense of Watson as a man estranged from his own generation. At 45, with two children at home and with his athleticism and vigor intact, he seems, at times, to be the Oldest Member.

The public has been aware of this grimmer, more austere Watson for less than two years. First there was Watson's harsh handling of the autograph-seeking Scottish golfer Sam Torrance at the Ryder Cup ("Menu-gate") 22 months ago. Next came Watson's criticism of comedian Bill Murray for what Watson and then-PGA Tour commissioner Deane Beman considered inappropriate antics during the 1993 AT&T Pebble Beach National Pro-Am. Finally, and most tellingly, there was the "Gary McCord flap"—named for the part-time Tour player and mustachioed funnyman who lost his Masters TV gig this year after Watson, offended by on-air quips during the '94 tournament about "bikini wax" and "body bags," sent a handwritten demand to CBS director and producer Frank Chirkinian to "get rid of him, now."

But those who know Watson intimately insist he's not ready for the wing chair by the window. "He's not stoic, he's not humorless," says Bruce Edwards, Watson's caddie for the better part of 20 years. "But he's a shy guy who wants to let his clubs do the talking."

Edwards has been at Watson's side on many a Sunday, victory within reach; he has seen him try to hit the perfect shot over waste and fen. One time—Edwards thinks it was on the 18th hole at Pebble Beach during a Bing Crosby Pro-Am—Watson hooked a critical approach shot into the Pacific. And while another golfer might have dropped his club and turned away in disgust,

Watson, his mouth a tight line, watched, without blinking or moving, the whole flight from impact to splashdown.

"Why didn't you react?" Edwards asked afterward.

Watson's reply: "Because that's my punishment."

These days, when he sees his boss taking punishment, Edwards rises to his defense. "Tom is the big brother I never had," he says. "He's shown me how to win—not just in golf but in life."

Asked about McCord, Edwards says, "It's not the steak anymore, it's the sizzle. And Gary McCord is the sizzle. I remember walking onto the 18th green [at Doral] one time and hearing the sound of a kazoo coming from the TV tower. Tom said, 'That's just McCord, trying to be funny.'" Edwards shakes his head. "It's become a carnival out here, a circus. You look at the way society's going, where there's no respect for anything."

Equally distressed by the McCord backlash is another longtime Watson friend, former U.S. Golf Association president Sandy Tatum. "Tom is *anything* but stuffy," Tatum says. "He can be scatological, he can be epithetical. Tom, unfortunately, may be out of step with the taste of the American public. But that certainly doesn't mean Tom is wrong."

Tatum, who has played as Watson's amateur partner in the Pebble Beach Pro-Am since the mid-1970s, got a preview of the McCord affair when Watson denounced Murray for antics with the gallery in '93 that included Murray's waltzing of an elderly woman into a bunker without her consent. Many Tour players defended Murray, but neither Watson nor Tatum bought into the performer's reprise of his *Caddyshack* role. "When Murray picks up a woman and throws her into a bunker, I think that's way across the line," says Tatum. "And Tom's the kind of person who would think so. And *say* so."

Tatum sees a clear distinction between public decorum and private fun. He recalls the time 12 years ago when he, Watson and golf architect Robert Trent Jones Jr. were designing the Golf Links at Spanish Bay, just up the peninsula from Pebble Beach. After a day's work the three, joined by cartoonist Hank Ketchum, shared a late dinner at Pebble Beach's Club 19. "We had a delightful dinner," Tatum says, "with copious quantities of some very good wine. And toward the end of the meal, Tom disappeared for a bit, then returned with a little grin on his face. It's 11 o'clock, and he's got a wedge and three golf balls. 'Come on,' he says. 'Let's go play The Shot.'

"This is February following the June that he'd won the U.S. Open by chipping in at the 17th to beat Jack Nicklaus"—known ever since, in Watson's circle, as The Shot.

"So out we go to the 17th green. Pitch dark, there's no moon. We have a hell of a time trying to decide where The Shot was played from. Everybody's got an opinion, and Tom's doesn't matter a whit; nobody's interested in what Tom's got to say. But we finally get it all sorted out, and we spend almost half an hour playing The Shot. And it was absolutely hilarious. I've got to tell you, Tom would not have won the Open that night." After midnight, Watson challenged Tatum to a pitching duel at the 18th green. The contest culminated with the two men hitting wedge shots over the old tournament scoreboard.

"So there's not an iota of stuffiness," adds Tatum. "But a round of *competitive* golf is a serious obligation, and Tom thinks of it that way."

Indeed, Watson is rarely seen wisecracking, a la Fuzzy Zoeller, or flinging rubber snakes in the manner of his friend, Lee Trevino. Watson's tournament demeanor is so focused, so *dour*, that one understands why the Scots have practically granted him honorary citizenship. "I always felt as if he played with blinders on," says Nicklaus, who served as Watson's foil in four of the greatest duels in golf history—Turnberry 1977, Augusta '77 and '81 and Pebble Beach '82. "Tom reminds me of Ben Hogan in that respect," says Wadkins. "I played a lot with Ben Hogan, and he'd say, 'I don't like to play jolly golf.' I don't think Tom likes to play jolly golf either."

Friends say the two Watsons—the midnight prankster and the gimlet-eyed competitor—have coexisted since he was a teenager in the early 1960s. He was "Flytrap Finnegan" to a small group of grown-up golfers who let him into their Saturday-afternoon game at the Kansas City Country Club. ("That was a misnomer," Watson says, "because Flytrap Finnegan was a yappie, loudmouth caddie from the Toonerville Trolley, a cartoon strip. I was shy and didn't say a word.") At 14, Watson was the Kansas City Match Play champion; his father, Ray, was an accomplished player as well, having advanced to the fourth round in the '50 U.S. Amateur. So the tone of those Saturday outings was at once collegial and competitive.

"I learned how to needle and how to take the needle, how to

laugh and have fun," Watson says. "But all the people who played golf with my dad were serious golfers—*serious* meaning they loved the game. Every time they hit a golf shot they were there for one purpose only, and that was to hit it the best they could."

To this day Watson counts as close friends an extraordinary number of men who, like Tatum and legendary golfer Byron Nelson, are 10, 20, even 30 years older than he. At the same time Watson is close to only a handful of active Tour pros (Wadkins, Ben Crenshaw and Tom Kite come to mind). His wife, Linda, recalls attending a birthday party in New Orleans in the 1970s for former U.S. Open champion Ken Venturi. "We were, like, 25 years old, and everybody in the room was 40 or above," she says. "At dinner, Bob Rosburg said, 'Tom, how'd *you* get here?' And Tom said, 'In my Chrysler.' " On the road, the Watsons socialized with Tour couples like the Murphys (Bob and Gail) and the Cerrudos (Ron and Madeline), who were five to 10 years older—until, as Linda notes, "a lot of them went out on the Senior tour."

When asked about these friendships, Watson says kiddingly that "old people are better storytellers." But he plainly values the insights and judgment that accompany age. His own judgment, although fallible, benefits from a sense of obligation and discipline that was drummed into him by his father. Throw in the fact that he has lived his life within the leafy, Republican-dominated neighborhoods described by novelist Evan Connell in *Mrs. Bridge*, and Watson's conservatism seems preordained.

It was not. Watson's older brother, Ridge, general manager

of a winery in Carmel Valley, Calif., is a former Peace Corps
volunteer with a Thai wife and a view of the world that he describes as more "anarchic" than Tom's. His younger brother,
John Marshall, is a New York interior designer and former actor
who gleefully baits his brother on visits home. "The first thing
we do at the airport is get in Tom's four-wheel-drive and argue,"
says John. "Which appalls the rest of the family, but it's fun."
Even Linda, who was Tom's childhood sweetheart, rolls her eyes
over the ideological gap in her marriage. "Yes, he *does* listen
to Rush Limbaugh," she says playfully. "There's a big group of
players who do, and I laugh at them all."

Ironically, as captain of America's most recent Ryder Cup
team, Watson had to stamp out an embarrassing Ditto-head
Rebellion, which threatened to inject Limbaugh's views into
the biannual match with the professional golfers of Europe.
On Sept. 20, 1993, Watson visited the White House with 11
other wealthy Republican golfers, who tugged at their ties
and squirmed during a prematch send-off hosted by President
Clinton, a golfing Democrat. Several players had threatened to
boycott the ceremony because they found the higher marginal
tax rate onerous. Furthermore, Payne Stewart had blurted to
the press that Paul Azinger, son of a Vietnam veteran, didn't
want "to shake the hand of a draft dodger."

The President ignored the widely quoted insults and warmly
greeted the team in the Rose Garden, shaking hands down the
line. Watson then gripped a golf club and said, "You know, Mr.
President, the golf grip is a lot like politics. If you hold the club

too far to the right, you're going to get in trouble on the left. If you hold it too far to the left, you're going to have trouble from the right. But if you hold it in the middle . . ."

Clinton, amid laughter, finished the thought: ". . . you'll get it just right!"

Watching Bill Clinton and Tom Watson stand shoulder to shoulder while camera flashes popped, one could only wonder what common ground they, as prominent baby boomers, might have found. For starters, they might have agreed that theirs was a generation forced to make personal decisions with divisive, polarizing consequences. Clinton's famous letter from Oxford, voicing his loathing for the way American military might was being applied in Vietnam, candidly weighed the cost to his political future if he followed his conscience. Two decades later Watson would struggle just as mightily with a different choice—whether to sanction, by his silence, acts of bigotry in his own backyard. Hindsight tells us that the politician acted more forthrightly than the golfer, but hindsight rarely takes in all the factors influencing a life-defining decision.

In that regard, it's interesting to hear Watson reflect on his college years. It has been reported, inaccurately, that he marched against the Vietnam War. And he has long been teased for casting his first presidential ballot for George McGovern, a Vietnam dove. ("You're an idiot," Ray Watson told his son.) Less well-known is the general discomfort Watson felt at Stanford, where the verities of Kansas City's sheltered neighborhoods seemed under constant attack. "I was somewhat of a fish out of water," he says, "and yeah, I was unhappy at times."

One pictures the four-time Missouri amateur champion escaping to the Stanford Golf Course, a challenging and secluded layout in the foothills above the campus. Watson is remembered there as a somewhat solitary figure. A spring and summer golfer at home, he had to be prodded by golf coach Bud Finger to qualify for the team during his first autumn at Stanford. And although he was the Cardinal's No. 1 player for three years, he won only the Stanford Invitational and the Fresno State Classic.

Richard "Pooh Bear" Jay, the teammate with whom he played the most practice rounds, remembers Watson as a mischievous friend and a gifted but unpolished golfer. "He would shoot 68 with two balls out of bounds," says Jay. "He'd usually have at least one disaster hole every two or three rounds." Clem Richardson, who roomed with Watson on golf trips, says his friend spent a lot of time in front of mirrors, analyzing his swing. "But he had other interests. Most of us in those days were pretty idealistic, and he cared about what was going on in the world."

Watson's only volunteered memories of this period involve his predawn drives down the coast to the Pebble Beach Golf Links, where the starter let him play free as a dew sweeper. On these spiritual excursions, Watson would fantasize he needed pars on the last three holes to win the U.S. Open—against Nicklaus, no less.

"In many respects Stanford was disappointing to me," Watson says. His name is attached to an annual benefit tournament for the Stanford golf team, but he has not attended for several years.

His college teammates say that when they approach Watson at tournaments, he is invariably gracious but distant. And they are puzzled by the grumpiness of his recent pronouncements. Jay, who is mainstream enough to have served on the USGA's mid-amateur committee, says, "I disagreed with Tom on the Gary McCord business. I almost wrote him and said, 'Hey, remember—it's only a game.' I feel as if Tom's really missing something, not getting together with old friends to reminisce," says Richardson. "But he seems restricted, confined. I don't know . . . maybe we represent something that he'd sooner forget."

Taking it as far as it will go, one might argue that Watson, uncomfortable with the deep antagonisms of his time, resigned from his generation and adopted the values and viewpoints of his father's peers, the World War II and Korean War generations.

"Where is common sense?" he asks, sprawled on a living-room couch at his home in Mission Hills, Kans. "We're trying to teach this younger generation the right values, but we see institutions breaking those values down. I'm not talking in a religious sense, but hey, it's O.K. to teach the Golden Rule in schools. It's not a religious rule, it's a *human* rule."

To Watson it's also common sense that malpractice lawyers should not have doctors in a headlock, that sports agents should not manipulate athletes' careers for personal gain, and that business owners should not have to fill out dozens of forms for alphabet agencies. "It's not the spirit of the law any more," he says, decrying the American propensity for litigation. "It's the economics behind the law." Before he went to college, Watson worked summers for the rental-rug department of Gateway Chemical, a janitorial-supply company owned by his grandfather, Searcy Ridge. "When I was working there, all you had was a delivery slip for chemicals. Now you've got 20 to 25 pages of EPA and OSHA forms you've got to fill out for that chemical. That's what's stifling small business."

Almost in the same breath, Watson tells how he was going to school, one fall day in 1957, when the earth shook to an explosion. "We looked up, and there's big black smoke downtown. That was the chemical company going up in smoke. BOOM!" The Gateway Chemical fire actually damaged a neighboring business and nearly killed a welder trapped in the basement—suggesting that maybe the single delivery slip wasn't adequate.

"There's middle ground," Watson says, smiling.

Middle ground, in fact, is where Watson tries to stand. He likes Rush Limbaugh, but he also listens to Cokie Roberts and National Public Radio. He disarms critics with contrarian positions (he supports the legalization of recreational drugs) and unexpected opinions. ("I think Clinton's doing a heck of a job as a caretaker President.") He reads several newspapers a day, consumes letters to the editor like candy and parks the television on CNN or C-SPAN. Tell Watson you just returned from a Mexican vacation, and he'll ask what you think of the latest developments in the PRI-Salinas scandals.

"I think he's a person with a highly developed critical nature," says Jones, the golf course designer. "And that can occasionally be misinterpreted, when something isn't diplomatically stated."

The middle ground is where Watson lives. His family's home of 17 years—an unspectacular two-level with a swimming pool in the backyard and neighbors close by—is in the middle of a city that thinks of itself as "the heart of America" and serves as a test market for companies pursuing the "average consumer." His just-completed country house, 25 miles away in rural Kansas, looks out on a fishing hole and is served by gravel roads. Asked why he has never followed the example of most Tour pros and moved to a warm-winter climate, he looks puzzled and says, "Friends. Family. Both sets of parents live here. My high school friends still live here. What would I want to move away from them for?"

Reminded that people *do* make such moves, he shakes his head and laughs. "They're fools. I think they're foolish."

THE PROBLEM with criticizing Watson is that he knows himself better than you know him. In the late '70s, when he was winning four or five tournaments a year, Watson heard ad nauseam that he fussed too much with his swing, that he made golf harder than it had to be. He countered that his swing was not sound—as evidenced by the number of times he had to play around trees and from behind cart paths. Almost two decades later, every round he plays is vindication, because from tee to green he is a better ball striker than he was in his prime.

The problem with *Watson* criticizing Watson is that he shows no mercy. Faced with the erosion of his putting skills over the last decade, Watson has pursued his lost stroke with a passion bordering on delirium. He is convinced his misses derive from a faulty setup or swing-path malignancy, so he shies away from gimmicks like the long putter or the cross-handed grip.

Mark McCormack, founder and CEO of the International Management Group, recalls the same thing happening to his client Arnold Palmer. "Arnold putted cross-handed on the back nine at Turnberry during the 1977 British Open, and he shot a 29," says McCormack. "The reason he wouldn't stay with it was pride. He thought he was strong mentally and shouldn't let putting conquer him. I think Tom's the same way."

Watson, hearing of McCormack's view, shows no anger. "I *am* hardheaded," he concedes. "I'm stubborn in the sense that I think I can make it work. I *will* make it work. But it's not fair to say that I won't use the long putter someday, or putt cross-handed or sidesaddle. But my problem is simply making a good, consistent stroke under pressure. I can't do it right now. The club goes straight inside. Closed and inside."

Even Hogan couldn't win when the three-footers started looking like 30-footers. Watson's last Tour victory was the 1987 Nabisco Championships of Golf, and although he has threatened to win many times since—including serious runs at all four major titles—his putter, particularly on Sundays, has betrayed him. The short putts that rim out make the galleries gasp, but it's the long putts that don't reach the hole that differentiate Watson at 45 from Watson at 30. "I know if he could be as aggressive as he used to be, the fear would leave him," says Edwards, his caddie.

But Watson can't be, and the fear probably will never leave him.

Have the years without victory changed his personality? His Tour colleagues don't know him well enough to say. Davis Love III, an eight-time winner, admits that Watson used to intimidate him. "You didn't know if he was in a bad mood or a good mood, or if he was kidding." Mark McCumber, who calls his one-shot victory over Watson at the 1981 Western Open "one of the highlights of my career," describes Watson as "a man on a mission"—insular and hard to know. "I remember playing with him in the Western Open in '81 or '82, and they had lost the greens; it was hard to tell between ball marks and spike marks. A lot of guys on Tour, if they don't know for sure, they say, 'Fix it.' I remember asking Tom, on a green that was just brutal, 'Is this a ball mark?' I was starting to fix it, and he matter-of-factly said, 'Nope.' He knows what he sees. You may not agree with his interpretation, but I respect immensely that he's willing to make a stand. A lot of people aren't willing to do that."

IN APRIL Watson played in his 21st Masters. His role was not prominent this time (he shot 284 and finished tied for 14th), but the week provided personal resonance in the form of Stanford freshman Tiger Woods, the 19-year-old golfing phenom. Woods, who qualified for his first Masters by winning the U.S. Amateur, spent the week in the Crow's Nest—a tiny dormitory, traditionally reserved for amateurs, in the cupola atop the Augusta National clubhouse.

Watson had slept in that same Crow's Nest 24 years before, when he was a Stanford senior. At the time, the top eight finishers in the previous year's Amateur qualified for the Masters, so Watson, who had finished fifth, got to bunk with Tom Kite and national amateur champion Lanny Wadkins. "Tom kept screaming in his sleep all week," Wadkins recalls with a chuckle. "I didn't know what he was on at Stanford, but it wasn't what we were on at Wake Forest."

If Watson talked to Bobby Jones in his dreams, he doesn't recall it; but there were other reasons why a young man might toss at night. In 1971, thousands of American men below the age of 25 were conscripted into the Armed Forces, most of them to see duty in Vietnam. Many more, of course, were not called and did not serve. Watson's student deferment expired with his graduation, but his birthdate—Sept. 14—was a late draw in the Selective Service Lottery. That made military service extremely unlikely.

Watson had already made his career choice. Midway through his senior year at Stanford, in December 1971, he telephoned Linda and blurted that he wanted to try tournament golf—a prospect so unwelcome to her that she rejected his proposal of marriage after graduation. ("I had eight years invested in the relationship, but I did not want to be a professional golfer's wife," she says. "I didn't want my husband to be a stranger to my children.") When she did consent, a year and a half later, it was with the understanding that Watson would play the Tour for only five years. Neither she, nor anyone else, could anticipate that he would win 32 Tour events and eight major championships in 14 years.

Watson himself sometimes comes up short in the anticipation department. Having been spared the hard choices over Vietnam and the draft, he married a Jewish woman; he embraced in-laws who are Jewish and began his married life under their roof in Kansas City; and he hired his Jewish brother-in-law, lawyer Charles Rubin, as his business manager.

These developments had certain members of the Kansas City Country Club screaming in their sleep. Founded in 1896, the mansion-bordered private club had long offered its socially prominent members sanctuary from unwanted associations. If Watson didn't fully understand the implications of this tradition, he got the picture when his parents told him the club would not be the best place for his wedding reception. (Tom and Linda celebrated their nuptials at the predominately-Jewish Oakwood Country Club in Kansas City, Mo.) As the son of a member, however, and with his golf exploits bringing distinction to the club, Watson's domestic arrangements were tolerated. He was granted junior membership soon after graduating from college. Later, in the wake of his major championship run, proud club members hung a large painting of Watson in the club's Tap Room.

Since Watson's college major was psychology, one can assume he understood the extraordinary position his club membership put him in. He seemed to fumble for rationalizations as his two children reached school age. As if to quiet voices in his own mind, he started an annual junior golf clinic in Kansas City's Swope Park, giving away golf clubs and bringing smiles to children of diverse backgrounds. More significant, in 1980, with Charles Rubin's help, Watson launched an annual one-day golf exhibition for Children's Mercy Hospital of Kansas City—an event that has brought the world's best golfers to the heartland and raised more than $6 million for society's most vulnerable. Watson's visits to Children's Mercy, hospital insiders say, are notable for his involvement with the children and his avoidance of publicity.

Then came the Shoal Creek controversy of 1990, ignited by the PGA of America's decision to play its championship at a whites-only Alabama country club. Shoal Creek may have shaken Watson's irresolve, but his public pronouncements either dodged the issue or emphasized the more positive connotations of the word "discrimination"—e.g., discernment. (In a careless moment, he even said that both blacks and whites needed to "chill out.") But when progressive elements at the Kansas City Country Club put up H&R Block founder and chairman Henry Bloch for membership, Watson ran out of wriggle room. Upon learning that his club's secret, five-man membership committee had blackballed Bloch, who is Jewish, Watson wrote his letter of resignation, ending two decades of accommodation. "His ox was finally gored," observes *Golf Digest* columnist Tom Callahan. "With Shoal Creek, he was in the chorus of unenlightened voices that said it was a private club situation."

Today, Watson will discuss his resignation only in the broadest terms, his voice dropping almost to a whisper. "It was a very personal decision," he says. "I just didn't feel my family was welcome. It was time to say, 'Hey, let's be fair to people. Let's not judge people on the basis of race or faith.' "

Watson's reluctance to say more is explained by the effect the resignation had on his parents—particularly his father, a Kansas City insurance broker. The elder Watson, who still wears a 1950s-style crew cut at age 76, was baffled and enraged by his son's action. The two were not on speaking terms for months, and Tom had to turn to the Rubins for emotional support. Tom also got the cold shoulder from most of his father's golfing pals, including those who had welcomed him to their Saturday-afternoon games in the '60s.

The Kansas City C.C. dispute drew attention to Watson's family situation, which was troubled even before the Bloch nomination. Ray Watson is a recovering alcoholic who quit drinking some years ago, but his behavior in galleries reportedly became so disruptive that his son insisted he no longer attend tournaments. This was a blow to the proud father who had already distanced himself from the independent lifestyles of his other two sons.

Ray and Tom have since reconciled. Last August, Ray traveled to Tulsa to watch his son play in the PGA Championship at Southern Hills Country Club. In January, Tom and Linda met his parents in Hawaii for a 50th wedding anniversary celebration, with grandchildren Meg, 15, and Michael, 12, filling out the entourage. Tom and Ray played golf as of old—reliving, no doubt, the time when during a visit to their summer home in Wallon Lake, Mich., a 12-year-old Tom played his father in the club championship at

Wallon Lake Country Club and lost on the 20th hole. "We had a great time," says Ray, "except I can't play a lick anymore."

Ridge Watson says the hometown rumor mill exaggerated his family's rift. "I think Dad was probably not wildly pleased [by Tom's resignation], but it certainly didn't change the way we behaved at family gatherings." But another close observer describes the months following the Bloch episode as "horrible, a nightmare." Neither the Watsons nor the Rubins will discuss the matter, seeing no gain in public confession.

Meanwhile, changes in the club's membership policies—Bloch and other minority members were ultimately admitted—opened the door for Watson to return. When he did so, it was without fanfare. "We think it's time for healing," he says. Previously, he had discounted the possibility of rejoining, saying, "It would revive the publicity."

And publicity is something he has had more than enough of. Watson seems only to have to open his mouth or uncap his pen, and controversy follows. "It's getting old," Watson says. "Linda says, 'Keep your mouth shut. You don't open your mouth, your feet can never get in it.'"

SO YES, Watson continues to take his punishment. If at times he seems to be frozen in his follow-through, it's because he must watch life's every shot find fairway or hazard, depending on the judgment that he has displayed.

"I don't make excuses," Watson says. "I just think society is so excuse-oriented. 'It's not my fault. It's not *my* fault!'"

He shakes his head. "You make excuses, you're not fooling anybody. That's what I learned playing with my dad," he says. "If I hit a shot that ended up close to the hole and didn't hit it solid, Dad would say, 'You hit it off the toe' or 'You hit it fat.' There was no getting away with excuses, so I never made any.

"That's what I love about the game of golf. It's yours. It's *yours*." A thin smile visits Watson's face, as some imagined shot clears all obstacles and rolls toward the flagstick.

"It's nobody else's," he says. "It's yours."

POSTSCRIPT: *Reading this piece a decade later, I get the sense that I caught Watson at the edge of a precipice. His mother, father and a nephew died within a few years. Chuck Rubin suffered a debilitating stroke. Bruce Edwards succumbed to ALS, otherwise known as Lou Gehrig's disease. On top of that, Watson divorced and remarried. But he continued to play golf and play it well, winning five senior majors before his 58th birthday. During the third round of the 2007 Senior British Open in Muirfield, Scotland, I was standing just off the 17th fairway when Watson hit a three-iron shot that he followed with his eyes, as in the story above, until it landed 15 yards short of the green—at which point he turned to his caddie, Neil Oxman, and said, "Didn't my ball look beautiful against that dark sky?"*

Swing Master

The hat, the swagger, the name: Slammin' Sam Snead was a
legend who was at one with his game

*Acting on a tip, I was the only journalist on the scene when Sam Snead
died at his Virginia farm. I use the expression "on the scene" loosely.
Not knowing how much time Snead had—and not wanting to pester
his family—I drove by on the highway every hour or so, looking for
signs of his passing. I wrote a line or two of this Snead obit on the top
of a donut box while parked at the mountain cemetery where he would
soon be buried.*

———————————

ON A MOONLIT NIGHT, SAM SNEAD SAID, YOU COULD TURN
your headlights off and drive those old Southern roads for
half an hour without meeting another car. Barns and dark-
ened farmhouses flew by in the milky light. Telephone poles
provided a visual rhythm. "Cows would be sleeping in the
middle of the road," he once told an interviewer, "and you
had to be careful because they were black and black-and-tan
and blended into the road." Moving at speed in the night
was intoxicating for a young man like Snead, born before the
Great War in the Back Creek Mountains hamlet of Ashwood,
Va. Another Southerner, the novelist Thomas Wolfe, wrote
about trains hurtling through "the huge and secret night, the
lonely everlasting earth. . . ." Snead, with his golf clubs and

clothes piled in the back of his Model A Ford, must have felt like a moonshiner hauling white lightning.

He was never a deep thinker, Snead, but he knew that his life was extraordinary. When he died last Thursday at age 89 at his home in Hot Springs, Va., flags at the nearby mountain golf resorts were lowered to half mast and tributes poured in from around the world. No golfer between Bobby Jones and Tiger Woods—not even Arnold Palmer, whose swing was too much a wild swipe to inspire imitation—was as iconic as Snead. With his coconut-straw hat and long, syrupy swing, Snead was the only golfer that casual fans could identify at a distance or in silhouette. His follow-through spoke like poetry; the club face finished parallel to his shoulders, and his balance was so exquisite that he could hold the pose indefinitely. "I try to get 'oily,' " he explained in his 1986 autobiography, *Slammin' Sam*. "Oily means a smooth motion. It's the feeling that all your bones and muscles are so in sync, any movement you make is going to be smooth and graceful."

Legend has it that Snead developed his swing on the family farm in Virginia, hitting stones with clubs he fashioned from branches. Later, when he wasn't hunting squirrels, doing chores or playing banjo in the family band, Snead caddied at the Cascades and The Homestead golf resorts, just up the road. After high school he took a job repairing clubs at the Cascades for $20 a month plus playing privileges. He didn't own a set of real clubs until he was 22, but he entered the Cascades Open in 1936 when he was 24 and finished third, earning a whopping $358.66 and landing a professional's job at the fancy Greenbrier resort, just across the West Virginia border. A year later he won a PGA Tour event on just his second try, shooting four rounds in the 60s at the Oakland Open. (When Tour promoter Fred Corcoran showed him his photo in *The New York Times*, Snead innocently asked, "How'd they ever get my picture in New York? I ain't never been there.") Before he was finished, Snead would win a record 81 PGA events, the last at the '65 Greater Greensboro Open, at the age of 52 years and 10 months—also a record. "Quit competing," he said, "and you dry up like a peach seed."

Snead's reputation rested on conventional measures of greatness—he won the Masters and the PGA Championship three times each, the British Open once, was the Tour's leading money winner three times and played on seven U.S. Ryder Cup teams—but his appeal transcended the records. He had an alliterative name, like Mickey Mantle, and a marketable swagger, like his friend Ted Williams. "Any guy who would pass up a chance to see Snead on a golf course," Jim Murray wrote, "would pull the shades driving past the Taj Mahal." In his prime Snead promoted headache powders, tires, deodorants and cars. His Wilson clubs were used by more golfers than any other brand. There was even a chain of Sam Snead Motor Lodges—for travelers who disliked driving at night as much as Snead did.

Above all, he was voluble. Depending on the company, Snead would kill an hour or two swapping blue jokes or debating the best way to skin a deer. He'd even jaw at his golf ball. ("Now stay put, you little fooler, this ain't gonna hurt none at all.")

He claimed that he swung in three-quarter time, and with a bit of urging he would leave his table and join a nightclub combo, playing trumpet on tunes like *Honeysuckle Rose* and *The Sheik of Araby.*

Snead's travels gave him plenty to talk about. He'd tell you how he was bitten by an ostrich in Argentina and how, on his first visit to St. Andrews, in 1946, he mistook the Old Course for a vacant lot. How in '38 he escaped injury from a lightning bolt that killed two golfers standing beside him and how he played two holes barefoot during a practice round at the '42 Masters. How he survived a small-plane crash in Iowa, and how he turned down an offer to be flown in a twin-engine plane by Palmer, a licensed pilot, saying, "Thank you, Arnold, I don't fly with learners."

Snead was four days shy of his 90th birthday when he finally came to the end of the road. Hours after his death a gibbous moon floated over the Back Creek Mountains. It was almost bright enough to drive by.

POSTSCRIPT: *The cows-in-moonlight quote I owe to Snead's biographer, Al Barkow. For more of Snead and other touring pros of the barnstorming era, I highly recommend Barkow's oral history,* Gettin' to the Dance Floor. *(And don't skip the eloquent and insightful forward by Jaime Diaz.)*

✿

A Fond Farewell

At the birthplace of golf, Jack Nicklaus let go of the game, and
the fans at St. Andrews embraced him more closely than ever

*Starting in the mid-'90s, I drew the This-Might-Be-the-Golden-Bear's-
Last-Major assignment so often that you could read my skepticism between
the lines. ("Nicklaus is retiring, not!") But when the day finally came—at
the birthplace of golf, no less—I felt strangely unprepared.*

"Don't cry because it's over, smile because it happened"

—ANONYMOUS

I WAS SMILING LAST FRIDAY AFTERNOON WHEN JACK
Nicklaus stood on the little stone bridge and waved to us.
And when I say us, I mean the thousands of spectators who
packed the grandstands on the Old Course; the hundreds more
standing on tiptoe on the narrow street that runs along the
18th fairway or leaning out of windows or peering through
binoculars; and the unseen millions watching on televisions
around the world.

We were there to see Nicklaus wrap up his tournament career
with a nostalgic last visit to St. Andrews, which is not only the
birthplace of golf but also the terrain upon which Nicklaus won
two of his record 18 major championships. To mark the occasion,

the Royal Bank of Scotland had issued £5 banknotes bearing the golfer's image—an honor previously accorded to only two living persons, Queen Elizabeth II and the Queen Mother—while less-well-heeled entrepreneurs hawked ball caps bearing a Golden Bear logo and the words JACK'S FAREWELL.

The real currency was emotion. Five-time British Open champion Tom Watson, Nicklaus's playing partner for two days, teared up as he walked off the 18th tee alongside the man he beat in the famous Duel in the Sun at Turnberry in 1977. ("What Jack has accomplished has been unsurpassed by anybody who has ever played the game," Watson said afterward.) Luke Donald, the talented young Englishman who rounded out the threesome, was amazed to see people cheering Nicklaus from rooftops and hotel balconies, while a contingent of Tour players lined up in front of the Royal & Ancient clubhouse to, as Donald put it, "clap him in."

But I was smiling. I figured that Nicklaus—even a 65-year-old Nicklaus with surgery scars and a titanium hip—still had something left for his fans. That was apparent early on Thursday morning, when Nicklaus and Watson both birdied their first hole of the tournament. (A spectator yelled, "Another duel in the sun!" To which Jack wryly replied, "So far.") It was confirmed on a later hole when he smacked a nearly full-length version of one of those high, fading tee shots he once employed to power around doglegs and soar over trees. I smiled even though Nicklaus three-putted five times on his way to a first-round 75, a score that made it unlikely he could achieve his declared goal of surviving the 36-hole cut and playing on the weekend.

Granted, my chin quivered a bit when Nicklaus showed up hatless for his second round. I'm old enough to remember his crew cut, the brutal 'do he wore when he was a beefy 22-year-old getting his first professional win at the 1962 U.S. Open at Oakmont, beating Arnold Palmer in an 18-hole playoff. (We didn't love Nicklaus then. We called him Fat Jack and prayed he would give up golf to pursue his original career choice: insurance salesman.) Sans chapeau he looked like the Nicklaus of the '60s and '70s, the dressed-by-his-wife styler with blond bangs, loud trousers and a signature gesture (raising his putter to the sky as a putt toppled) that camouflaged his essential nature as a plodding tactician.

Nicklaus had worried last week that his game might disappoint, that he might go out sloppily. "I didn't want to finish shooting a pair of 80-somethings," he said, and I smiled when I heard that. After parring number 17, the famous Road Hole, Nicklaus was only one over par for Friday's round, and all he had left was the quirky 18th hole, a short, flat par-4 as homely as a car park. The only ornament on this hole is the Swilcan Bridge, a little stone arch that players use to cross a ditch—sorry, a burn—100 yards or so off the tee. We all knew that Nicklaus would pause on the bridge to acknowledge cheers and be photographed, and we knew that the image would be iconic, something to be viewed by golfers until the end of time.

When Nicklaus stepped onto the bridge I was standing far away—maybe 250 yards off—looking back across the double fairway from the 1st tee, so I felt no compulsion to weep. It was different down by the burn, where history and sentiment had people snuffling in hankies and rubbing their eyes. (Watson, asked if Nicklaus's retirement would leave a hole in the game, said, "I don't think you can call it a hole. He leaves a mountain behind. A mountain of championship victories.") The Open Championship, momentarily stalled, resumed when Nicklaus and his entourage moved off the bridge, although the ovation continued until he reached his ball.

But here's what you have to remember: Nicklaus never wanted to be anything but a competitor. Now that he had survived the bridge and the sun-splashed moment had been bounced off a satellite to five continents, he went back to work. Using a putter from the fairway, he rolled his ball through the shadowy hollow known as the Valley of Sin, up the slope, past the pin—"Oooooh!" went the crowd—and 15 feet beyond. (Applause.) Watson and Donald quickly putted out, clearing the stage.

A hush fell over the crowd. As Nicklaus lined up his birdie putt with help from his son Steve, an occasional male voice punctuated the stillness. ("One more time, Jack!" "You can do it, Jack!") The old golfer bent over the ball the way he always has—like a question mark, his right shoulder lower than his left, his left foot turned out. That's when my eyes got blurry and my chin trembled again. Suddenly it was very important to me, to all of us, that Nicklaus make his putt, that he end his career with a birdie and a round of par at St. Andrews. He took his putter back, brought it forward, the ball ambled down the slope . . . and dropped into the hole to one last roar from the crowd.

Jack lifted his putter, some startled seagulls wheeled in flight, and a couple of big tears arrived to anoint my smile.

POSTSCRIPT: *The Monday morning after the Open, I walked to the St. Andrews branch of the Royal Bank of Scotland and bought four of the Nicklaus banknotes. I keep them in a safe deposit box in Kansas City, and considering how far the dollar has fallen of late, they're probably the best investment I've ever made.*

ॐ

Happy to Be Home

With a little help from a gang of regulars at Bay Hill,
Mr. Palmer became Arnie again

Until I met Arnold Palmer, I didn't realize he was a golf nut. That sounds silly, I know, but most touring pros approach the game as a discipline, a business or a penance. Not Arnie. To the King, a day without golf is the proverbial day wasted. A month without golf? Unthinkable.

———————

CHANGE YOUR VIEW OF ARNOLD PALMER FOR A MINUTE. Stop thinking of him as an icon. Get past your sense of him as a rugged individual, chiseled from anthracite and baptized in Pennzoil. Picture him instead as just one of a group of guys—not a man apart. Share his pleasure as he settles onto the seat of a golf cart in the Florida sun, a Coke in one hand and a hot dog in the other.

"You eatin' hot dogs again?" The question comes from an old pal rolling by in another cart.

"First one since I've been sick!" Palmer says, managing to chew and beam at the same time. At 67 he radiates health and contentment. Eight weeks after having his cancerous prostate removed by surgeons at Minnesota's Mayo Clinic, he's playing golf and flashing the famous smile. As his buddies are quick to testify, "He's still the same old Arnie."

He is. And, of course, he is not.

His good friend and dentist, Howdy Giles, chauffeured Palmer around Orlando's Bay Hill Golf Club in late January, when the golfer's outdoor activity was limited to putting and kibitzing. "I'm with Arnold in the golf cart," Giles says, "and maybe 40 guys come up and say, 'Hey, Mr. Palmer, how ya' doin'?' When we got back to the clubhouse, he said, 'It pisses me off. Before the surgery they called me Arnie. Now it's Mr. Palmer.'"

Nobody dies from too much deference, but Palmer had a point. His cancer seemed to be robbing others of their vitality. A sickroom mentality froze smiles. "Arnold Palmer is the John Wayne of golf," says Jim Deaton, Bay Hill's head pro. "You almost imagine him with a six-shooter and a wide-brimmed hat. We wondered if he'd come back with the same swagger."

Clearly Palmer faced a challenge. He needed to reassure himself—and others—that a tiny gland could not bring down a legend. He needed to regain his stamina. And he needed to restore not just a golf swing but a *persona*.

He needed the Bay Hill Shootout.

PICTURE A CLUB within a club. The Shootout is a subgroup of Bay Hill's roughly 400 members, with a few dozen celebrities, touring pros and ex officio stalwarts thrown in. For a lifetime fee of $200, Shootout members gain entrance to a daily tournament, along with an inexhaustible supply of bonhomie and nonsense. When Palmer bought the Bay Hill Club and Lodge in 1969, he started the Shootout. But he still had to pay his $200 to join.

The Shootout's "commissioner" is Lee Havre, a retired car dealer and banker from Ohio. A wiry character with a cola-colored mop of air, Havre has lunch every day at 11 at a table in the Bay Hill dining room, where he trades jibes with friends and dodges questions about his age. ("Lee," a club member once said, "I'm going to cut off one of your arms and count the rings.") Players who want a spot in that day's Shootout, which usually begins around noon, leave him messages or swing by his table. Havre then retires to the starter's shack, by the 1st tee, and makes up teams. Each team gets an A player (like Palmer or Tour veteran Steve Lowery), a B player (a 75-to-80 shooter, like Havre), and so on down to the D players, who shoot in the 90s. Team scoring is by individual scores—no handicaps—or by three-ball aggregate, with each player anteing up $30 to $50 for the winners' pot. Side bets between individuals or partnerships liven up the action and keep the little gray cells occupied.

If the Shootout were a novel, Dan Jenkins's name would be on the title page. The roster of regulars includes Tom (Two Beer) Bernier, Pete (Zorro) Groux and Bob (the Hammer) Jack—an attorney whose knees click like castanets and whose golf bag is decorated with the scales of justice, tipped to the right. One player got his nickname when Deaton, unable to pronounce the name off a list, called out "Ron . . . Alphabet?" Ron Azarewicz thrust his hand in the air and said, "I'm here!" Now his bag tag reads RON ALPHABET. Another regular, Dick Simmons, once missed a putt so badly that an onlooker sniped, "Try to get it closer than Edward Scissorhands." To his chagrin, Simmons is now stuck with the name.

"We're just a bunch of kids in grown-up bodies," says Jack. And like most kids, they love their toys. The 14-club limit is waived for Shootouts, and some players carry more hardware than a True Value store. (Havre's bag recently choked on eight Callaway metal woods, 12 Top-Flite irons, a putter and an orange ball retriever.) In the same spirit of excess, wrinkled golf gloves dangle like Tibetan prayer flags from the roof supports of their carts.

It was to this temple of male bonding that Palmer hastened after his January surgery. In the early days of his recovery, when swinging a club was forbidden, he followed Shootout matches in his cart, snapping eight-frame-per-second sequence photos with his new Nikon F-5 camera, which he purchased from Nikon vice president John Clouse. ("That camera's meant for professionals," pointed out Giles, an accomplished photographer. "Well, I'm a professional," deadpanned Palmer.) By late January, Palmer could leave the cart for short walks and practice his chipping with the banter of his buddies in the background.

On Tuesday, Feb. 25, the waiting ended. Palmer told the commish that he was ready, and Havre—who shares Palmer's birthday of Sept. 10 and who, coincidentally, had his own prostate removed eight years ago—wrote "A. Palmer" on the pairing sheet. Palmer shot 80 his first time out, and although the score was not released, word of his return spread around the world through the media. Within days he had fired a pair of 70s over the familiar Bay Hill layout.

Most of his rounds, though, were sloppier, with spells of weak hitting and aimless putting. "I don't know if I'm tired or my brain just goes out," Palmer said in mid-March, walking down the 3rd fairway. His caddie, Mike Sturgill, cruised the right side of the hole in a cart laden with two green staff bags and 40 or 50 clubs. "I ask the doctors about it," Palmer went on, "and they say, 'Be patient.' But they say that about everything."

On the practice range that day Palmer seemed almost nostalgic. He hit long irons and watched the balls draw toward the target, as remembered, and then drop 15 yards short. "Not a lot of steam in them anymore," he said, sighing deeply.

"The steam will come back," said George Nichols, chairman of the Arnold Palmer Golf Company.

A couple of swings later Palmer got his body through the ball, and the shot pleased in the remembered way, dropping far down the range. "There it is, George," he said. "There it is."

Palmer's friends were used to his swing moods (not to be confused with his mood swings). When he returned to his Bay Hill condo last fall, after a summer of pallid competition at his home in Latrobe, Pa., Palmer found himself being outdriven consistently by Shootout rivals such as Bill Damron, father of Tour rookie Robert Damron. And never mind that Damron was doing it with an overlength driver that couldn't fit sideways in a pickup truck. "I don't like to be outdriven, even if it's by John Daly," Palmer told Deaton. "It bothers me."

"You could see the determination in his face," recalls Deaton. Focusing on his legs and his shoulder turn, Palmer added flexibility exercises to his already vigorous workout program. "And within a week," Deaton says, "he was hitting it noticeably farther."

So competitive is Palmer that it matters little to him whom he's playing. Payne Stewart, who lives nearby and sometimes plays in the Shootout, brings a gleam to Palmer's eye, but so does a cackling contractor with a deep tan and a pale left hand. "This is good for me," Palmer says. "There are so many good players at Bay Hill that you can always find someone as good as you are."

Palmer's caddie puts it more strongly. Watching his boss crack up with laughter over something said on the 6th tee, Sturgill says, "This is more important to him than being on tour. He loves these people."

THEY LOVE him back, of course.

By early March, Palmer was certain he would be strong enough to play in next week's Masters, extending a string of appearances unbroken since 1955. He was almost as confident that he could play in the Bay Hill Invitational, the Tour event he hosts every March. "Look out, Tiger Woods!" he crowed, watching a practice putt curl toward the heels of Sturgill's toed-out feet.

Palmer's Shootout pals saw his comeback in a different light. They were less concerned with what Arnie was scoring than with what he was saying. They studied, not his spine angle at address, but his posture in moments of reflection. And as far as they could tell, Palmer's comeback was well ahead of schedule. He had resumed part of his exercise routine, which includes 300 to 500 stomach crunches before breakfast. He was back behind his desk every morning, answering correspondence and making business decisions. He filmed a Pennzoil commercial one morning, made a cancer-awareness spot the next. He asked a staffer to rent a helicopter for a quick jump to a golf resort near Tampa so he could look in on his Arnold Palmer Golf Academy. ("You can go with me," he joked. "That way I know you'll get a good helicopter.") Palmer swore to his friends, as he has for years, that he intended to slow down. "I'm really going to this time," he told Havre. "I'm going to play golf every day. I'm going to go to the movies when I want to."

"But I haven't seen any signs of it," Havre says with a snort. "He hasn't changed. Never will change."

Palmer's vitality is of more than passing interest at the Bay Hill Lodge, where the likelihood that resort guests will see Arnie is a bigger selling point than the speed of the greens. Framed photographs and paintings of the King hang everywhere, and Palmer memorabilia fill display cases. It's common for a 20 handicapper on the range to find himself practicing alongside a man who has won four green jackets, two claret jugs, a U.S. Open and 60 Tour events.

The Shootout guys are no less awestruck. Says Deaton, "Even though they're used to him, there's a change in the electricity when he's here."

Recognizing the effect Palmer has on people, Havre judiciously juggles the pairings. Sometimes it's to please Palmer, who may request that he be teamed with a visiting friend or celebrity. Just as often, golf with Arnie is arranged for sentimental reasons. Havre recently paired Palmer with 29-year-old Patrick Sugrue, a Bay Hill assistant pro who caddied for Palmer at last year's

Bay Hill Invitational. "I never thought I'd get to play with Mr. Palmer," said Sugrue, following the older golfer's every move with the eyes of an acolyte. In the same group, but from the opposite end of the age and power scale, Sprint Telecommunications executive Don Poynter echoed Sugrue's enthusiasm. Yes, Poynter confirmed, he was recovering from five mild heart attacks, open-heart surgery and the recent replacement of a toe joint—but the sun was shining, the grass was springy underfoot, and he was playing golf with Arnold Palmer. Poynter grinned. "You don't think I've died and gone to heaven?"

Two weeks before the Bay Hill Invitational, this theme of grown men chasing ecstasy on borrowed time turned intense. Havre paired Arnie with 37-year-old Jay Williams, an insurance agent who had recently had a seizure and collapsed at the Bay Hill pool. In four days, Havre told Palmer, Williams would have a malignant brain tumor removed. Thinking optimistically, Williams had gone to Circuit City that very morning and bought a 60-inch television. During his convalescence, he planned to watch the NCAA basketball tournament and Palmer's return to tournament golf.

"What a group!" Palmer said, walking up to Williams and the rest of his team on the 1st tee. "I've got two sick guys"—he counted himself—"and I don't know about the other two." That produced grins, none bigger than Williams's, and set the tone. A half hour later, walking off the 4th green with a birdie, Williams was practically floating. "It doesn't get any better than this," he said in poignant parody of the beer commercial. Watching

Palmer stride back to the blue markers on number 5, Williams added, "That is probably the finest human being on the face of the earth."

To be human, alas, is to be frail—less durable than a silly nickname or a silver trophy. In his Shootout rounds Palmer stopped from time to time to observe the water turkeys on a pond or to stare up at an interesting aircraft, following the white fuselage across the blue ceiling until it dwindled to a dot and vanished. "We think we're indestructible, but we aren't," he told Havre.

That's something Palmer's fans should keep in mind next week as he walks in the shadows of Augusta's tall pines. The hills will be steeper than he remembers, and the greens a little too fast for his old nerves. But the bigger tests—the challenges of restoration and reconnection—he has already met in the company of friends.

"You think I can hit Finsterwald?" he asked one morning. Palmer stood on the clubhouse end of the range, a driver in his hand, and stared at his old Tour rival, Dow Finsterwald, warming up at the opposite end, 320 yards away. Palmer turned to his entourage, grinning mischievously. "I'd love to bounce one in his pocket."

Mr. Palmer was nowhere in sight. But Arnie was back, and ready to give it a rip.

POSTSCRIPT: *On a subsequent visit to Bay Hill, I was surprised to find my Palmer piece made into a shiny plaque and hung in the men's locker room. "We put it up," a member told me, "because it's the Arnie we know and love."*

NOVEMBER 18, 1991

❧

A Journey to the Western Isles

An inquisitive traveler to the Hebridean island of South Uist
goes in search of a nearly lost golf course

*Readers of my Golf.com column were baffled in the summer of 2007 when
I ranked a course they had never heard of as best in the world. My choice
made sense only to those* SI *readers who remembered this story from my
first year as a full-time golf writer.*

IT IS A MATTER OF ARGUMENT, AMONG THE FEW MODERN-
day Hebrideans who give a damn, whether Old Tom Morris actually laid out the golf course at Askernish, on the island of South
Uist, as has been claimed. Old Tom was 70 years old in 1891, when
the course he designed at Muirfield, near Edinburgh, opened. A
journey west to the Outer Hebrides from Morris's home in St.
Andrews, on the eastern coast of Scotland, involved rail, donkey
cart and ocean steamer and required three days in fair weather,
considerably more in foul. As it took only a few hours in those
days to design a course—it was mostly a matter of the expert
pointing at this hummock or that swale and directing someone
to drive stakes into the sandy soil where the holes should go—it
strains credulity that a graybeard golf professional would tax
himself so for a nine-hole course on such a remote island.

"But if he were a fisherman," a craggy old Scot offers, "Old Tom could have come to the Outer Isles for the salmon and brown trout and delegated the golf course to a lad."

Right. A lad.

STANDING ON the 1st tee at Askernish in May of last year, with soft green grass curling over the kilties of my golf shoes, I saw no evidence that Old Tom—or anybody, for that matter—had laid out a golf course, in 1891 or since. There were no fairways, no greens, no discernible hazards—just a flat meadow covered with dandelions and tiny daisies. Ahead were some high dunes; beyond, presumably, was the beach. Behind me, on a wire fence, hung a score of dead crows, their black beaks open and gleaming in the late-morning sun. Bits of dirty fleece dotted the turf.

"Where are you aiming?" my wife, Pat, asked. She was studying a pencil-drawn course map that had come with the clubs she had borrowed at the estate office.

I wasn't aiming. My plan was to belt a drive in the general direction of North America, find the ball and then pick an attractive target for my second.

"Someone's coming," she said.

There was the sound of an engine from the rutted gravel road behind us. A small pickup bounced through the gate, passed in front of us and parked near a sheep pen. Two young men jumped out and began unloading material—golf flags, tee markers, a mower. One of the men, a slight fellow with short black hair, waved cheerily in our direction. We waved cheerily back.

Mentally, I was making notes for a tournament yearbook: "The first hole at Askernish is a par-4 of indeterminate length and inscrutable shape, with trouble behind in the form of the North Atlantic and Newfoundland. The prudent shot off the tee is a hole in one, since any ball landing either in fairway or rough is inevitably lost. The green, while not severely undulating, is invisible. This accounts for last year's average stroke total for the hole of 24.2. . . ."

My drive split the middle of the meadow and disappeared in daisies. Pat elected not to hit at all until she was sure we were on a golf course, so we set out together, Pat dragging a pull cart, me with my light nylon bag slung over my shoulder. The men waved again, and we waved back. The mower sputtered and roared to life, spewing smoke.

We found my ball after a brief search. Pat stayed behind to guard it, while I walked ahead to find a green. I had gone some 150 yards when I noticed a subtle elevation of the turf, perhaps a foot high and 30 feet in diameter. I walked onto this terrace and searched among the daisies until I found what I was seeking: a crude burrow. You might call it a hole.

I dropped my tweed cap on the spot and strolled back. "Maybe we should come back when those men are finished," Pat said.

I was having none of that. I said, "We'll never have a better opportunity to play golf as it was played a hundred years ago on genuine linksland." I took a seven-iron and turned to face my target. Or what I thought was my target.

"Where's my hat?"

Pat put her hand to her mouth and began to laugh.

I was between a snort and a chortle myself. I was tempted to go back to the hotel, get out the letter and read it again.

"Here's a story idea for your book," the letter began. *"What I envision is a pilgrimage to the last remaining links course in its original form in Scotland. It would be about an area that is true Scottish beauty—isolated, glacier-torn mountains and not the postcard-puff hillocks you see in Wales. The story would be about downing a few stiff ones with the local crofters, their sheepdogs parked diligently between their feet at the bar; about the salmon fishing that goes on in those parts, a subject that has left the locals little more than poachers on estates owned by huge tobacco [conglomerates] and guarded by thugs-for-hire from London's vicious East End. There is no shortage of stuff to write about on a trip to this early outpost of Scottish golf."*

And then, a nice note of caution: *"I would not expect the golf course per se to be a pristine links."*

Poised with my seven-iron on the *machair*—the sandy land or "sea meadow" that comprises the west coast of South Uist—I had to agree. The only structure in sight, a ruin, really, was a glorified shed that had been battered into disuse by winter gales.

The words of young Peter Voy, the local factor for South Uist Estates, were clearer now. "One of the problems of the Askernish course is that it's not owned by anyone," he had said before sending us out. "The machair is subject still to crofting and common grazing. There is a committee for the golf course and people who play golf, but there are no real enthusiasts. Last year the course about collapsed completely. The thing almost disappeared."

This conversation took place in Voy's office in a stone building a few hundred yards back toward the main road. Voy's unruly black hair contrasted nicely with his neat tweed jacket, checked shirt and tie. He had spent 18 months on the island working for South Uist Estates Limited, a family syndicate based in England.

The island and the estate, Voy explained, were one: a 21-mile-long, seven-mile-wide ribbon of machair, moorland, sea lochs and mountains. Ninety-nine percent of the land was subject to crofting tenure—*crofter* being the British term for tenant farmer.

"The landlord gets a rent of 20 to 30 pounds per croft per annum," he said, "but to all intents and purposes the crofters have most of the rights of occupier-owners." There was "sport" on South Uist, but golf was not the first thing that came to mind. "For fishing and shooting, it's paradise."

Askernish—which was spelled AISGERNIS in Gaelic on the little white sign by the main road—was not strictly a golf course. It had been a grassy airstrip from 1935 to '39. Currently, it served as the local site for the annual South Uist Highland Games. By and large, Voy said, the crofters were content to share the machair. Yes, there had been complaints about the "excess of enthusiasm" by some army golfers at a recent summer solstice tournament—Voy wouldn't elaborate—but the British Army no longer used the course. Yes, a few crofters grew agitated at the sight of mowers on the machair, fearing the loss of their winter's keep. And yes, there had been some conflict when the golfers put up electrified wire fences to keep the sheep off the greens.

"That was very controversial," Voy said. "The sheep kept getting caught in the wires."

If that were so, I offered, the crofters might not be that excited about the coming centennial.

Voy raised his eyebrows.

"The centennial," I said. "One hundred years of golf at Askernish, from 1891 to 1991."

Voy tipped his head back in understanding. "Ah! I was going to say, *what* centennial?"

SO I STRUCK with my seven-iron. Not against Voy; against all hope of hitting the green.

"Nice shot," Pat said. "I hope you find it."

We did find the ball, 20 yards from my hat. From long grass, I chipped to within 20 feet of the burrow, the ball rolling no more than a club's length on landing.

I was enthralled with the daisies, hundreds of tiny white blossoms no taller than my putter blade. The ground was rough and bumpy, and my first putt—hammered with the force of a croquet stroke—ripped through the flowers, changed direction twice and bounced over the hole before stopping abruptly. Pat was laughing again as I tapped in for a 5.

All this time, the mower buzzed behind us like some lazy spring bug. Taking the ball from the hole, I looked back.

I blinked.

The daisies had retreated and a golf green had emerged, not 30 yards from where we had teed off. The putting area was

nestled charmingly against some grassy dunes. A deep sand
bunker yawned behind. A red flag lolled atop a pin planted
firmly in the freshly mowed turf.

THE CAPTAIN of the Askernish Golf Club was Peter Steedman,
an accountant. I found him in his office at Uist Builders Limited,
two miles north of Askernish, on the road into Lochboisdale
(pop. 300). A professorial man with wispy white hair and a
carefully knotted tie, Steedman had the sad air of a golfer in
exile. He sat behind his desk and regarded me with disbelief.
Outsiders rarely came asking about the golf course.

"Enthusiasm for golf here is not as it is on the mainland,"
he said, choosing his words carefully. "Fishing is the main
attraction. We get help from local hotels, but basically it's a
do-it-yourself course."

Pressed for details, he obliged. The membership numbered
about 35. The annual fee was £30 male, £20 female and £5
junior. Hotel guests played for free.

When I asked for the daily greens fee, he took fully 10 seconds to answer. "Uh, five pounds, I think. Yes, they put it up
this year."

Steedman's interest in the game dates from his childhood
on the mainland in Scotland, where he had played regularly
at the Falkirk Tryst Golf Club in Larbert, Stirlingshire. This
Steedman admitted freely. Otherwise, he was a bit reticent. On
the subject of the rowdy army golfers: "That's a bit of a sore
point around here." On the pavilion (his and Voy's term for the

ramshackle clubhouse, which has since been leveled): "It's in a state of refurbishment at the moment."

As for the legitimacy of the Old Tom Morris legend, he shrugged. "There's a certain difference of opinion on that."

THERE SEEMED to be a difference of opinion about everything related to Askernish's past, seeing as how there was no documentation. When I asked Voy if he had any records concerning Old Tom and the building of the course, he shook his head.

"The only thing we have is this," Voy said, pulling a ledger from a row of ancient books behind his desk. He turned pages until he found what he wanted.

"This is a very strange piece of paper. It's an extract from a legal document dated 1922, and I think the best interpretation of this document is that, concerning golf, if there is sufficient goodwill, good and well. But if the crofters say no, it'll go to Land Court to be decided." He looked up. "I'm quite certain the court would hold that the common grazing would prevail over playing golf."

The paper he showed me was signed by Lady Gordon Cathcart, widow of John Gordon of Cluny, who bought the island in 1838. I knew nothing about Lady Cathcart.

Of Old Tom Morris, I at least knew the basic biographical data: four-time British Open champion (1861, '62, '64, '67); father of Young Tom Morris (winner of four Opens himself by the age of 22, dead tragically at 25); professional and greenkeeper at Prestwick and St. Andrews; designer of Lahinch, Royal County Down, Muirfield, the New Course at St. Andrews and a few dozen other layouts in the British Isles. But it was impossible to compare Askernish with, say, Muirfield, and conclude that they were the work of the same man. Nowhere on Askernish was there a bunker like that guarding Muirfield's 13th green—six feet deep with a vertical face. Nowhere on Askernish was there a green like that on Muirfield's par-3 16th—ringed by seven diabolical bunkers.

Later, I read in *The Road to Mingulay*, a book about the Outer Hebrides by the noted Scottish author, columnist and broadcaster Derek Cooper, that Lady Cathcart had ruled South Uist with "imperious disdain" until her death in 1935. It was a remarkable example, Cooper wrote, "of the tenacity of the wealthy."

SHOWING A certain tenacity of my own, I returned to Askernish the next afternoon. Pat dropped me off by the dead crows and took the car to look for seals somewhere south of Lochboisdale.

The machair was now dotted with flags. The daisies had been cut, giving the place the appearance of a small-town municipal course in America.

Another surprise: a golfer, preparing to strike his ball from the 1st tee.

He introduced himself as Steve Peteranna, general manager of the Dark Island Hotel on the island of Benbecula, 17 miles to the north. Peteranna, in his 30s with dark, curly hair and a mustache, wore jeans and a handsome wool sweater. He was descended, he said, from an Italian carpenter who had been shipwrecked on the island in the 18th century.

We played together for an hour or so—indolent, meandering golf under a high blue sky. Peteranna knew his way around the course and could make sense of my scrawled course map. There were only nine greens, he said, but alternate tees offered various angles of attack to make up 18 holes. "There used to be another green out there." He pointed to some dunes along the beach. "Rabbits ruined it."

I had heard about the rabbits. They had so overrun the course in the 1960s that the desperate crofters had infected them with a virus called myxomatosis. "That just about made them extinct," Peteranna said of the rabbit virus, which promoted runaway skin tumors on the animals. "The rabbits died a long, slow death."

The rabbits were on the rebound, thanks to a belated ban on germ warfare. On the 4th green, Peteranna addressed his putt, glanced at the hole and then backed away. There were *two* holes, inches apart—one man-made and one the apparent result of tunneling under the machair. From a few feet away they were indistinguishable.

Peteranna confirmed his target and then stood over his ball again. "The gentleman who made up the disease committed suicide," he said. "Felt a bit guilty, I think."

When Peteranna left to go back to work at the hotel, I had the course to myself. I played several balls, stopping occasionally to look back toward the mountains. I strolled along the edge of the machair and enjoyed the sea air. Along the beach, the dunes fell off as if cut with a knife, leaving low cliffs. Birds swooped and pecked at seaweed. Waves lapped gently at the sand.

Was this the machair as Morris had found it in 1891? I continued to be puzzled by the relative lack of features, the land's docility. A modern architect, looking at Askernish, would order up a half dozen bulldozers to give it that "genuine Scottish links" look.

There was also the mystery of the soil itself. Linksland, we are told, is hard and bumpy. At St. Andrews, instead of divots I left mere bruises on the fairway; at round's end, my wrists and elbows were sore. But here at Askernish, the ground was green and yielding. My pitching wedge cut the machair as cleanly as a turf knife and threw up Augusta National–like slabs of grass.

But the biggest mystery, as I told Pat at dinner a few hours later, was the missing 14th tee. "It's not there," I said. "I looked."

The dining room of the 20-room Lochboisdale Hotel, four miles southeast of Askernish, afforded a picture-window view of the sea loch, and at 9 p.m. on this late spring day, the rocky foothills and the ferry slip were still bathed in afternoon gold. It wouldn't get dark till around 11, so we lingered over coffee, enjoying the warmth of an open peat fire. The hotel menu, to our delight, was quite sophisticated—fresh salmon, local venison and other Hebridean specialties served with delicate sauces and fresh vegetables.

After dinner we moved to the cedar-paneled lounge, which was equally warm and cheery but bereft of crofters with sheep dogs at their feet. Of the dozen or so people at the bar, perhaps half were locals and only one, a fortyish man in a leather jacket, was a golfer. He was Charles Bruce, a local construction worker.

Bruce had a workingman's fatalism about golf and a long memory for indignities suffered at Askernish. "I've lost 50 balls there in the chickweed and buttercups," he said plaintively. "It's tame now, but in six weeks time, you hit it anywhere off the fairway and you won't find it. And the rabbits! They pick the ball up and sell it to the next guy!"

A waitress and a barmaid had joined our group. There was also a young man in a white tunic, who leaned against the kitchen door, listening. The words HEAD CHEF were embroidered on his toque.

Bruce said, "But if it's the golf course you've come for, it's Angus you'll want to talk to."

The chef straightened and nodded a bashful greeting.

That's when I recognized him. He was one of the young men who had driven onto the course with the flags and mowers.

Angus Johnstone was the greenkeeper at Askernish.

ON THE THIRD day, Askernish touched me. I was practicing on the machair, hitting short irons into the 9th green, when I suddenly became aware of my solitude. With the warm sun at my back, I wandered over to the boundary fence and took in the surrounding crofts: the green meadows filled with grazing sheep, the stone cottages, the bare brown mountains beyond the main road.

Travelers to the Western Isles invariably remark on the special quality of the light, the depth and texture of the colors. It's as if the landscape were made by an artist laying on translucent glazes with a knife. The sounds—lambs bleating, a lark's song—seem similarly layered. The buzz of an insect catches the ear as surely as the sharp squeal of a seabird.

My eye was drawn to the wreckage of the pavilion, a few yards away. The sign was weathered, but still readable: ASKERNISH GOLF CLUB, EST. 1891. HONESTY BOX IN CLUBHOUSE DOOR.

The honesty box was long gone; the door itself, I saw upon closer inspection, dangled from broken hinges. Tentatively, because I didn't know what constituted trespass, I nudged the door open. The floor of the entry was mostly rotted away; what remained was covered with bird droppings. Beyond, in a room the size of a small house trailer, pieces of guano-splattered furniture were strewn about. On the near wall, a framed photograph of two old-time golfers caught my attention. There was a typed caption: "Two Founder Members of Askernish Golf Club: The Late Alec Macdonald & Alec MacIntosh, Captain and Secretary."

To cross the treacherous floor I had to balance on the floor joists. I poked my head into a room no bigger than a closet. Light leaked through holes in the roof. I could make out a few rusty golf clubs propped against the wall. On the floor, in bird poop, lay a tarnished plaque: ASKERNISH CLUB CHAMPIONS. The champions were listed for 1980 through 1985, and no further. Also on the floor, and even more pitiable because it looked older, was a trophy engraved, THE WOODEN CLUB—NORTH V SOUTH, ASKERNISH GOLF CLUB.

I reflected on the words of Peter Voy: "They're doing a holding operation until some messiah comes along."

To restore my spirits, I withdrew from the pavilion and played a hole or two, stopping now and again to catalog the sweet smells and sights of Hebridean spring. The sun seemed hardly to have moved. (There is a saying in the Hebrides: "When God made time, he made plenty of it.") When I spotted two figures back on the 1st hole, walking toward me with bags slung over their shoulders, I went to meet them. I needed reassurance that Askernish was not haunted.

How do I describe Michael MacPhee? I remember him in jeans and sweater, in his 20s, a slightly built crofter with dark stubble and eyes shaded by a white tennis hat. Strange garb for the keeper of the flame of Askernish.

I watched him swing: a smooth and easy pass with the arms, but with insufficient weight shift and leg drive. The sort of swing one might take at a rock if one had only a shepherd's crook.

"Myself and Donald Macinnes there"—MacPhee nodded to his bespectacled companion, an insurance salesman—"we're about the only regulars now. The holidaymakers come out still, but the old members have lost interest because the course is in such a state. It's not been right since Dr. Robertson moved away to Edinburgh."

I learned more about Ken Robertson as I followed MacPhee and Macinnes around. The great man was MacPhee's doctor when he was young and needed a kidney transplant, and years later Robertson infected him with the golf bacillus. MacPhee painted Robertson as something of a Renaissance man, a dabbler in photography, painting and book illustrating. Robertson had adopted Askernish as his own—nurturing the greens, mending the pavilion, staging tournaments and introducing school-children to the ancient game. "He had this course beautiful," said MacPhee wistfully. "He had it really looking like a golf course should look."

Unfortunately, Robertson had retired and removed himself to Edinburgh. I didn't have to ask when this had happened; the event was recorded at the pavilion in language any archaeologist would understand.

The two young Scots continued their friendly game. The competition dated back 10 years and was still keen, judging from the occasional baleful look MacPhee directed heavenward. ("The language can get very bad, very blue," Macinnes said.) They favored match play almost exclusively, honoring the time-honored Scottish belief that no round of golf should be spoiled by one or two bad holes.

MacPhee added: "And he still can't beat me!"

They had answers for most of my questions about the machair: the rabbits, the horizontal rains of winter, the ancient cattle pens overgrown with springy grass. MacPhee explained the dead crows on the fence: The gamekeeper traditionally displays his trophies to show the lord of the manor he is doing his job.

On one hole, MacPhee was searching in the long grass for his ball when he exclaimed, "Oh, look!" He turned back the grass so I could see the tight brown nest I had almost stepped on. In the nest were three tiny blue eggs.

"Be starlings," Macinnes said.

Of Old Tom Morris the two young men knew considerably less. The prehistory of Askernish—that dismal era preceding Robertson's Camelot—was to them the stuff of musty books and graveyards. If 1991 marked a centennial, though, they assured me there would be a celebration. "Just the two of us," MacPhee said, smiling at the thought. "This golf course is our pride and joy."

On we walked—the Scots playing their ancestral game, the American observing.

"There's a rumor that he's coming back," MacPhee said, preparing to hit off the 9th tee.

I was watching my wife drive through the gate, the windshield flashing gold in the falling sun. Swooping lapwings formed a crown above the car.

"Who's coming back?"

"Dr. Robertson," MacPhee said. "I heard that he may come back soon."

IF OLD Tom Morris designed Askernish, he may have designed the South Uist roads as well. The island's principal north-south highway is a one-lane road. Cars and lorries race toward each other at turnpike speeds before braking suddenly and pulling off at passing bays positioned every quarter mile or so.

I drove eight miles of this shared fairway after lunch on our last day. My destination was the hamlet of Bornish, where I was told I would find the Catholic Church of St. Mary's. Voy had offered its pastor, Canon Angus MacQueen, as the ultimate authority on the local links. "He's chairman of the historical society and a great local character," Voy said. "And he plays golf."

St. Mary's rectory, a stone house behind a picket fence, stood on a hillock 100 yards or so above the church. No one answered my ring, but I heard voices out back, and that's where I found Canon MacQueen. A gray-haired, barrel-chested man in his 60s, the canon was bent over a concrete walkway, tending a collection of purple and lavender seaweeds. He wore only shorts and sandals. A few feet away a young man in a bathing suit sat in a lawn chair, sunbathing.

"This is milk pudding," the canon explained, once we had gotten the introductions out of the way. He separated the ingredients for me—carrageen moss, seaweed and water. It wasn't clear to me if this was a pud one ate or a pud one employed as a garden mulch. It's still not clear to me.

The canon's house guest was Peter Boyd from the nearby isle of Barra. "Just in to play some golf at Askernish," Boyd said cheerily. "It's a beautiful wee course."

The priest agreed. They had, in fact, just returned from a morning round. When I asked if it was true about Old Tom Morris designing Askernish, Boyd jumped in: "Oh, yes, definitely." How did he know? "I saw it in writing in a golfing magazine."

Canon MacQueen shrugged. The historian in him plainly distrusted such a source. "I'll tell you what I know of its history," he began, "but it's not much, I'm afraid."

Alas, he spoke the truth. He told me some things I already knew—that Askernish was a landing strip for mail planes in the '30s, that the Highland Games pitched their tents there every July—and something I didn't know: "Barra used to have a very picturesque nine-hole course until the early 1950s, but it closed for lack of interest."

Boyd looked up. "Was there not a banker that looked after Askernish?"

The canon nodded, still bent over his pretty weeds. "The semi-colonial types always looked after it—doctors, lawyers, bankers, that type." Robertson had been the last in this succession, and no doubt the best, but the privatization of record-keeping had robbed the course of its past.

"He *is* coming back," the canon said, meaning Robertson, "but only on holiday."

I felt a pang of disappointment for the young crofter MacPhee. No messiah would restore Askernish this spring.

We chatted a while longer. Finally, the shirtless priest held out his arms in apology: He had nothing more to offer. The historical committee was preparing a history of the island, but they had not yet researched Askernish.

"No one can afford the time."

Nor could I—afford the time, that is. After thanking the canon and Boyd, I drove back to Askernish for one last round. Pat and I were taking the car ferry from Lochmaddy to the Isle of Skye at dawn the next day.

I had not given up looking for the lost 14th tee, and I finally discovered it, miraculously. My pencil-drawn map had it immediately adjacent to the 5th tee, but it was atop a wall of high dunes defining the golf course's southern boundary. When I reached the top of these dunes, puffing a bit from the weight of my clubs, I froze in my tracks. Behind me was the gentle meadow of Askernish; ahead, stretching south along the sea, was Ballybunion! The terrain was suddenly as violent as a storm-tossed sea. Canyons wound through grassy dunes carved by winter gales. Sand spilled down dune walls. Shadows collected in sinister pools. If this was not the closest thing to Ballybunion, on Ireland's southwest shore, I was damned.

There were no fences and no signs—and no witnesses—so I teed up and drilled a two-iron shot into the area I immediately dubbed Askernish Old. There was no guesswork about this shot, as there had been that first day with Pat. I saw a golf hole in the wilderness. I visualized a fairway on the valley floor leading to a natural greensite in the shelter of some dunes, 400 yards away. If Old Tom Morris once stood where I stood, I'm sure he saw the same hole, and I bet he sent his lad scampering down the valley with a wooden stake and a red ribbon.

For the next hour or so, as the sun settled over the sea, I enjoyed Askernish Old. I played winter rules, improving my lie on the imaginary fairways and taking two club lengths' relief when my ball rolled against a dead sheep. I assigned myself an automatic two putts on each imaginary green, except where I spotted a natural hole or burrow, in which case I tried to chip in. This, surely, was what golf was like in its formative stages—the salty wind, the sky, the mingled odors of wet wool and manure, the golfer creating his own course as he went along.

Amazingly enough, I lost no balls on the Old. Coming in, I hooked one onto a sandy cliff above the beach, but I made a stance and blasted safely back to the machair for bogey. I mentally signed my scorecard for a course-record 23—for five holes.

When I got back to the 14th tee, I looked across the meadow and saw two figures atop a grassy ridge that served as the 3rd tee. I recognized the shapes as MacPhee and Macinnes, the crofter and the insurance salesman. We waved at each other: two young Scots on one dune, one no-longer-young American on another dune, met by someone's century-old impulse that *this* linksland, *this* stretch of machair, should be a golf course.

Was that someone Old Tom Morris? I'd like to think so, but one might just as fairly credit the design to Angus Johnstone or Robertson or Lady Cathcart or to myself—to the rabbits and sheep, for that matter. The lesson of Askernish is that a golf course is a brief compact between man and terrain, with terrain ultimately holding the upper hand.

I teed off, and my drive seemed to hang in the air forever.

POSTSCRIPT: *Many years after this piece appeared, a greenkeeper from the Scottish mainland went out to play on the machair. He, too, looked south from the 14th tee and saw a golf course in the wild dunes. As this book goes to press, that greenkeeper, Gordon Irvine, is well on his way to turning the old sea meadow into an 18-hole links course. Eleven of the holes represent Irvine's educated guess as to how the dunes holes looked in Old Tom's time.*

I returned to South Uist in September 2007 to meet the members of the resurrected Askernish Golf Club on that nibbled shore where the "compact between man and terrain" has, against all odds, been renewed. But that's another story.

Acknowledgments

WRITING CAN BE A LONELY ENTERPRISE, BUT COVERING golf for a national magazine is not. Some of the prose in this collection was composed in media tents in the inspiring company of a couple of hundred journalists. So I must first offer thanks to all the neighboring writers who took a second to feed me a fact ("Hal Sutton's on his fourth marriage") or to ask why I was slumped over my keyboard with my eyes closed. I owe a particular debt to those current and former SPORTS ILLUSTRATED writers who have sat with me at majors for the better part of three decades: Rick Reilly, Gary Van Sickle, Jaime Diaz, Alan Shipnuck, Michael Bamberger, Chris Lewis, Rick Lipsey, Cameron Morfit, Farrell Evans and Seth Davis. Thanks, guys, for setting the bar so high . . . and for conceding me the bed without a footboard when we share a house at the Masters.

I am also indebted to the communications staffs of golf's tours and governing bodies, the people who give us a place to work, a place to eat and an interview room for grilling suspects. They are too many to list here, but I'll thank them by remembering two departed friends: John Morris, who set a standard for warmth and civility during stints at the USGA and the PGA Tour, and the guileless and amiable David Earl of the USGA.

I must credit the photographers who worked with me on these stories, even if the list is long. The magazine is called

SPORTS ILLUSTRATED, after all, and I wrote every word in this book with the knowledge that a world-class lensman was backing me up with the proverbial thousand words worth of imagery. I benefit, as well, from access to the photo shoots, where profile subjects tend to speak more freely than they do for a reporter brandishing a recorder or notebook. Anyway, sincere thanks to Fred Vuich, Robert Beck, Bob Martin, Darren Carroll, John Biever, Bill Frakes, David Walberg, Jim Gund, Rich Frishman, Todd Bigelow, Jacqueline Duvoisin, John Iacono, Heinz Kluetmeier, David Bergman, Warren Little, David Cannon, Al Tielemans, Simon Bruty, Lane Stewart, Peter Read Miller, Ron Modra, John Burgess, Ben Van Hook, V.J. Lovero, David Klutho, J.D. Cuban and Matthew Harris. I have also worked with a host of great photo editors, but I'd like to pay special tribute to SI's Miriam Marseu and Porter Binks, who have coordinated our coverage for much of the GOLF PLUS era.

Must I thank Google? Probably, but I owe a bigger debt of gratitude to the SI sports librarians, who have been answering my queries and faxing me clips for 29 years. (Big thanks to Joy Birdsong, Natasha Simon, Helen Stauder, Angel Morales and Linda Levine.) Ditto for the many red-eyed reporters who have stayed up all night in the Time & Life Building checking the facts in my stories.

I definitely have to thank Robert Creamer, the legendary writer-editor who drew me into the SI fold. Bob gave me the opportunity to work for a succession of gifted and supportive managing editors, starting with Gil Rogin and continuing with

Mark Mulvoy (the golf-daft Bostonian who turned me into a golf writer), John Papanek, Bill Colson and our current ME, Terry McDonell, to whom I am especially indebted because he green-lighted this collection. I have been just as lucky in my draw of golf editors. Over the years, my sleepy late-night prose has been slapped awake by Myra Gelband, Mike Bevans, Roy Johnson, Joe Marshall, Greg Kelly, Mark Godich, Jim Gorant, Bob Roe and the incomparable Sarah Ballard, who was herself a distinguished golf writer. And then I got really lucky. Since 1995 my immediate boss has been SI Golf Group editor Jim Herre, a tough editor (by reputation) who hands me sweet assignments, boosts my confidence at regular intervals and treats my phraseology with unwarranted respect. Jim is my idea man, and for that alone I'll probably mention him in my will.

Finally, I'd like to thank Gorant, Stefanie Kaufman and Kevin Kerr, the talented editors who turned these digital wisps into a book, and the inimitable David Feherty, whose boisterous introduction provided me the best push start I've gotten since I sold my '52 Chevy.